What Horses
REVEAL

What Horses
REVEAL

From First Meeting to Friend for Life

KLAUS FERDINAND HEMPFLING

Translated by KRISTINA McCORMACK

Trafalgar Square Publishing

First published in the United States of America in 2004 by
Trafalgar Square Publishing, North Pomfret, Vermont 05053

Printed in China

© Klaus Ferdinand Hempfling 2004

ISBN: 1-57076-285-6

Library of Congress Catalog Control Number: 2004110559

Picture credits

Colour photos: Felix von Döring - Kosmos (page 152); Anastazia Joergensen, Frederiksberg (pages 50, 172); Gabriel Kärcher - Sorrel (pages 101, 115); Christof Salata – Kosmos (page 152); Christiane Slawik, Wurzburg (pages 58, 74, 76, 78, 79, 80, 82, 83, 84, 85, 88, 89, 90, 92, 94, 95, 96, 97, 98, 99, 100, 102, 104, 106, 108, 109, 110, 113, 114, 116, 118, 120, 121, 122, 123, 124, 125, 149, 151, 170, 173, 175, 176, 177, 181, 182, 183, 186, 187, 188, 190, 191, 193, 194, 196, 197, 198, 199, 200, 201, 203, 205); Sabine Stuewer, Darmstadt (pages 75, 76, 81, 86, 91, 108, 112, 117, 119, 120, 122, 126, 171, 180, 202, 204) All other 335 colour photos come from Klaus Ferdinand Hempfling's collection and his videos: *Coming Together* and *Dancing with Horses*.

The illustrations are by Cornelia Koller, Schierhorn (pages 59, 61, 71, 137, 146, 163,). The b/w illustrations (page 48) were drawn by Malene Hempfling.

Designed by Judy Linard
Color separations by Tenon & Polert Colour Scanning Limited, Hong Kong

An Accompaniment

The old monk sat in his armchair. Without taking his gaze from the void into which his thoughts seemed dreamily to sink, he said softly:
'You want to learn from me. That is good! But you demand explanations, descriptions, specifications – that is not good! For what use is it to make many words?

'What represents normal these days – and only because the masses have established it as that – is also moving, within its limits – within the boundaries of the ordinary. Within the boundaries of that of which the masses feel capable – and every small mind that determines this era.

'But that which you seek, and with you ever more people, is far removed from this.'

Klaus Ferdinand Hempfling
From: 'The Message of the Horses'

Contents

The Game of the 26 Cards
What Horses Reveal

Continuous Renewal
The First Encounter

26 Characters, 26 Paths
How to Shape Horses Correctly

Conclusion
What Are You Going to Do with what You have Learnt?

The Mysterious Gateway into the Realm of Mankind

Up through the Fires

The precise recognition of a horse in just a few seconds, the transformation thereafter in the few minutes of the first encounter, and the subsequent careful transition to ground and ridden work, is the foundation and heart of my work. How do horses reveal themselves in so short a span of time? What is the secret of my work? And, is that even something that can be taught or learned? This book illuminates some aspects of the world of horses that have until now lain in shadow. It sheds light on the questions to which more and more horsepeople require answers.

of this World

- How do I truly recognize my horse?
- How does a deep understanding develop?
- How does a lifelong friendship develop?
- Which path does this book take toward the goal?
- What am I being offered by it, and where can that lead?

Let us begin our journey immediately with a look at the work.

Campeon 13 fights out of desperation because it is the last means available to him. But the human (the author) does not enter into this fight, and thereby achieves a situation wherein both horse and human are winners.

The story of Campeon 13 will be elaborated upon in this chapter, and with it the introductory message of this book.

A Revelation for the Existence of Mankind

This horse is named Campeon 13; 'campeon' means 'champion'. He was, at the time the photos were taken, only nine years old, yet his expression seems to show nothing of youth but only sadness and suffering. His fearfulness and his pain now know only one path, that of aggression. The soldiers of this Spanish breeding facility (with several hundred stallions) were, by order of the state, required to get on well with him, but had, out of fear, banned him to the farthest stable, until, that is, the day that I was scheduled to appear for a demonstration. Then everyone was reminded of the presence of this horse and also of others who had to endure a similar fate. It was these hopeless and frightened horses that were given to me for this demonstration; and this was also true of almost every demonstration I did elsewhere.

The soldiers were basically nice people and I quickly became friendly with one of their officers. What they did to the horses was, for the most part, done unconsciously, was outside the limits of their perception and sensibility. Most of them sought the horses' friendship, but did not find it.

The primal battle

We will return to Campeon 13 shortly but, for a moment, I would like to remain with the soldiers. They are part of a tradition that began with the warriors, the elite of their forebears. Among the Celts, the Teutons and the Vikings, these warriors were also knights. On their long hard path to becoming such a knight – a cavalier – they learned something of the primal battle, of the most important fight in the life of a man, namely, the fight with himself. They learned that the powerful forces and strengths of nature, instinct and evil can never be subdued with force, but solely with the unimaginable depths of creativity which only true humanity can bring forth. For our forefathers in the occidental world, this process was once symbolized by oneness with horses because, according to these ancestors, when a person encounters a horse he encounters his own dark side and, at the same time, the spark of hope in himself. And that was considered worth finding.

In time, however, the warriors became merely soldiers, and the horses, those disguised bearers of hope and good fortune, became primarily symbols of war, vanity, gambling sports, superficial entertainment, and power.

A completely new system

For many years I have used this system of communication and many thousands of people have witnessed these encounters with horses. In this book I will not only describe a completely new system for truly recognizing horses – any horse in the world – but will also describe how to get the deepest insights into their natures and patterns of behaviour. In addition I will disclose to everyone how they can, from the first moment, arrive at the deepest connection and understanding, and from there follow the path of which, currently, only children, and those who have not totally lost their child-nature, dream. This is an honest and sincere attempt to further true communication with horses but, once again, time will judge the outcome.

After some minutes of fighting, Campeon 13 now seeks only closeness to the person who responded to his aggression with closeness and understanding. Now it is possible to recognize a horse that is essentially good-natured, and seeks nothing more than connection and exchange. This horse that up to this point had shown all human beings nothing other than rejection and aggression now devotedly follows the author on a loose lead rope. Nothing remains of the danger that was there at the start. What actually happened in these minutes? What effected the transformation? How can something like this be learnt? Look at the precision of the person's bearing in each photo. His attention is continuously focused on the horse; there is devotion on both sides!

Example 1: Campeon 13

What is actually happening here?

As can be seen in this series of photos (and in a more cohesive way in the video *The First Encounter*) Campeon 13 transforms himself in just a few minutes from a dangerous aggressor into a closeness-seeking, totally devoted fellow being. This horse has revealed himself to me and to the spectators. And this revelation is, as is nearly always the case, also a revelation for the existence of mankind. What is happening? How do horses reveal themselves? And, what does it mean when horses do reveal themselves? No matter what and how is happening, the owners and caretakers often no longer recognize their own horses. Something strange, something different, deep, new, and often also unfathomable, has revealed itself to them.

The search for mutuality

If a picture says as much as a thousand words, what then do a thousand pictures say? You will find almost that many pictures in this book. I have begun with three photo-sequence examples from my practice. They may, at first, seem like exceptional cases but believe me they are not. We will look at a great many horses on the following pages, together with methods, forms, ways of interacting with them, and points of view. These days many breeds have come to symbolize very particular riding theories and, for the most part, I am not interested in that. I would much rather we looked at one horse – his eyes, his nature, his suffering or, even better, his good fortune – and then another horse. For me it is first and last about the relationship between a human being and a horse, nothing more. If a person truly strives for integrity, humanity, truth and inner awareness, and if he is prepared to question himself again and again, that is enough for me, and it is certainly enough for the horses, because they seek mutuality, not differences.

Fifteen minutes of truth: when aggression comes of sorrow

In this book you will learn why Campeon 13 reacts as he does, and can react only that way. I put this example at the beginning because I wanted you to see something important right from the start. How many people say that in a particular situation they had to react in such and such a way because other beings provoked that response? Look again at these pictures so that, instead of a fighting horse, you see a dancing horse. Can you not then immediately see how the person is dancing? Is there not an unusual peacefulness, harmony, and rhythm in these pictures? However aggressively the horse conducts himself, the person apparently remains completely unperturbed by it. Softly, gently, yes almost tenderly, he lets the horse act and only controls the situation with him. And the horse, does he have any other choice but to finally give himself in total trust to a person who behaves this way? Is it not then only a question of time? I believe it is.

What will you make of this?

Initially you will get an overview, an *impression* of what happens during these encounters. Then, what actually takes place on many levels will be documented. Having come to the end of the book you will look at these first pictures again in a different light in order to read in every detail, information that right now is still invisible. But we have not got that far yet. In the course of the following pages I will list and describe minutely what the whole thing amounts to. Whether for you too it will become a dance, an act of clarity, peacefulness, consequence, presence and flowing communication with the world and with the horse, is not in my hands.

Expression and form

You will begin to understand why, for example, even this horse, after some minutes of aggression, so directly seeks close contact with me, and you will realize that this has completely different underlying reasons from those you might expect. What is important here is that this happens in such a connected and concise way. The person's expression and demeanor do not seem to change from beginning to end. Everything that is initiated seems to emanate from me, and even in the first and second photos it is written in my face and bearing that the result will soon come, indeed that it must come. I am aware of the outcome right from the start and throughout the encounter.

Study the first and last pictures of the sequence and you will have to agree how similar the two are as far as my expression and demeanor are concerned and yet, in the first picture, the stallion is trying to conquer and even injure me. It is very serious, for both of us. The horse fights for his dignity and to finally be understood. His expression is one of deepest sorrow and I struggle to ensure that the horse does not confuse me with whoever is responsible for his sorrow. And that is how sorrow, misunderstanding and danger become trust, devotion, and reliability.

I will try to teach you this, to teach you what I am able to teach, as well as I can.

The person's bearing and expression are very similar in both these pictures. Even in the first photo you can see how calmly and quietly the person responds to the horse, although he tries repeatedly to attack. How different the horse appears in the second photo – a moment selected from the end of the sequence. Now he expresses exhausted peacefulness and gentleness. The person, however, remained the same from beginning to end. Even under repeated attacks from the horse his expression and demeanor remained demonstrably relaxed and gentle. In the chapter entitled 'The First Encounter' we will work on this in great detail.

Example 2: 1000 Kilos of Concrete or Childlike Over-enthusiasm and Misdirected Strength

No one at the military station knew exactly when this Breton stallion had last left his box. No one now dared to open the door anymore, because no one wanted to have a 1000 k (2205 lb) creature at the end of a lead rope with only one thing on his mind: to crush the person at the other end of the rope.

The *plaza* (square) in front of the stables was unsecured and unfenced, and a horse such as this can easily drag a dozen men through the dust. How is it then that one man is able to handle the horse, to withstand his massive attacks and, finally,

to have this horse follow behind him, like a little poodle, on a slack lead rope?

When you study this example it is made very clear that all of this has virtually nothing to do with raw, pure bodily strength, but rather with a certain quality of energy and inner power.

These photos show how calm the person remains. Here again we can see a dance, softness, and extraordinary tolerance. This is no longer play but, as so often in my work, it is about my safety and the safety of other people. You may sit in the fragrant big

city temples and speak of energy and power, of calmness and inner knowledge. With a horse like this, action demonstrates where promise and illusion lie, and where far-reaching results are really to be found.

By the end of this book, you will know why something like this can occur. You will know what kind of a horse this is, how he feels and behaves, and what he expects from human beings. You will have learned what you need to act with integrity with this horse as well as others. And you will know what a long road it is to that point. It is my hope that you will also know how wonderful each single step on the path can be. If you grasp that, then this book will have fulfilled its purpose.

Not one of the soldiers trusted himself to go into the stable with this 1000 k (2205 lb) Breton stallion. They all knew that as soon as the door was opened an explosion would follow. But what happens when you react to the explosion in a different way from that which the horse expects? In the end, this stallion-giant follows me like a lamb. He lets himself be touched everywhere on his body, and follows me on a slack lead rope all over the military base. Even this horse now exhibits nothing but gentleness and trust. How do we arrive at such openness in such extreme circumstances? What lessons are there in these encounters even for 'totally average' horsepeople? Once again I ask you to please study the person's inner and outer demeanor in the photos. As we shall see, this is another element necessary to success that goes along with the recognition of the horse — even, and perhaps especially, in such extreme cases.

Example 3: a Hopeless Case? Devotion and Sensitivity Instead of Sentimentality

This delicate creature would barely allow herself to be handled or touched. She was anxious and frightened. Only by being completely cautious could anyone approach her, but touching, blanketing, or problem-free saddling were not possible. The picture sequence on these pages shows something very significant. Instead of leaving the horse alone to have time to become accustomed to me, I immediately lay my arm across her back.

Two things become apparent straight away. Firstly, the results show, even after just a few minutes, that my choice was probably correct. The horse stands there absolutely quietly even as I lay the saddle blanket over her eyes and ears. And she follows me, lightly and dancer-like, even as we pass very close to the crowd of spectators. Secondly, you can see that the horse desires to be close to me from the very start.

As with the first two examples, I have deliberately put this example at the beginning of the book in order to steer you away from premature assessments and all too easy misinterpretations right from the start. Throughout this book, this point will become very significant. Indeed, it is one of the most important keys to success. We will learn how to touch horses in their sense, how to handle them, how to respect them with every movement and how you recognize and acknowledge their total dignity. However, we will also learn how genuine emotion has nothing to do with muddled, maudlin emotionalism and sentimentality – quite the contrary. Superficial friendliness helps you sell vacuum cleaners and win elections. But only with clarity, righteousness, and genuine, relevant empathy can you win the soul of a horse and the miracle of life.

What specific transformations horses undergo in the first minutes of their encounters with me is something that only the owners of the horses can assess, not the spectators. Even when, as here, the horse reacts with total shyness and nervousness at the beginning, a spectator cannot truly know how momentous the step is that leads to the calm demeanor and inner peace this particular horse displays when I lay a saddle blanket on her head. Formerly, that action would have sent her into a complete panic. Important to note in this example is the directness with which the problem was approached and solved. Here too the horse is following even the most subtle signals after only a few minutes. In Chapter 5 I will address in depth the subject of 'spontaneous healing'.

Do Form, Structure and Quality Still Exist Today?

In the pictures on these pages we see Janosch cantering around me. And he is doing that with only a rope looped loosely around his neck. The amazing thing is that the horse is completely correctly positioned to the inside for the entire time, even at the canter. And he is cantering in circles of 2–4 m (6¹/₂–13 ft).

People have always said to me that that is not the way it works, that a horse must be 'correctly' positioned to the inside with reins or some other device, particularly at a canter because, if left to himself, a horse always bends to the outside in canter. This is also true, but it is only true for as long as it is not made clear to the horse through thorough, high-quality work that he can better carry himself and his rider if he bends to the inside. That is an example of quality, form, and structure.

At this stage it is also important to emphasize the following: some of my readers were and are of the opinion that openness, tolerance, and the reference back to our forebears also means libertinism and a policy of 'anything goes'. However, 'anything goes' ends in chaos and superficiality, both of which are totally opposed to the true life and the true spirit of horses.

At the point where people leave the common, superficially standardized path – where they seek alternatives, even alternatives for a different way of life – there they all too often also leave the quest for form, structure, and quality. My way, my path, with horses is a genuine alternative and it still exists worldwide probably *because* it is grounded on form, structure and quality.

We will come back to this theme repeatedly in the course of this book. Right now I just want to make it clear that liberation from a thought structure that all-too-easily says 'I do it this way because it was always done this way' to truly self-responsible and aware action does not mean throwing all rules overboard. That would only lead to personal and, as you see so often these days, social chaos. More accurately, it means that the rules should be examined very closely, and the fact that nature and harmony are powerful, very formal structural concepts which exist according to very strict laws, should be recognized. That human freedom is grounded in these laws is one of the mysteries that the horses allowed me to see.

Here you see clearly how the horse at liberty tries to present himself, in action and expression, with a correct inner bend. A horse wants to please himself and his rider or trainer, and steadily develop a mutual understanding. But, instead of allowing this to happen, most riders hinder the natural development of their charges. We must learn to do little, in fact almost nothing, but to do it at the decisive moment.

In this picture sequence Janosch is cantering around me in a circle of 2-4 m (6'/₂–13 ft)with only a rope looped loosely around his neck. Note the correct positioning to the inside that Janosch exhibits in these pictures. This example should suffice to show that freedom, trust, understanding and harmony do not mean that great achievements are not possible. Quite the contrary is true. This book will demonstrate that it is precisely the inner qualities that are necessary in order to bring forth outstanding achievement without the use of force.

Junque's Progress: when External Form Ultimately Evolves from Inner Connection and Clarity

It is important to establish an inner connection with a horse right from the very start but, unfortunately, so many well-meant efforts to build inner connections in reality often result in a much greater vacuum. That is very sad because then the good beginnings fizzle out and what

Three phases in the development of the stallion Junque are very easily recognizable in the pictures on this and the following pages. It is amazing to compare the starting point to the results several years later. This photo comes from the book *Dancing with Horses* and shows the first phase, i.e. a horse that is very much on the forehand and moves in an unbalanced way, totally without flexion or bend. (See also the photos on pages oo and oo.)

remains is usually resignation. I will try to steer you away from that.

Thus, while attempting to develop a life of integrity with our horses – which could be described as one side of a coin – we forget that the other side, for example just an external usefulness can also be developing. And it is dangerous if any problems that arise are unacknowledged because they can lead to further problems. However, if you are aware of these pitfalls then they can be avoided in good time.

The advantage of superficiality

If, for example, horses are given the most common types of training, of whatever kind and for whatever riding style, it can

be assumed that the majority of these horses will later function pretty much in a certain way. Twenty, thirty, or more, percent of horses, however, will not achieve certain goals, or will for other reasons, perhaps because they rebel too much, be deemed 'unusable' in the end. This is virtually calculated into the equation, it is part of the horse-training business. What counts in this case, from the very beginning, is an animal's usefulness, and the tried and true methods that have a great probability of giving the anticipated results and value. This is not the way I operate, or think, but, in fairness, these methods must be given their due for the relative clarity and simplicity with which everything occurs. There are more or less clearly formulated methods, recognizable stops on the way, and standardized goals. If you are satisfied with that, then you, at least, will not too easily go astray.

Well-camouflaged lies of life

For those of us who want to adhere to inner values it is not this desired external usefulness that counts the most. We must, however, be very careful because at this point some well-camouflaged lies of life, into whose fine web it is easy to fall, can arise. In the relationship I have with horses, there emerges from the foundation of deep trust an immediately visible effect, a visible 'usefulness' that is in fact very important. On the one hand, therefore, I say that the relationship and inner values are the important things, and that outward

The second phase: in these three pictures taken about a year and a half after the first photo, things already look completely different. It is hard to believe that this is the same horse because now the horse is free in his movement. He looks significantly shortened from front to back, with his proud, upright carriage, and his good neck position. The hind legs step far and powerfully under the weight of his body.

'usefulness' should be disregarded but, on the other hand, I say that the outward transformation that springs from within, the 'effect', is so significant. This sort of 'usefulness' develops in a manner that is very different from that which is commonly known. All this appears to be contradictory but it is not.

Because this seems so incomprehensible to some, we address the topic at this point, right at the beginning of the book.

The same horse

Let us look at the pictures of my Spanish stallion, Junque, on these pages. Junque featured a great deal in my book *Dancing with Horses* and the first photo (opposite) is taken from a sequence on page 136 of that book. This picture shows a horse with a relatively poorly set neck, fairly flat movements and, in addition, there is no bend or flexion to be seen. He is heavily on the forehand, contracts his back tightly, and is not at all balanced in his movements.

The next three photos were taken about a year and a half later when the overall impression is completely different. A major horse magazine published these photos, indicating that the story would be about the same Junque seen in *Dancing with Horses*.

Thereupon letters to the editor arrived, some of which even spoke of a deliberate deception; the readers thought he could not possibly be the same horse. Some mentioned the fact that the mane, which in the original photo lies to the left, lies to the right in the more recent photos. This 'phenomenon' is quite simple to clear up. Purebred Spanish horses must wear their manes to the left, even when the growth is actually to the right, as Junque's is. But, because I place no value on such superficial 'fashions', naturally the horse now wears his mane on the right side.

But, even if some do not want to believe it, it is indeed the same horse. The very one that can be seen with me on the cover of this book.

The free play of the movements

How differently the stallion moves and carries himself here (above). It is still a far cry from the lightness shown in the following photos, but it can already clearly be seen how the whole horse is differently proportioned. The neck is set higher, the shoulder is more angled, the back shorter, and the neck is elevated and well formed. The horse is free and well balanced and carries himself nicely on the hindquarters. Elevated steps already hint at piaffe and passage. The pictures on page 25 finally show a dancing horse with a free forehand and free play in his movements. In the video, *The First Encounter*, the progression through the three phases can be seen in motion, and in unison with my actions. Such changes are possible exclusively through careful and specific, consistently sequential exercises.

Is it only an excuse?

With regard to the work that follows, I would like to begin with this example: all of these pictures speak of a deep inner connection between horse and man. That is the starting point, the path and the goal, all in one, and is the main purpose, the reason and the reward for my action. But the proof of the rightness of this path is also the physical, visible effect. It is the external appearance of the horse. And these connections are all too often forgotten, or not even noticed. Many people cannot, therefore, even imagine that outwardly visible successes come to be when your attention is directed completely and totally toward inner values, because, very often, these are not recognized by those who strive for inner qualities of whatever kind. But, my experience in this respect is that, if you strive for inner values, you are only genuinely doing that, and in the right way, if positive changes are also seen on the outside, for example in well-being, strength, energy, expression, form, and beauty.

That is demonstrated in the photos by Janosch as well as by Junque. When people say 'the whole thing does not look so great on the outside because we are striving for inner values', it is only a lame excuse. True inner values also always impress themselves on the outer form.

Seek that which truly nourishes

Let me reiterate that I maintain, and all the pictures on these pages can unequivocally verify, that unbelievable 'miracles' on the outside are possible only when inner values and forms are developed. Only then can something develop externally without our doing anything that is specifically 'use' oriented. It grows as, for example, a thriving tree grows in size and magnificence. It happens all by itself when the conditions are right; and this book is about the conditions. We do not, therefore, want to forget about the external, on the

contrary, we want to further it, and enjoy it, and bring the living to life; in order to do that we must seek that which truly nourishes. The egg yolk comes first, then the egg white, and only then the shell. And only when the yolk and the white are large, will the shell also be large. The shell is never there for its own sake. It adapts itself to the shape and mass of the contents it is there to protect. I do not want to build a big shell with a lot of tricks, only to always live in fear that the fragile, hollow structure could collapse in on itself at any time. I want to concern myself with the yolk and the white – in other words, the content. Because, when that is fully developed, I will also have a great egg that can truly nourish. Therefore, this book – to stay with the analogy – speaks of the shell, but only peripherally. Our subject is primarily yolk and white. But we must not forget that we ourselves must also be checked and measured by visible results.

Joy, form and aesthetics

Inner progress, then, is also always outer quality, it is also always quality of life, wealth, enjoyment, joy, form and aesthetics. Ascetic deprivation is as strange in the eyes of horses, and just as harmful to life, as use-oriented exploitation, unadulterated external vanity, or self-consuming libertinism. In my opinion, my way with horses is the absolute simplest. It always orients itself to the centre, to the wholeness of the inner and outer being.

The third phase: in these photos taken about three years later, Junque demonstrates the most beautiful carriage and magnificent elevation and collection. The horse has been consistently worked from back to front. The horseperson, by his own example, shows the horse through which ways of moving he can better strengthen and balance himself. Carriage, elevation, and collection are consequences of suppleness, strengthening, and of active hindquarters. At no time is the horse constrained or trapped by reins and lines. This example demonstrates that the outer result is a significant consequence of inner values. Inner content reveals itself in the outer world.

Is it Always a Piece of Cake?
Truth and Conflict

The pictures in this sequence surely belong among the most exciting of photos. During filming in the wilds of the Pyrenees, Janosch resisted when we came to a dry creek bed. Unsaddled and unbridled, the horse could now do whatever he wished. Only the inner authority and power on my part, along with the signals of my body language, can restrain the horse on the spot and eventually persuade him to walk through the creek bed. What is important to me at this point is the fact that even conflicts in precarious moments bring harmony if they are handled in a certain way. External posture and signals are one part of this correct handling, radiating power and presence are the other. Please note again, from one photo to the next, the person's calm firmness as he, with no other aids at his disposal, makes his dominance in this situation understood by the horse.

Living and dying, uniting and quarreling, parting and approaching are not all, as I had to learn, necessarily opposites. On these pages you see pictures that show me 'quarreling' with my horse, Janosch. During filming, I wanted to ride the horse through a dry creek bed, in order to demonstrate certain things there. I am sitting on the horse without saddle, bridle or reins. Now truth shows itself in the middle of this quarrel. There is nothing with which I could hold the horse at that moment and he is very well aware of his power. You can see here, in what I consider a unique document, how the horse leaps over the little creek bed in order to consistently resist me. Bent forward with my thighs on the horse, all that is left to me to control him is my body language. What is it that keeps an unsaddled, unbridled horse of this calibre, out in the freedom of a wide Spanish plain, in place — wildly and unhappily wringing his tail? It is most probably our mutual 'argument protocol'. Naturally I quarrel with my horses, with the people who are dear to me, with life, and with the earth, even if I avoid quarreling with the heavens whenever possible. Many

people quarrel with each other with the underlying belief that they can always separate, always end things. I try to quarrel in such a way that my co-quarreler and I can come together again in total harmony as quickly as possible.

My belief is that everything that exists has its own legitimacy. I do not want to miss a single one of my many combative and instinctive aspects, but I am also happy about every time I have transformed these combative and impulsive aspects into creative activity. Smothered desires are murdered power.

At the end of my little quarrel with Janosch, that we have mutually conducted using only the mildest means, there stands a quiet, self-subduing horse. I remained composed, quiet and tender, but nevertheless very definite. Janosch knew very well that he could run away with me to wherever he wanted but, in the end, he realized once again that, in overcoming, there is to be found new power and new trust in himself and in life. Two gentlemen have quarreled and both have won. Let us take that with us on the path that lies ahead.

From First Encounter to Friend for Life: what Awaits You in this Book?

Using the book *Dancing with Horses* as a foundation, I will convey to you the art of truly recognizing horses so that you can then encounter them directly in complete trust. I have been doing this professionally for fifteen years (perhaps I am more like a 'professional child' who begins every day like a young boy on Christmas morning). I have encountered thousands of horses and their owners in my clinics, and so much goodwill, so many good intentions, that it was very difficult for me to understand why the fruits of that were often so shattering. Today I know that goodwill and good intentions are just enough to begin the journey, but, on their own, are not nearly enough to arrive at the destination. For that, pluck, clarity, perseverance, and the ability to differentiate and discriminate are required. In addition, you need the drive to continue asking questions until the answers are truly gratifying and bring true happiness, no matter how often you might founder, because success comes down to being good at finding questions, not at finding answers. He who does not continually question, dies without hope long before his actual physical death. And he who is unrelenting and good at finding and formulating questions, finally realizes that the answers are his life itself – the fulfilled days of his existence.

Weeping, not fighting

To make this successful journey requires a childlike and steadfast faith in the goodness and validity of this world and a steadfast will to stand out, to be unique, while also being reserved and mild. The devil loves nothing more than the loud 'speechless' masses.

When someone with these qualities runs into that symbol of all symbols, the horse,

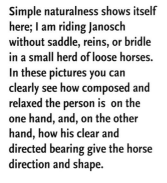

Simple naturalness shows itself here; I am riding Janosch without saddle, reins, or bridle in a small herd of loose horses. In these pictures you can clearly see how composed and relaxed the person is on the one hand, and, on the other hand, how his clear and directed bearing give the horse direction and shape.

the unicorn, the Pegasus, the ferryman and guide of all souls, then he needs only to close his hand to grasp the truth. Horses are among us so that that can occur.

As I see it, therefore, being with horses is a 'conscious forgetting'. There are questions upon questions, there is curiosity and the all-encompassing drive to understand, to see, to perceive, to feel, to discover and to know. But in the encounter with one horse, none of that exists anymore. There is only unconscious consciousness and the forgetting of everything irrelevant. Space expands into the boundless and time flows into insignificance. Then, finally, Campeon 13 can simply weep, rather than fighting all the time, and in this weeping lies deep healing.

Similarly, Phaeton, the fearsome Breton stallion giant can then finally do what he actually wants to do, namely, follow along like a good-natured friend. To follow that person who finally came to the point of forgetting about questioning in order to simply live the answers, those great gifts of heaven.

Is this book an instruction manual?

By working in this way, togetherness with horses is brought back to its intrinsic naturalness. It is relaxed play that wraps itself around the earnestness of existence. I would like to encourage this and I would like to present my questions and the answers that life revealed to me. This book seeks to be an example, and perhaps also a paradigm, but not an instruction manual.

Here you see Janosch and me in relaxed play. The distinction between work and 'horsing around' is lifted. The horse is repeatedly sent out on a wide arc and then brought back to me. It is important at this point to strive for normality and uncomplicated simplicity.

My Gateway into this World: a Beginner on the Run

Too many go through this world and seek the great, the fantastic, and even the ultimate good fortune without noticing that they continually trample on the traces of it. All that they seek basically lies right in front of them, within reach. In the most minute detail lies the miracle, in every moment is the eternity of creation. Everything is already at hand and in effect. With everything in their power, the horses want to nudge us towards these truths, which are so simple, yet so far removed from the human world.

It was not long after the time that I had wandered throughout the Spanish Pyrenees. Shortly after Franco's death, that land was still raw and relatively untouched; something horrible always has something good in its wake. Wide expanses of the land were completely uninhabited, and the inhabited parts were mostly still under the fragile, delicate veils of that time, leaving the land barely enough power to assert itself. In the streets of Pamplona, the true nature of Spain (so ably described by Hemingway) could still be sensed. The north, a green paradise, still resisted everything oppressive, everything that sought to impose measure on the immeasurable. Nature and mankind seemed to have preserved a remnant of uniqueness and a pure, deep-rooted pride that allowed me to forget my own ancestry. Driven by a vague yet powerful longing to let the invisible, the tender, the mysterious become visible in myself as in every person, I continued the quest which actually began in my earliest childhood. I

searched for that freshness, that dew which in the very early morning lets the hundreds of finely spun spider webs glow so clearly in the still low-lying, mild sun. You dared not disturb them then when they stood out from their surroundings so bright and sparkling but later, in the routine of the day, the magic had vanished, and you tore through the webs without even noticing them.

The old woman

I was always aware of this mystery, a way of being that, like the magic of the morning, was present even though the 'fresh dew' of this way of being did not let itself be seen, could not let itself be carried over into the routine of life. I, therefore, left that which I did not like anyway, in order to seek that which does not appear to be available in this world, and so, one day, I entered the oddly scented, dimly lit rooms of a woman who some sought to know their future. I was ashamed of myself; uncertain and silent I sat myself down on a chair. The woman looked at me for a long time, with an expression as incredulous as it was friendly. A smile lurked in her expression, as though she wanted to conceal it from me. Finally, she began to laugh and, after a while, she said, 'But you are a horse – you are two-thirds horse'. At the time I had not had any contact with horses; that came about three or four years later, when I was twenty-nine years old.

There was not much I could make of that statement, or of some of the other things the woman told me. In fact, none of it made much sense, but she confirmed my path, and just said that I would soon see.

Everything is already there!

I wrote my first book when I had only been with horses for two to three years. That was one of the main points of criticism, particularly in my homeland; how could a beginner trust himself to write such a book? Today, that is forgotten, but I do not think it should be forgotten. A book has been, and still is being, read around the world, and thousands of people are trying to follow its message and methods — trying to teach themselves according to something that an upstart beginner has written. And they are successful doing that.

What I had tried, and am still trying, to do, is describe that magic by which you must be seized when you do not start the day with stress and plans, but rather with that childlike outlook that allows you to see the dew drops on the otherwise invisible strands of the impossibly fragile webs. I do not need to weave the webs; I do not need to conceive them, they are already there. If you wait for the right time and take yourself to the right place, then, without fail, the magic provides eternal newness, that which is forever untouched, even in the hidden rooms of no-longer-conscious perception.

In this book I describe much that is new from this mysterious world. This book too, like the first one, was completed in barely two months. And with the totally new system of describing the character groups of all the horses in this world, I have once again found something, not made something. Again, I stood in awe of the miracle of that reality which the people around me just hurriedly crossed over and disturbed. I merely posed a number of questions and would not let go of them until the dew of the night laid itself silently but very tangibly upon the otherwise invisible answers in order to let them shine in the light of the ever new day.

Yesterday's paths

Since that afternoon with the wise woman, twenty years have passed, and not so long ago I drove once more on the roads through the Pyrenees, through the north of Spain, through the land that had been my home. Today it is praised for the exemplary fulfillment of one of the standards of the European Union. This standard stipulates that each member nation has a maximum of six percent of its population employed in agricultural pursuits. Well, if that is praiseworthy, then Spain should be praised. But, on the gigantic buildings that now line more than a thousand kilometres of the once so-green coast, I can find no more sparkle, even in the early mornings.

With the change from the second to the third millennium, perhaps I was allowed to become an eyewitness to that gradually fading trace of an irreversible transformation that would prove that truth exists. And that is perhaps the strangest of the effects of my work, because I have never wanted proof of truth. I always believed very steadfastly in its existence. Nevertheless I collided with great force with those beings that carry the proof within themselves, and today I can state with certainty and authority, 'Give me a horse and I will lead before your eyes the proof that God exists.'

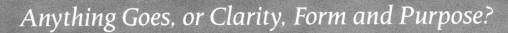

Anything Goes, or Clarity, Form and Purpose?

From Chaos Into Harmony

This book aims to describe and fathom the depths of the nature of horses, and to describe it so densely and practically that the secret of the horses' nature is revealed to anyone who truly asks. Anyone can then find his way from the first encounter to friend for life. But what exactly should one seek? In any event, answers to still-open questions can only be found in the daily practice and lead to fulfillment when we are sure of where we stand now; that is the starting point for our new journey. As we will see, it is a journey from chaos into harmony, because the time is ripe for a further giant step.

This is a very typical situation with a stallion after some minutes of our first meeting. The strength, respect, beginnings of trust, and unconditional focus on what is happening in the moment, hold man, horse, and space together. Body and spirit must find a solid standpoint from which to allow strength, integrity, and harmony to be brought out of the present moment. How should a person experience and perceive himself in order to take himself to a different quality of life? I will elaborate on that shortly.

At this point I am trying to bring to your attention the fact that both chaos and harmony are established at the beginning of the relationship between person and horse. That fact is not actually part of the consciousness of many people. The following three photo sequences show some everyday situations. In these particular cases, everything turned out well. However, in addition to the risk of accidents, the beginnings of great misunderstandings between human and horse, and possibly mental and physical injury, are established in these everyday situations. For that reason, in all my clinics, and above all at my school, I place the very highest importance and value on the good beginnings of relationships.

In the first picture sequence we see a rider briskly shoved aside by her horse as she is attempting to saddle him. A horse should allow himself to be groomed and saddled without being tied up. The behaviour shown in the photos indicates an extraordinarily bad relationship between horse and human. With amazingly little effort, such behaviour can be easily avoided. Important: any further efforts founded on behaviour like that illustrated, are absolutely in vain. First, a trusting relationship between horse and human must be established, which makes such situations impossible.

Let Us Continue Clearly and Honestly – the Horse is a Chaos Machine

Before we come to grips with the details of my new 'horse recognition system', the first encounter, and the question of how I truly keep my horse as my friend, I would like to lay a pair of large foundation stones in the form of two rules. A single wall of our building can be quickly improved and repaired, but a wobbly foundation is a danger to the entire structure, so let us begin prudently.

Horses could confidently bear the name 'chaos machines' because they certainly bring a high degree of endangerment, frustration, and chaos. In contrast, posed horses in glossy photographs portray an image that people yearn for; they hint of freedom, happiness, and harmony. This broad spectrum of extremes within horses is not recognized these days and thus not taken into account. It is certainly not beneficial and can lead to many problems. In order to examine and solve these problems, we need to go to their roots.

To begin, I want to establish the first simple rule on this topic.

Rule 1

Being with horses means summoning the courage to endure chaos, and finding the power and the wisdom to overcome chaos, over and over again.

As a horseman, I can only demonstrate uncommon results. These give me the right to teach. But, if the results are uncommon, and the teaching is uncommon, then the individual steps that lead to these results are also uncommon.

I would like you to reach the stated objective and, for this reason, I will confide another thoroughly unknown horse truth: not everyone is meant to be with horses.

Many people are afraid of horses – boys

and men above all. In this regard the clichés about the strong man, the courageous protector, often break down. Cows, for example, are also large animals, yet the fear of horses, unfounded as it may be, is for many much greater than that induced by bovines. This does not arise by chance. In ancient cultures, it was often the case that only certain high-ranking individuals were permitted to ride and handle horses. This was because it was known that a high degree of self-knowledge is necessary in order to be with a horse in such a way that the horse's inner nature is not damaged. Today this idea seems almost absurd, yet if it is given just a little thought, then the truth of this old precept will reveal itself to

anyone. At this point I would like to give you the second rule.

Rule 2

He who is not conscious of the fact that in all eras and in all cultures the horse stood, and stands, for chaos and raw instinct (the devil has a horse's hoof), will find himself in a burning house only to be amazed that it can sometimes be very dangerous, and that he might in fact burn up — both internally and externally.

And so, fear of the horse is a deep-seated, primal foreboding. For example, even the most peaceable people frequently become scolding, and even striking, brutes in a

Here the problem is haltering and bridling a horse. It is hard for anyone to conceive just how deeply negative is the impression made on horses by the human behaviour illustrated here. Everything that might possibly have been achieved in other areas would most certainly be disrupted within seconds by such situations. We have to learn to deal with this in a fundamentally different way, to learn to conduct ourselves in a manner that would never allow a situation like this one to arise. But that requires a totally different, totally new inner attitude.

In these pictures we see the grey gelding nearly run over his owner in order to get to the paddock as quickly as possible. Unfortunately, in my professional practice such chaotic and dangerous situations continually confront me. What is always lacking in these cases is a basic understanding of how to interact with such challenging and powerful beings as horses. In my work with horses, I do not directly address these symptoms. The first encounter is all about establishing the relationship so firmly that all eventualities are bound into the state of trust.

why does this personal weakness become so quickly and clearly visible solely through interaction with horses? Or, expressed another way, why do horses have the ability to magnify our character traits?

A guide out of chaos

On the following pages I would like to familiarize you with an important part of the horse's soul while we discuss something of the true nature of chaos and harmony. If you bring this knowledge into the relationship with horses from the very

1. Klaudia's stallion stormed out of his box at every opportunity. This problematic behaviour carried over into leading and riding, bringing with it many undesirable characteristics. The sequence pictured here shows how it is possible to, in minutes, build a relationship with a horse that provides connection and security, and thus nips in the bud any misbehaviour on the part of the horse.

2. Long before the actual work with horses, the students in my school learn things that at first seem meaningless. However, the results that arise from our preparatory work, give evidence of great harmony, and prove the value of these 'unlikely' steps.

3. Tranquility and time are the first requirements. Here the person is clear, composed, and calm. Everything that emanates from him is as powerful as it is gentle and sensitive.

4. This is the only correct way to hold a horse in a problematical situation.

beginning then you will start from a completely different point.

So, what is it that horses teach us? What can they do that hardly any other beings in the world can do as well? It is the recognition of chaos and harmony and the path from one to the other. Now, chaos in interaction with horses is anything but beautiful, but it is not necessarily extremely oppressive. Chaos in life, however, can be dangerous, suffocating and deadly. The horse is, so to speak, a classroom for us, the 'practice session' so that we can recognize the nature of chaos and harmony and apply

stable or on the backs of their horses, and do what they would never do with a cat or a dog. They do things that they could otherwise never reconcile with their sense of dignity and understanding of humanity. They recognize that fact, and perhaps even resolve never to do something like that again, only to behave in exactly the same way on the next occasion or the one after that. In the end, the reason behind this is most certainly a personal weakness. But,

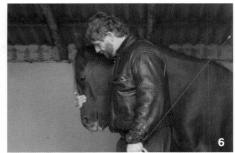

what we have learned to life. This is the path from rider to knighthood.

Why is it the horse in particular that has this task? Why do we feel so drawn to the horse, despite all the difficulties that arise? What exactly is harmony from the horse's point of view? How can we create, and how can we apply, that in our lives?

Combined with the inner power of the person, this has a harmonizing and powerful effect. Only after some minutes do I open the box.

5 and 6. In the meantime the horse appears to be very much calmer. The person's body, the whip and the lead line create a clear boundary for the horse. The right hand is laid purposefully on the chest of the horse and signals him to step backwards. To reinforce this signal, the whip vibrating in the hand can be used. The horse is kept in the box, as he has been up to now, by the still closed stable door.

7. Now the person has become an insurmountable barrier for the horse. Light signals keep the horse in place. The most important thing, though, is that the horse builds up a fundamental trust in the inner power and fairness of the handler. Then it will never come to a fight or a dangerous situation.

8. Here, the horse that previously always shot out of the box as soon as the door was opened, has learned to stay in the box with the door open, even when the person steps several metres away. In only a few minutes, peace and harmony have replaced chaos and danger.

9 and 10. Only now can the horse be carefully taken out of the box. He is very relaxed and carries his head quietly and low. Even leading is no longer a battle. Of his own volition, the stallion maintains a natural distance between himself and the person.

Dear Mr. Hempfling,

Given the current state of my life, I see no other possibility but to separate myself from my dog, Amanda. Is one of your friends, or, preferably, are you, looking for a dog? I hope that you will not find my request a burden because, in turning to you, I am restricting the circle of people to those who act exclusively in a dog-oriented way. My Amanda has had to endure my rage, my scorn, and my boundless self-pity long enough.

With best wishes,

Bettina

My first book, *Dancing with Horses*, is read all round the world, and consequently we receive letters, comments, and inquiries from everywhere. From time to time I take the above letter to my clinics to read aloud. Ostensibly, a young girl is trying to get rid of her dog because she is not treating it well. This is a strange letter, is it not? Somehow, something seems not quite right. Why in the world must this poor dog feel only the rage, scorn, and boundless self-pity of this girl? I am sure you already suspect the truth behind the letter, which is that I have merely changed the word 'horse' to the word 'dog'. But what is inconceivable, and what makes this letter take on a shocking meaning, is that now you immediately understand what is going on. In fact, it seems perfectly understandable that a young girl wants to get rid of her horse so that it will no longer be subjected to rage, scorn, and self-pity every day. What in the world is happening in the relationship between human and horse?

Significant truths in a short letter

A girl seemingly wants nothing more than to have a horse of her own, but then wants to give her up and place her in good hands, that are apparently better for the horse than her own.

As simple and childlike as this letter comes across, there is so much truth in those few lines, and, at the beginning of our new journey into the world of truth between human and horse, it is worthwhile taking a closer look at this letter, to understand it on a deeper level. Because this letter is anything but unique – quite the contrary in fact – it transmits a message which either appears openly, as it does here, or hides within the most varied phraseology. What important information can be taken from it?

1. The girl loves this horse named Amanda.
2. This girl wants only the best for the horse, under any circumstances, even to the point that she would rather give up her beloved animal than keep Amanda in her, oppressive for the horse, presence any longer.
3. Bettina knows her own weaknesses very precisely. Never mind for the moment whether or not these are in fact as aggravating as she thinks. The fact is that Bettina is very critical of herself.
4. Bettina also knows, or senses, that her behaviour has negative consequences for the horse. She perceives that her horse is suffering.
5. She has tried everything to bring her behaviour towards the horse under control in order to make a different life for her. Such a cry for help usually comes only at the end of a long, tortuous evolution.
6. Bettina also recognizes that her behaviour is symptomatic and is connected to a particular state of life. That is a very deep insight.

7. Apparently, Bettina is not in a position to alter her behaviour in the near future, or the state of her life.

It is remarkable that, in connection with a horse, this all seems very familiar to us – we are no longer faced with an unfamiliar event as we were when the word 'dog' was substituted. Here we are faced with a known and comprehensible reality.

It is also very significant that Bettina knows about herself and her situation. She also knows about her horse in this situation. She knows that it cannot go on, that something must happen. But she does not know what or how!

It all comes down to the path

The people who come to me looking for advice, whether from my books or in person, are those who, like Bettina, are very aware of their situations, or at least have an inkling, and who want the 'other' but do not know how they can achieve it. The search is not, therefore, about fundamentally new insights, but rather about the path, where it begins and precisely how it evolves. So many know of the journey, have ideas of the goal, but neither know where to begin nor in which direction to proceed.

They are driven hither and yon by vague notions, hopes, dreams, and a precise or diffuse vision of a way of being, with or without their horses, that is formed and guided by a depth and integrity different from that which is considered to be the norm. And with that we come to another very important message from Bettina's letter. She makes clear, between the lines and in the lines themselves, that, one way or another, her horse too has something to do with her life's situation. Apparently there are two meaningful components.

1. Unlike what would be the case with a dog or a cat, for example, the horse suffers very directly and visibly in the current situation. The horse is a bearer of suffering, a whipping boy, even a lightening rod, despite the fact that Bettina makes every effort to spare Amanda from all of that, as well as from herself. Amanda seems to draw out Bettina's rage, her scorn, her boundless self-pity just as a lightening rod draws the lightening. In other words, a horse, like virtually no other creature, lets our negative aspects become apparent, and then suffers to a high degree himself because of them.

2. Bettina apparently believes that her life in the company of her horse cannot change, or could only change very slowly. She also very consciously wants to take the step described in the letter, in order to attain for herself, above all without the horse, a different clarity. It seems that with her horse certain life circumstances have become so entrenched that they are no longer readily altered.

Being with a horse is something fundamentally different from being with animals that do not also create images within us similar to those of the horse, like the eagle, the dolphin and the elephant do. As with horses, there also seems to be something very special about these animals.

Why the Horses Follow Me

The photos on these pages demonstrate harmony. There is a beautiful interplay between human and horse, there is trust and there is similarity in the movements of both. You have the feeling that it is simply right. What you see here nearly always occurs after just a few minutes. More and more often it happens before I have done anything with the horses, before they have been moved or touched in any way. I will come back to that later. The important thing is that not only do the horses follow me, but that they also do it in a very calm and devoted manner; this can be seen in all the pictures. Why do the horses follow me and why should, and will, they follow you? The answer to this question will surprise you.

In addition to the horse's peace and calmness, these aerial-view photos show something else. The horse's head is always lowered, even in the turns. Man and horse find themselves nearly perfectly on a line and the amazing thing is that the horse does not seem to need even a second to react. It is as though both are following a previously established path. The person does not appear to be searching for or thinking over his next move, and neither does the horse. That is exactly what I experience when I lead horses. In these pictures it sometimes even seems as though the horse determines the way and I just happen to be walking a step in front of him. In most of the photos you can clearly see that I, too, have my head lowered. Nevertheless, the total expression of my body is clear and definite. If you contemplate the expression of the horse and then the expression of my face and body, however, does it not seem to you that you really do not see a difference? Is not my expression on the whole very similar to that of the horse?

A path without consequences, consequences without a path?

If we believe our forbears, then life is a series of events, all of which are connected with each other — all of them! Today this simple perception has almost totally disappeared from the consciousness of humanity. If the horses follow me, if harmony visibly results after a short time during those occasions, then, according to the ancestors, this is no more and no less than the consequence of all the events of my life before this. If the horses follow you, it is likewise the consequence of your life's events.

I, for example, was on my own at a very young age, and because of that my childhood had a different, larger meaning than is usually the case with most people. The primal trust that I developed during my childhood let me discover very early on this interconnection of which our forbears speak.

To this day I have been able to preserve much of my childhood by, for example, retaining a real consciousness that every consequence, every manifestation of life is always the inevitable result of whatever comprised the path to that point. That is form, structure, and interconnectedness as opposed to 'anything goes', falling apart, and the belief that individual occurrences, even tragic ones, happen by coincidence like the defects of a machine.

To a modern person his destiny is like a plaything of arbitrariness. To my mind, that is a shocking idea. I do not live that way and I never want to live that way, because, in the end, fear greets every new day: at the moment of awakening there is already an undefined anxiety rather than a childlike joyful anticipation of new life and surprises. With that joyful anticipation, fear has no point of origin, no destination, and no hope of taking root.

Horses smell and sense that fear and shy away from it because they want to be led by someone who is self-aware and on a path that will give both person and horse direction and proportion, and, therefore,

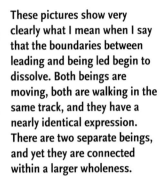

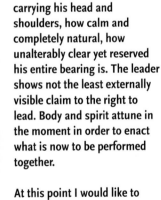

These pictures show very clearly what I mean when I say that the boundaries between leading and being led begin to dissolve. Both beings are moving, both are walking in the same track, and they have a nearly identical expression. There are two separate beings, and yet they are connected within a larger wholeness.

In conclusion, please take the time to study the relaxed manner in which the person is carrying his head and shoulders, how calm and completely natural, how unalterably clear yet reserved his entire bearing is. The leader shows not the least externally visible claim to the right to lead. Body and spirit attune in the moment in order to enact what is now to be performed together.

At this point I would like to refer once more to the individual leading positions and body postures in this sequence of photos, which are easy to learn and imitate. The individual leading positions are described in detail in my book *Dancing with Horses*.

form and awareness of the future.

Thus, if the horses follow me, it is the consequence of a path. It is neither coincidence, nor is it an occurrence that stands alone in and of itself. If it is seen that way, then only the tricks, the shortcuts, are being looked for and those will not be found here with me.

Abel and the sheep

I will now take a giant step back, not quite to the time of Adam and Eve, but almost. The biblical image of the first shepherd, Abel, will, surprisingly enough, help us here. Abel stands as an unusual contrast to his brother, Cain, who ultimately slays him. It is possible to interpret the biblical images in a natural sense, which is very different from today's usual interpretation. Thus, following this line of interpretation, Abel is a shepherd in the original sense; and for shepherds, the question of who actually leads is posed. Does the grass pull the sheep? Do the sheep flock to the grass? Does the grass lure the shepherd so that he then leads the sheep to it?

To this day the concept of the shepherd has a calming effect on people because it is an ancient primal image of life. It therefore occurs right at the beginning of the Old Testament, because the life of the ancient shepherds is the result of a number of events that, together, dissolve the distinction between leading and being led. Who leads who is neither important nor discernible. What is important is life and survival, and, at the same time, form, content and harmony. Where the shepherd was with his sheep, the grass grows greener and juicier than before. And the sheep nourish the shepherd and his people. In the flight of the starlings, no one knows who actually leads whom, and yet the artful choreography is there to see. Heaven, earth,

grass, sheep, and shepherd become one event that can only be explained and understood in its interconnectedness and in its entirety.

We will shortly discuss further why Cain, the planner, the earth shaper and boundary builder, in the end slew his brother.

Does the horse walk behind me or do I walk ahead of the horse?

This is the simple question. What would you make of the following very unusual thought. What if I do not bring the horse onto my path and lead him, but, rather, I simply put myself on the horse's path and walk two metres ahead of him? Am I leading the horse? Or, am I simply walking his path a few steps in front of him?

Again and again during my encounters with unfamiliar horses, I let them follow my hand as though they are being hypnotized. The pictures show that. But what if, in fact, I am actually following the head of the horse, only I am a second in advance of the horse's movement? That seems totally absurd, but that is, in a specific, exaggerated way, exactly what happens. I put myself in a world at one with the horses, as the shepherd is at one with the sheep. In my case there is a comparable interplay: leading and being led blend into a shared experience. I lead the horse, the horse leads me, and we are both led in that place and time. Only in that way can what seems to be impossible occur. We are simply on a shared path. We each reveal ourselves.

What is chaos?

Cain was the first agent of chaos in the Bible, and his path begins and ends with a murder. Why is he an agent of chaos? Because he disrupts the interplay of the powers for the sake of his own ideas. He wants to plan, to change, to build walls around his estate and create his own measure. Everything which does not serve that purpose is destroyed – even something as close to him as his own brother.

When I am with horses, all planning, every elevation of my self-assertion simply ceases, because if harmony is to exist between us it can only occur if I give myself over to this greater primal rhythm and lead in the moment of being led, although the boundaries between them dissolve. Chaos, consequently, is nothing more than the arrogance of man made visible.

Without doubt, the person seems to make the horse follow with his head even the smallest of his movements, as if bewitched. But now, look at what is going on completely the other way around. Imagine that the person was trying to very quickly move his body as the horse's head was signaling him to do. Could that not also be read from these pictures? And that is one of the secrets of my way of being with horses, because, basically, the one happens at the same time as the other.

Is it all a Question of Power?

I have compared my way of being with horses to the original life of a shepherd. He leads and assumes responsibility without relying on his own potential strength.

Abel was the first original shepherd in the canon of images in the Bible. Cain powerfully changed his piece of the earth, and he saw himself as having developed so much power that he even believed he could decide about the life or death of his brother. If you continue to follow the biblical images it becomes clear to the alert observer that Abel and Cain are, in fact, one person. The murder plays itself out within a single individual and it is symbolic of so many murders that occur within all of us.

I want to stay with this ancient image one more moment, because in my association with horses I feel very at home with this image in particular. No matter how the individual relates to this primal image, it seems to me to be very helpful in making this subject matter, which is so difficult to put into words, a bit more comprehensible.

The cycle begins

Before the murder, both brothers bring a sacrifice to the heavens. But only Abel's sacrifice is graciously accepted. Why is that? Abel, so it is said, sacrificed the best part of the sheep: the fat. In all ancient sources, fat is the symbol for the material world. In our time the symbolic images of Beuys* and his butter mountains come to mind.

Abel offers as a sacrifice the matter, or substance, and what is left over is the spirit, or soul. Cain however sacrifices those parts of the fruits that come from the middle of the earth. The earth, too, is a symbol of the material, but the seed represents the spirit.

That is what Cain sacrifices. Cain renounces the spirit, he renounces the inner power that would connect him with that primal event that we have been talking about all this time. But God does not want that. The sacrifice that pleases Him is one of matter so that the spirit can rise. After the sacrifice, Abel symbolizes spirit and Cain is symbolic of matter. However, the spirit cannot exist without the body. Therefore Abel goes to his brother and trespasses on his land. Cain then merely repeats his earlier deed and again slays the spirit, his own spirit and a cycle begins. The cycle of chaos is an unconscious act of the human being, because, whenever he can, he puts his conception of the world ahead of the integral way of being which can only exist in interconnectedness with all the qualities and aspects of creation.

The two forms of power

This image, therefore, puts human generated and managed power and diminished, purely materialistic thinking on one level, just as connected, harmonious existence, within the laws of creation, is on a level with the spirit or soul. And this brings us to the ancient symbol of the horse.

The horse symbolizes these two types of existence, as well as the two forms of power. Both reside in the horse, and both ways of being are possible with horses. And, if one listens to the ancient sages, then this is true, at least in our culture, only of the horse. Only a human being who rides can be depicted as either one or the other, as either a mere rider, or as a knight. If a person who rides is not a knight, then he is just a rider. This seeming banality is important and

* Joseph Beuys (German, 1921-1986) was called one of the most influential of postmodern artists. He was shot down over the Crimea during World War II, and found by Tatar nomads who saved his life by rubbing his body with animal fat and wrapping him in felt. These materials later featured prominently in his work.

very meaningful because, if we sincerely follow the directives of our forbears then this literally means: the mere rider is on the path of external power, and therefore on the path of disruption of his soul!

For that reason, all the old writings warn against devoting yourself to horses without being tested first. According to the Bible it was strongly forbidden for the Israelites, the shepherds, to be with horses. King Solomon was the first to bestride a horse, because he was a king of wisdom.

Only when a person possesses spirit and soul, in other words, true wisdom, can he be with a horse in such a way that turning and leading are not forced or strained by external forceful aids, but rather can be experienced together as an interplay of creation.

It is purely for that reason that I can be as I am with, for example, the Breton stallion we saw in the pictures on pages 16–17; purely because I renounce every form of external physical power. That is the only reason why I remain uninjured and why even 'destroyed' horses follow me. Like the ancient shepherds, I give myself to a gentle play, to a world of wholeness, to the world in which the horse, too, exists. And, after a few minutes, we begin to move and dance together. That is actually all there is to it. We then walk on the same path, in approximately the same tempo, and together we are part of a greater whole.

Those who build only upon their purely human power will, in the end, only come to undesirable results with horses, even if they are not totally defeated by the problem. But horses like the Breton stallion show us more than clearly the true cause of chaos.

When the abstract becomes concrete

With that Breton stallion, I seem to be more powerful than all the soldiers, but in fact I am completely powerless; I lead him as Abel led the sheep. I would gladly make this clearer for you if I could, but I cannot. It is that 'something' that Bettina seeks, that Bettina lacks, and that Bettina senses exists. How you arrive there, how the first steps should look, how we can recognize every individual horse from certain physical characteristics and thus realize how to proceed in our work, I will discuss in the course of this book. With horses the abstract becomes very concrete and abstract possibilities become very real, as do seemingly mystical dangers. The fact that aeroplanes fly does not mean that primal laws have been overturned.

The true image of rider and horse

Horses, as we have already said, are symbolic of instinct and matter. Man has the choice. He can give precedence to either the material or the soulful-spiritual aspect of his existence. If Cain or, more particularly, a Cain-person, is with a horse, then matter comes to matter. Like two identical poles, they bounce off each other. It never amounts to a true encounter; Bettina described that briefly and succinctly in her letter – suffering and chaos ensue. However, if an Abel-person, a spiritual person, is with a horse, he can direct matter by means of the spirit, by means of the soul. Now the antagonists come together. Now opposites find each other in order to truly meet. The spiritual man directs matter.

Naranjero and Fear

Let us summarize: the horse invokes both unbounded fascination and a subtle, seemingly unfounded fear in mankind. In many, the horse invokes a desire for an inner understanding and communicative connection, but likewise he seems to unleash powers that are as negative as they are hidden.

We are on the trail of the mystery of the horse and his place in the mythologies of the world. If you follow the research of anthropologists, horses effected and advanced the development of mankind to its present form. And surely the horse did that because he mirrors humanity and all its possibilities.

We have spoken about how the horse reflects our character traits, and he conforms to the following typical human pattern.

Never frighten

We all came into this world with a greater or lesser feeling of powerlessness. Parents who are not conscious of this fact plus a rough environment can reinforce this experience until it becomes pathological. The rule among the ancient peoples was, therefore, that children were never to be frightened in any way, or to have their courage carelessly taken away, otherwise, it might never return. A child who feels himself powerless, will naturally develop a number of fears, which, in the world of unaware adults will find nothing to alleviate them but will instead find many things and situations to confirm these fears. Consequently, there is a growing certainty that only with every increasing self-assertion can life be mastered. Only through self-assertion can you take care of yourself, can you give yourself to your

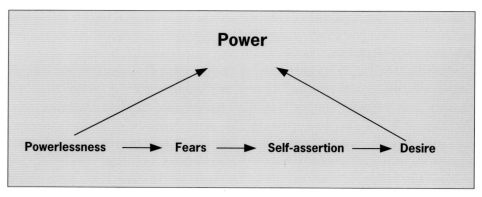

The triangle illustrated here shows the fundamental limitations of the unaware person who functions almost exclusively within these points.

If a horse is forced into this pattern through the manner in which a person interacts with him, then fighting and chaos ensue.

desires and fulfill yourself. Only through accumulation of power can you protect yourself from becoming oppressed. Only in this way, so you believe, can you conquer your fears and dispel powerlessness. So, the desired goal and consequence of all actions is power, no matter how subtly or overtly it expresses itself.

A person only realizes that this does not work when he truly seems to have acquired external power – when he wins the lottery, or acquires a prestigious title – because the wish to become even more powerful does not end there. But, what does come is the fear of losing what has been achieved. No matter how great the supposed power is, the fear and the feelings of lingering powerlessness remain victorious in these unconscious structures.

Do I have power over Naranjero?

On the same day that I dealt with the Breton stallion at the military stud in Barcelona, I also had to deal with Naranjero, the most 'studdish' of all the stallions at the breeding farm. He had severely injured many of the soldiers and attacked several mares so fiercely that they died; however, there was great reluctance to do without his genes. The pictures opposite and below show me with the stallion near a mare heavily in season. With my little finger I jiggle the bay horse into the immediate vicinity of the mare. With a 'normal' stallion that can be a dangerous undertaking but with an animal like this one, it can be almost deadly.

Why did I do this? Because it demonstrates exactly the opposite of the type of external power of which I have been speaking this whole time, the type of power that grows out of powerlessness, fear and desire that begets itself within human beings and fails with certainty when steps of true integrity and conviction are demanded of people. Truth has been captured in these pictures. You can believe whatever you wish about my way of doing things, but there is no getting around these results.

Horses want to, and must, show us the way out of the limited viewpoints that I depicted in the small 'triangle' diagram; that is their assignment. **For harmony lies first in conquering fear itself, then in the necessary devotion to life, and in the renunciation of external power and external desires. In the meantime there is only chaos.**

Naranjero was truly one of the most impressive stallions at the military station, but also the most 'studdish' and therefore the most dangerous. He was brought to me last. They wanted to save the 'hardest nut to crack' until the end. In order to push the whole thing to the very limit, I asked that a mare in season be brought into the yard. Holding a slack lead line with my little finger, I led the highly excited stallion into the immediate vicinity of the mare. Only someone with a death wish, or an idiot, or someone who truly knows what he is about would do such a thing. Why am I so certain about what I am doing? Why does the stallion give me so much power over him? What is it about this power? In this picture sequence, too, it is evident how a gentle dance evolves, even in such a dramatic situation. Please note the subtle body language, how grounded the person is, his clarity, and the always-loving expression displayed toward the threatening, fearsome, horse.

The Snake: the Hidden Aspects of Our Existence

To our forbears the horse was sacred. Most importantly, they knew the two sides of his nature. For them, the horse was an animal encompassed by the symbol of the snake, and the snake brings fulfillment or destruction depending on how it is handled. These Celtic coins clearly convey the likeness of a horse to a snake.

A horse 'entices' a person to exercise power; the urge that exists in every human being to make himself safe through the use of strength, whether overt or hidden, is, so to speak, inflamed or increased. Frequently you also get the impression that riders are truly convinced that horses actually earn the punishment they receive. This explains the very strange transformation of many people as soon as they want to achieve something with a horse.

The horse tests and challenges us and, for whoever is not grounded, there exists the danger of doing and thinking things, developing conceptions and emotions that can only terrify. The mistreatment of horses is an accepted component of modern society.

We want to, and must, direct the horse. If we do not do that, not only is a relationship with him impossible but also potentially extremely dangerous. What leads a relationship astray is the superficiality of the desire to lead and direct. Things that a self-aware person knows how to apply with care through his inner clarity can be enforced with a shocking lack of gentleness by the unaware.

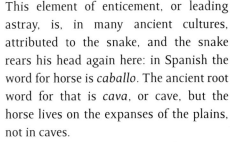

This element of enticement, or leading astray, is, in many ancient cultures, attributed to the snake, and the snake rears his head again here: in Spanish the word for horse is *caballo*. The ancient root word for that is *cava*, or cave, but the horse lives on the expanses of the plains, not in caves.

The inner nature of the animal is concealed in the Spanish word for horse. Often, ancient root words express something that lies concealed within a term. In this case, it is the spirit of the creature of the caves, the snake, the shadowy aspect. The first animal met in the Bible is the snake, with its seductive characteristics, and the ancient representation of the horse in our ancient cultures is also the snake. The Celts usually illustrated the horse with a simple line in a shape reminiscent of a snake. The illustrations here show that clearly. The top line of a collected horse also resembles a snake.

The two tongues of the snake

We find the snake on the staff of Hippocrates, the staff of physicians. (The fact that Hippocrates also carries the word for horse in his name ['hippo' from the Greek word *hippos*] is probably a coincidence.) However, the snake in this case symbolizes both death as well as healing. My observations on this topic end here. Whoever chooses to, can delve more deeply into the unbelievably exciting world of symbols and their inner significance. It was important to me to show in various ways that the horse is always met only in his extremes. It is important to know and assimilate that knowledge before coming

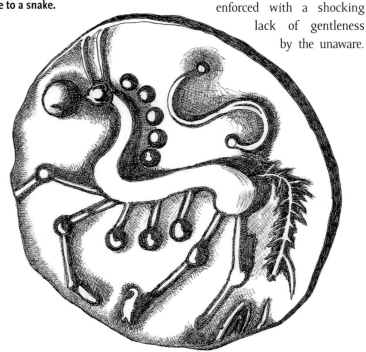

together with horses, because, whoever does not realize that he is not only symbolically with a snake when he stands before a horse, will, sooner or later, get his soul 'bitten'.

Even today life is still the ancient battle of the powers, the battle for predominance of matter or of spirit, and that is why the horse is so 'fashionable' again today, and so prevalent; horses lead us directly to the lost and concealed aspects of our being.

The top lines of the stallions here are shaped like snakes; the more pronounced this shape is, the more magnificent the impression. You may laugh at these mythological and ancient observations, but what if concrete results with horses support these apparently dusty old perceptions?

The Bitter Fruits of Love

It had just stopped raining. The reporter was waiting for us at the entrance to the small pleasure-riding yard, next to a young girl with a curious and expectant look. The reporter had chosen to write about my encounter with the girl's horse. Together we entered the stable, and there I saw a very introverted, disturbed animal tied up. The reporter immediately started to tell me about the problems that Mette was having with her horse but I politely stopped her. 'That is not necessary,' I said, 'everything is written in capital letters on that horse's brow.' I then began to describe and

Here I am at the very beginning of the work with Mette's little Icelandic gelding. Although Mette loves her horse more than anything, he runs away from her whenever he can. Despite Mette's affection, the horse is extremely disturbed and very sceptical about humans. A certain type of love and affection has a very obvious negative effect. What is the significance of that?

summarize the horse, Mette, and their relationship with one another. How that works is something I will describe in great detail in this book.

And so I did that which I always do. I tried to find the original reason why the horse behaves as he does, and why he can behave only as he does and not otherwise. In this case, as in nearly every case, the cause/reason lay in the nature of the person's demeanor and behaviour. It always upset Mette that she always had trouble catching her horse; whenever possible the little gelding tore away from her.

Mette became very quiet and thoughtful. My work began and after several minutes the horse followed me, and finally he also followed Mette. She could touch him and catch him with no problem and the horse followed her over large distances even without a lead rope. As the little horse came ever closer to me and showed his trust in me more and more, Mette could no longer control herself. The tears streamed down her cheeks and, sobbing, she said only, 'but I love him so much, I love him so'.

For a moment, there was silence, which I cut through with several clear and seemingly harsh words. I was trying to make Mette and the observers understand that love alone is not only not enough, but also that love alone is often worse than a purely matter-of-fact but knowledgeable relationship. Love, without clarity, responsibility, and pertinent emotional distance is often like a self-implosion. You 'love' something that is outside yourself, but fundamentally that very often means only yourself, your own needs, your own wishes and longings. Those are the bitter fruits of an isolated, a thoroughly questionable 'love'.

Today Mette has a different relationship with her horse. He no longer runs away when she approaches, he does not shy away from her affection. I would like to use this story as an opportunity to emphasize the three main dangers in connection with 'horse and human in chaos'. If the snake poison predominates, then no matter what omens of 'affection' or 'love' there are, three 'severe bites' lie in wait.

1. **Invisible or visible long-term frustration** This is very simple. The wishful dreams of a person about what it is like to be with horses are almost always far brighter than the reality he is able to bring about. Instead of continuous joy, the person then experiences a constant lack of fulfillment. The dreams are simply never realized. Aside from a few truly intimate moments, the feeling of frustation remains. If this continues for years, it can result in severe negative consequences for the person's psychological condition.

2. **Longstanding tension in anticipation of pain and disaster** Even this is a truly underestimated factor in the horse world. In most areas of life the reasonable person seeks to reduce his potential danger to a minimum. Naturally, something can always happen anyway, but you function in the knowledge that you have taken steps to insure your safety. But in most of my dealings with the riding world I discovered that most people were living with too great a latent risk, and, as a rule, they are aware of that. There is hardly any horse that I meet, with which I would immediately venture out into open country. The risk would be far too great for me because these horses are not usually well enough schooled. But, living a life in constant awareness of incalculable risk and danger, in connection with leisure time, recovery, relaxation, and nature, is a very serious stress factor. Never mind the fact that riders rank very near the top of accident statistics.

3. **Drowning in the feeling of inferiority** This has some relation to the previous point, but in an essential area goes far beyond it. The frustration mentioned above, where that which is striven for is still not actually achieved, even over a period of years, can alone naturally lead to a sense of inferiority. But in an area where leisure time and activity should increase a feeling of self-worth, there are in the riding world, exactly the opposite tendencies. We are interacting with a very special living creature and when this spirit, horse, is not handled and led in an integral and grounded fashion, he punishes us with contempt, and then actually despises us. He ignores us, fights us, laughs inwardly, and becomes sad, distant and actually contemptuous. Over the years, the human, whether he wants to or not, will see himself growing smaller in relation to this creature, even when he seems to dominate through external power and force. Inwardly, he is burning up and only superficial arrogance can give the appearance of a strong personality – one that is in fact inwardly devouring itself.

The horse coin has two large sides. Sadly, the majority of horse people act on the dark side, the side of the snake's poison. Even this, the fifth of my books, seeks to create awareness of this fact and indicate clear paths to bring you to the light side of the coin, so that you can comfortably establish yourself there permanently.

Like an Original Inhabitant of the Ancient World, I Fish, Hunt and Slaughter Sheep

Here you see a strip of the coastline on the south of the Danish island on which I live. Things here seem much as they did hundreds of years ago. We have displaced the original inhabitants in other lands, a deed for which we should feel guilty. On this island, however, we are the original inhabitants and, with my way of life and my actions, I try to let this ancient connection become a conscious one again.

Chaos heads toward darkness, toward death. When the whole is parted, broken into pieces and separated, then life is no longer possible. Horses are the symbol for the path out of chaos into harmony, into true life. Therefore horses are the symbol for healing, for the undivided.

If you want to understand horses and seek their revealing of themselves, then you must necessarily face life as a whole, in all its facets. In this spirit, life with horses radiates as though from a concentrated point to illuminate ever more areas. That is my life and it is only in that context that my works, my books, and my films can be understood. I am a 'writer', 'musician', and 'artist' as well as a 'shepherd', 'fisherman', and 'hunter'. In everything I do, as with the

horses, I try to find the trail of the original sources. We have a sheep and goat herd for wool, milk and meat, and daily fishing with a net also provides our nourishment, as does hunting for ducks, pheasants, rabbits, deer and other wild animals. In doing that, not only are we self-sufficient, but we also try to trace and relive all aspects of the laws of the ancient ones, our forbears. And that brings me to another important point.

Horses are mythology and history. From an anthropological perspective, horses are not to be overlooked. My forefathers lived here: the Celts, the Vikings, the Teutons, the Goths and the Cimbrians. I see myself as an aborigine of this culture. In being with horses, I found another connection to the forbears of our world; the Celtic world, and the world of the Teutons and Vikings, was the world of horses.

I have nothing against the fact that we live in so-called modern times. For me, this is not about a sentimental look into the past, but about an enlightened look ahead. It is easy to see the way when you draw a line between the present standpoint and the past; then, existence in the present moment suddenly has direction. From a platform built on the wisdom and acknowledgement of the ancient ones, and acceptance of the present, you can easily entrust yourself to the future.

This line between the present and the past is borne within the image of the horse. In him, nothing is 'off-limits' and nothing is covered-up. The horse is perhaps the most direct pathway and the most immediate contact point between the poles of our culture. In this sense I think of myself as a European, as a descendant of the world that, like no other, owes its existence and its cultural identity to the horse.

Here you see me on a morning's hunt for the midday meal. Hunting is not just hunting and riding is not just riding. Truth does not stop at the plastic-encased piece of meat at the supermarket. Hunting, fishing, slaughtering sheep – even death and killing must be seen in their greater connection to the whole. As I look at it, being with horses means turning to, and accepting, the origins and effects of everything as a whole.

Fishing is an important part of life here on the island. Our waters are very still. At least the coastal waters still belong to the small boats of the people who live on the coast. Several fellow residents and co-workers now get their sustenance from our direct activities in and with nature, and also our naturally kept sheep and goat herds are an important factor.

On The Path to Knighthood

To conclude this chapter, I list the ten most important qualities of a horseperson and you may be surprised to learn how horses 'define' them. These qualities are certainly not new, but their true backgrounds will seem to be new because they are so ancient that they have long been forgotten. This then is how a horse sees a noble human being and the qualities that distinguish him.

1. Constancy

A horseperson should possess constancy and persistence. But, does that mean a life path that does not change on the outside, one that knows no career lapses and changing, self-correcting sequences of events? The constancy that the horse seeks is that which always does what truly must be done now, even, and perhaps especially, when on the surface it might appear to others to be a sudden leap into the unknown. Thus true constancy is that which recognizes the necessity of the inner voice and follows it faithfully and unwaveringly.

2. Clarity

A horseperson should always strive for clarity. To the horse this means that the person does not care first and foremost about ordering his own plans, his own little front garden, but, rather, is always striving for clarity in recognizing how the external is connected to the internal, the inner qualities. This clarity allows him to act in the spirit of a greater connection.

3. Profundity and Depth

In the deep lies danger because the deep is unknown, sinister, and dark. Those who strive for depth all too easily lose themselves in it. Profundity and depth that are not matched with joy, lightness of being, and humour will quickly end in sorrow, loneliness, and bitterness. The profundity and depth that a horse seeks are also always connected very closely with patience, because patience knows that tomorrow is another day and that fanaticism seldom laughs at itself.

4. Power and Energy

Only when I realized that I first had to reveal all my weaknesses to the horse, and that, above all, the recognition and confession of my own powerlessness entitled me to be allowed to lead by being led, did the horses give me power over them. That is when I first sensed true power and energy.

5. Modesty

To a horse this has nothing to do with weakness, hypocrisy, cramped self-

Here you see me with Junque in the process of stallion training. Although he is in the immediate proximity of a mare in season he is held in place with only a loose rain attached to a simple halter, and so any battle with him would be hopeless from the outset. Inner values allow play, connection and experience to evolve out of danger and apparent lunacy. What, in fact, are the qualities horses demand of us 'on the path to knighthood' and how are these qualities seen by the horses themselves? That last point in particular conceals many surprises.

restraint, or formal politeness, and it certainly does not mean hiding your light under a bushel. Modesty from a horse's perspective means recognizing your abilities, how creation actually works in you, in order to simultaneously comprehend the source of this ability. That source does not lie in me. Life works through me in a certain way, and differently in someone else. So, true modesty is not a superficial, hypocritical external statement, but rather actual humility paired with proud inner presence.

6. Stillness

Today this concept is connected more with death than with life. In a horse's sense, stillness is a way of being that can, with the powers of space and time, realize equanimity, proportion, and timelessness even in the centre of the storms of life, even in the middle of active confrontations. It is neither the routine of a sanatorium nor is it early retirement. It is the spirit, grounded and rooted in itself, that remains steadfast and true to itself long after powerful floods have washed away the peace of others.

7. Courage

To a horse this has nothing to do with foolish derring-do, but rather with overcoming, as illustrated by this example. They stood in the face of the enemy and the young knight said softly to the old one, 'I am so afraid that even my armour is rattling'. For a moment the old one said nothing. Then he replied, 'Do you think that I will go into such a battle with someone at my side who is not afraid?' Again a brief moment passed. Then the old one added, 'But I would also not go into battle with someone who did not know how to overcome his fear. It is only for that reason that you do not hear my armour rattling'.

8. Joy

Joy in a horse's sense is not that feeling of excitement or butterflies in the stomach you get, for example, at parties; it means inner strength and power so that the human being can be calm, serene, full of good humour, and gentle on the outside. Fortunate is he who knows this state!

9. Devotion

From a horse's point of view, true devotion has nothing to do with that self-abnegation that seeks to be good, selfless, and noble. Horses will very quickly get aggressive with people like this and their devotion knows little of love or of good and bad. A horse's devotion is simple, it nourishes as matter-of-factly, as unconditionally, as the earth does. That is how radically the horses see it.

10. Resoluteness

With resoluteness even a thief will bring his misdeed to a successful conclusion, and we are destroying our world with resoluteness. The resoluteness that our horses seek is so different from that sort, because it has as a foundation all the previous nine points. Only when a person sees himself in perspective as a part of creation, and exists without wanting to be good, lives without repressing death, and acts for the sake of acting, not in order to win, then a resoluteness with which the horse can identify will grow in him. Then something enduring can occur – the circle of knighthood closes itself.

Strength and gentleness radiate from both man and horse, yet the strength is an inner one and the gentleness external. Both know their own strengths and weaknesses, victories and defeats. Both respect each other. But, according to which criteria have they found themselves? Is finding, recognizing and knowing a question of coincidence and whim?

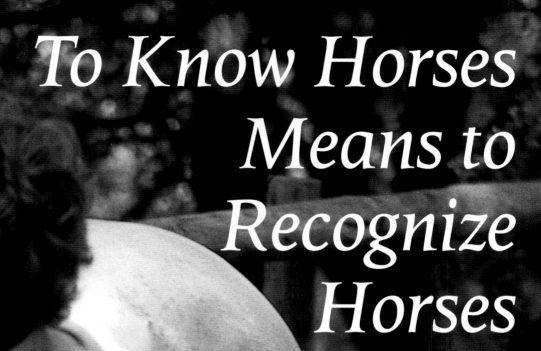

To Know Horses Means to Recognize Horses

From the Outside to the Inside and Back Again

How is it that people live together, and only when they are at the point of separation do they say, 'So that is who you are, I never knew you at all', but what they mean is, 'I never recognized you'. Who actually knows anyone, and who gives careful conscious thought to how they choose their environment, friends, pets etc?

Before I take my first steps with a horse, there is always recognition. During my years of working with people and horses, I have learned that most horsepeople spend their lives marking time because they do not complete even these first steps. But, how do you recognize a horse in just a few seconds? I have long sought for a way to explain and teach this very mysterious skill, and now maybe I have found it.

Get Out of the Vicious Circle: Show Me Your Horse and I Know Who You Are!

Toward what existence, whether human, animal or plant, do we gravitate and are we just drawn to a particular entity in order to avoid confusion? And what influence do we then have on the possible transformation of this entity? These questions are fundamentally important to relationships with people and with animals, even though, as a rule, they are barely considered. In order for us to come closer to the answers to these questions, we must focus on the following.

- What relationship exists between me and that being which I find either attractive or repulsive?
- How is it that similar problems, no matter what kind, seem to repeat themselves, as it were, in various different partnerships, and why is it that we always choose partners and a situation that seem to trigger and magnify these same problems?
- How likely is it that we can be successful in transforming a being, whether human or animal, to suit our conception should that be necessary? How sensible and ethical is such an intention?
- How is it possible to recognize myself and my counterpart, be it human or animal?
- What happens when I do truly recognize my counterpart, and what significant thing does not occur when I do not recognize it?

Here is an example. A man suffers from jealousy; he thinks his partner is continually going behind his back, and again and again he finds other instances in his partner's behaviour that make him jealous. Will this situation change if he has another partner? In all likelihood the answer is no. Is that because the supposed causes for his jealousy are just human nature, or only imagined, or is it because this person always selects partners who actually give him cause for jealousy?

The relationship with a horse is, as a rule, a very meaningful one in the life of a person. A horse demands more time, more space, more care, and more money, because of the way it must be kept, than nearly all other animals. The relationship between person and horse is, therefore, very sensitive, and for that reason it also leads to the kind of reactions I have previously detailed. The relationship with another person is without question the most complex, the deepest and many-

faceted one, but being together with a horse clearly reveals many problem areas that would remain hidden in normal social or private connections. How do we get clarity in these relationships, and how do we break out of this vicious circle that is so familiar to us all, and always seems to pose problems for us, no matter how often we change our social or geographic circumstances? Above all, on what are acquaintanceships, relationships, and partnerships grounded?

Two peas in a pod

The pictures on these pages show horse/human pairs that make a first important connection very clear: our animal, our partner, is apparently selected according to the criterion of similarity. This is not usually obvious to you but it is to everyone else. The horse/human pairs in these photos give the feeling of being very drawn to one another but look what happens when you try to place the individuals into new relationships with another horse/human. Immediately the impression is that somehow the new pairings do not work. In my thousands of encounters with such pairs, one thing has become abundantly clear to me: show me your horse and I know who you are, because this similarity is not merely external. It encompasses, above all, inner qualities, characteristics of spirit; and this

leads us to a very interesting, generally applicable law of nature.

In the illustration there are three points that are very close to one another. In nature, nothing is linear, everything is wave and circle shaped, even the boundaries of our universe and our similarities and differences. That which is very different from me is, therefore, not far away from me

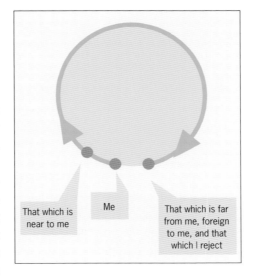

That which is near to me   Me   That which is far from me, foreign to me, and that which I reject

on the other end of a very long line, but it is in fact on the other end of a nearly closing circle! Thus that which is so different from me, which I completely avoid for this very reason, is as close to me as that which is nearly identical to me.

Someone who has always wished for a small dog gets a big dog, and someone who has always wanted a grey horse gets a

According to which criteria does a person choose his counterpart, be it another person or a horse? These pictures show clearly that the phenomenon of similarity apparently plays a very meaningful role in a close human/horse relationship. As we shall see, the choice of our closest intimates is made mainly according to one precept: in the search for our counterpart we are searching, above all, for ourself! Does not the ability to recognize your counterpart, be they human or horse, then take on an entirely different significance?

I am in the Pyrenees with a herd of half-wild horses selecting a horse for the filming of one of my videos. Repeatedly I observed that it was either the horse's great similarity to my own characteristics and behaviour that motivated my selection, or the fact that he was the exact opposite. In the extremes of heat or cold lie the stimulation and the attraction and in the in-between lukewarm, grey, areas lies the avoidance.

black one, and so on. Everyone is familiar with this phenomenon. From that we can establish the first simple rule. **For our intimate circle, we always seek that which is either very much like us or else the complete opposite, because both are actually very close to us! Both are in our 'neighbourhood', and both have something to do with our ultimate original nature.** One way or another, on the search for our fellow being, we are in truth searching for ourselves!

The two pillars of life: development and conflict

The ancient ones say that a person comes into the world as an unfinished being, so that he can, over the course of his life, develop into wholeness. In fact, this does not happen to the same extent in men and women, but we will disregard that here. And so, life is development and inner maturity. If this continued development does not happen then, internally, a person is already dead. But, as discussed, development and maturing only occur through conflict and chaos that must be unravelled and dissolved. Since we are always only seeking ourselves in a counterpart, naturally we are unknowingly

also looking for our possible development potential in the other. And, we also seek in the other those conflicts in us whose resolution makes possible maturity and development. In short: **if we seek ourselves in our counterpart, then we also always seek and find our own conflicts in him! Finding our own conflicts in the other also lets us find the potential for our own maturing and development.**

To return to our example: a jealous person will always find people that confront him with his problem – just so that he may overcome it! But, we have also said, if you believe the wisdom of our forbears, that there is no other creature that so profoundly confronts us with our problems as a horse. We therefore arrive at the following conclusion. **The horse confronts us with our problems as a human being in general, and through our own choosing of a very particular horse, we are then additionally confronted with our problems as an individual. The potential conflicts inherent in being with horses are, therefore, activated, but so, in the same proportion, is the potential for development and maturing.**

The great mistake

In my clinics I show people very clearly that their problems with their horses do not primarily have anything to do with the horses but rather with the people, because with me the horses will, in a very short time, behave very differently from how they do with them.

And now we come to a further important point. When I have the first encounter with a horse, the jumpy horse becomes calmer, the lazy one more industrious, the fearful one braver, etc. That is my job, it is a part of my profession. But, is the horse changed internally? Does the horse truly become braver, more industrious, calmer? No, absolutely not! What actually happens is shown in the following two diagrams.

The hooking-up of two creatures

On the left side of the left-hand diagram we see an example of a horse with all his potential pre-dispositions, his inner emotions, and his, at present, invisible qualities. We see that the horse is internally quite fearful as well as somewhat jumpy, unfocused, reacts with hypersensitivity to being touched, carries within himself a somewhat lesser

this, overplay it or renounce it, or act it out and acknowledge it. However, the fact is that man and horse will hook-up to one another at the point of their most prominent qualities! This is where they most frequently meet each other. Now look at the right-hand diagram: the fear of the man meets that of the horse and it multiplies. Why? So that the man will come to recognize his own fear very clearly. Through the horse, he will be forced to confront his greatest weakness. Since the man, who should provide leadership and set an example, is himself fearful, the horse will now pull out all the stops to present, and perhaps enjoy, the full spectrum of his fear.

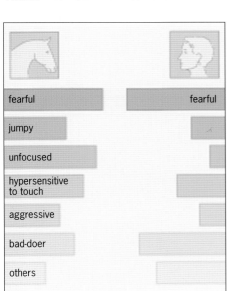

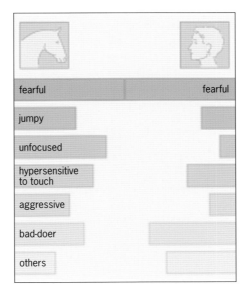

tendency toward aggressiveness and, lastly, is a bad-doer (unthrifty). The foremost quality is, and remains, fear. Now let us look at the right side of that same diagram. Here the owner of that horse is shown with some of his individual qualities. He too has a bit more of one quality and less of another. However, one of the most significant qualities in the fundamental composition of his nature is fear. He may hide or bury

During my clinics such a fearful horse 'changes' very quickly – but how does that happen? I instantaneously recognize fearfulness as the horse's most prominent characteristic. I recognize his nature and his character. I must do this with every horse, and in the next chapter I will describe in detail how that works. I see the horse before me as 'unlocked' as it is in the diagram we just saw. In the first encounter I approach the horse as a chastened being, as a person to whom the horse cannot hook-up with his weaknesses. I will explain how that works step by step in the chapter entitled The First Encounter. The most important thing is that I cannot remove even a millimetre of the horse's fundamental potential for fear! I am not God, none of us is God. I can only lead the horse to himself and take away his nervousness connected to hooking up to a person. I can do nothing more! **It is impossible to change your counterpart! With animals you can have a harmonizing, healing influence, and with people a harmonizing, healing and counseling effect. You cannot do more. Animals hardly change at all, and people change only through self-realization!**

Now it becomes clear how absurd it is to think that you can fundamentally change a horse and bend him to your will. It also becomes clear how important it is to recognize a horse – to immediately perceive all his inner qualities, to read him like an open book.

Reflect on what is being said here and try to extract the entire range of what is valid for you. I, who appear to transform horses in seconds and minutes as has been demonstrated, say that it is not possible to change the fundamental inner nature of an animal. All good animal handlers and trainers agree with me. A person cannot entice something out of a dog, a lion, a tiger

or a horse that is not clearly a predisposition or fundamental characteristic already part of them at birth. With horses, however, people attempt to do this again and again, even to the point of cruelty, and the inevitable breakdown. What is it, therefore, that is in me, what is in my horse? Why do I choose this horse and not that one?

If, at the end of this book, you recognize your horse, then you will have also recognized a good deal more of yourself. That is the only correct way to progress. You will also approach your own limits, and those of your horse and, above all, those you have in common, in a different way, because you will realize that the greatest problems are actually the greatest gifts – namely, challenges to personal maturity and development.

With my system of determining the character of horses I hope that:

- In a matter of seconds and minutes, you will be able to recognize your own horse and all horses you encounter.

- You will be able to perceive the traits of your horse with reference to your own nature.

- You will have at hand the ways and means with whose help you will be able to encounter the qualities of your horse and therefore, indirectly, also your own.

- Most importantly, you will get an overview of how broad the spectrum of possibilities is when you speak of horses and their possible characters.

- You will know as precisely as possible what is going on internally with your horse, so that, with this knowledge, you can achieve a mature and harmonious partnership.

When horses in a meadow, for example, meet each other for the first time they will quickly sort themselves out into small groups and pairs. They will quickly group together according to their similarities in appearance. Even among animals you can recognize the principle: in the search for your counterpart, you above all seek yourself.

- On the whole, you approach even the greatest faults of your horse with calmness, and react with wise, knowing restraint, because the qualities of your horse that you value the least are a bit like a caricature of your own nature.

- On the whole, and on all levels, you become more sensitive in your interaction with horses through recognition, understanding, and comprehension of their natures.

- In the future you will approach choosing a horse very differently and in a more grounded way, and thus avoid unnecessary mistakes for yourself and your future horse.

- You will learn how to support specific horses with particular characteristics and bring them into full bloom.

- You thoroughly understand where the greatest dangers lie with specific individual characters, and that you realize the points that cause certain horses to, as a rule, be misunderstood.

- You learn which person truly suits which horse. I would like you to also realize which horse truly suits you, because you can be confronted with your problems in conscious and unconscious ways. However, if you are clear about how things work overall, then you can interact with your horse completely differently from the very beginning. You do not have to make things unnecessarily difficult.

In its comprehensive inter-connectedness, my system for determining the character of horses encompasses the following:

- Appearance
- Character
- Aspects of health
- Aspects of carriage relating to the fundamental character of the horse
- Behaviour in normal situations
- Behaviour in stressful situations
- Behaviour toward his kind
- Behaviour toward people
- Suitability to the various human character types (which type of person will get along particularly well with which type of horse)
- Exercises and work programmes appropriate for each horse character group
- Association of the individual horse character group to colours, emotions, ways of moving, and even to rhythms, shades of colour, ways of expression, tastes etc.

How much is it possible to change your counterpart, your horse for example? Again and again we are faced with the temptation to 'correct' the nature of our partners, our children, our horses. Over the years I have been able to conclusively determine one thing: a frightened horse will always remain frightened, and a lazy one always lazy. The transformation that you observe in the horses I encounter for the first time has been brought about in a different way. Should you, therefore, place such a high value on the correct selection of a horse?

My Procedure: Recognizing, Knowing, Being

Before a person can say he knows his horse he must first have recognized his horse. That is a fundamentally different thing. Most people live with their horse, and also with friends and partners, and only think they recognize them. In fact, they are mostly following pre-established concepts. 'Learn to truly observe – yourself and your counterpart' is, therefore, one of the challenges of this section.

As a rule, the way things run in my demonstrations and clinics is that I immediately describe in all his particulars the horse that I, along with the guest observers, see before me for the first time. The effect is of someone reading something from a book. In fact, it is possible not only to recognize and describe very finely and deeply the inner state of the horse, but also to perceive directly, in the first moment, something of his relationship with people, with other horses and with his youth, and details of his behaviour, without having done anything at all with the horse. For various reasons, it is important to me to relay this information to the audience as soon as the horse is led in. Among other things, I do that to make clear that what will happen in the coming minutes is not arbitrary, is not a matter of trying things out, and is not a careful testing of the waters, but rather that there is a very clear and distinct message given, which is unequivocally determined and presented by the horse and his nature.

Who truly does recognize their horse?

Now we come to the important question of why it is so important to recognize your horse so precisely. To recognize a horse is something different from knowing him. You can only truly know a horse if you have first recognized his true nature. Unfortunately, that happens far too infrequently. A person who has not recognized his horse can be with the animal for years yet not know him. Sadly, it has been my experience that there are hardly any horsepeople who truly know their horses. How can that be? It is, very simply, just the way things are among people. As a rule we all have images and concepts, wishes and sentimental illusions. We all too easily cover a person we meet with an 'impenetrable paste'. We do not truly see, we do not want to truly see, and recognize who and how the other person really is. We want to transplant our concepts and images into reality and expect people and animals to respond precisely as we have imagined. People, like animals, will resist this, but such circumstances can continue for years – even though they are restrictive and agonizing. In the end, there is, not infrequently, the great silence and the loneliness within a purely external togetherness, or the final break. In between the initial non-recognition and the final break, misunderstanding reigns. Husband and wife, person and horse, student and teacher, parents and children, although they are together, are not with one another.

So many people have experienced how wonderfully horses have changed, and even healed, simply because I emphatically and clearly said what I had seen and recognized in their natures. That alone has a liberating effect.

What does it take to genuinely recognize a horse?

1. **Tying the subject to your own experience**   To recognize another being requires that above all you are clear about your own important fundamental characteristics. How can I recognize another being if I know barely anything about myself, only follow my own concepts, and those of the times that are 'fashionable'. Therefore, it is important that you always try to delve deeper into your own experience. Try to conquer the fear that prevents you gazing into the depths and then try to give your counterpart, be they human or horse, the same chances. That means that you must do the best you can to reveal yourself anew in order to see your counterpart as he is, and to avoid seeing in your counterpart only that which you dearly want to see in him. And that leads us straight to the second point.

2. **Recognition of the counterpart**   Learn to observe! In my clinics I occasionally carry out the following experiment. I ask my guests to close their eyes and picture their partner, their horse, or a good friend, clearly in their mind's eye. The result is often shocking. People who have spent many years with one another are not in a position to really describe each other. They no longer notice or observe, or get beyond their own skin. A friend of mine had been married to his wife for twenty years. In that time he had always had a full beard. He went on holiday alone and shaved off the beard, leaving only a small mustache. As his wife opened the door for him when he arrived home, she looked at him for quite a while, then said, surprised, 'My goodness, you've grown a full mustache'. The story is unfortunately true. In the course of this chapter I will give you only the most important tools you need to be able to recognize horses. Through my comprehensive descriptions, I will try to demonstrate how fine, how precise, an observation can be and what enormous conclusions can be drawn from it. I think you will be amazed.

3. **Bridge and Trust**   When you have mastered the first two important steps, then you will trust yourself. Recognizing a horse occurs in just a few seconds and it is this first impression that is so important! The things that take the time are the practice and the experiences that come before; you have to achieve certainty, acquire knowledge, and break up crusty old structures of thought. In the event, everything happens very quickly. You see a horse and in the same moment you have recognized him in his entire depth. He stands before you like a story, like a palace with many rooms in which you can wander and explore. Without this certainty, without this recognition, being with horses makes absolutely no sense for the person who wants to experience truth.

My System for Recognizing Horse Character Groups: The Principle of the 26 Character Groups

Every horse is an individual, and wants to be recognized entirely for himself, and I was confronted with the challenge of how to set out this tremendous field in such a way that anyone who wants to will find an entrée. The solution was in principle very simple, although it took years to arrive at it: I set myself the task of arranging all the horses of the world into twenty-six specific horse character groups and to naming these. Every horse will be found in one of these character groups. There you can find, for example, the King, the Minister, the Half-born One, the Frog, the Dove, and the Friend.

To ripen, a fruit needs the summer heat, so therefore I hope that with the following presentation, and the illustrations and photos, this broad, wonderful and important, but heretofore, inaccessible field will become familiar to every interested person.

Key points regarding procedure and methodology

1. My methodology

For this documentation of the character groups, I purposely chose not to use as examples any horses that I already knew. Nothing in the following presentation was available to me that is not now available to you as well, namely, the representative photographs. That was the only way I could make certain that no influencing background information could find its way, consciously or unconsciously, into the information. Thus the descriptions are absolutely 'original and virginal', and refer solely to the pictures to which we have common and equal access.

2. Beautiful or ugly, fat or thin

In judging a horse, even in public, I do not bite my tongue, I speak completely frankly. I know that by doing this I have deeply wounded certain horse owners and breeders, but there is no horse that I value or like more or less than another, and that is why I allow myself to describe the horses as I do, without apology. I can only truly recognize an animal if I can freely and honestly describe every trait without letting my perceptions be influenced or prejudiced by false sentiment. Only then can the horse reveal himself to me, be he fat or thin, ugly or beautiful, relative to current standards. He can reveal himself to me only if I understand him without an 'if' or 'but', whether it is my own horse or someone else's, so that I can then, with an open spirit, accept him exactly as he is. Do we not also wish for that total acceptance in the human world?

3. From detail to the whole

Someone came from Sweden to my Akedah School to take an entrance exam. A group

My system of recognizing the characteristics of horses gives a comprehensive overview. But you can only achieve this if you also understand how even the smallest detail influences the total nature of the horse. You will be very surprised by how individual character groups can be determined down to the smallest detail of a hoof or an eye and, vice versa, how the smallest details say something about the character of the horse.

sat in a small circle as she casually took from her bag a photo of her new horse to show us all. After a quick glance at the photo I said, just as an aside, that this horse surely had great problems with his hooves. At that, everyone in the circle looked at me in amazement, because only the horse's head could be seen in the photo, and their amazement did not diminish as the owner confirmed that the horse actually did have relatively small and weak hooves. I am certainly no soothsayer, and, in the course of the following presentations, you too will realize how deeply you can see into the spirit and nature of a horse, even if you know only one tiny detail, because everything is interwoven and interconnected.

4. Breed or character group?

This point will surprise some people: with respect to his behaviour and the majority of his traits, the horse's breed, with few exceptions, plays only a subordinate role. If you have, up to now, been searching the spectrum of the most diverse breeds to assure yourself of specific behaviour and qualities, this book will prove that it is not breed traits, but rather character-group traits that reveal differences and similarities among horses much more practically and precisely. We do find that certain breeds are more prevalent than others in certain of my character groups, but in the search for, and demonstration of, qualities of behaviour and appearance, the character groups are far more useful than breeds. A horse of the character group the Minister, for example, is first and foremost a Minister and behaves like a Minister be he also an Arabian, a Lusitano, a Friesian, or a Lippizaner. In fact, I think we can speak of this as a new dimension in the observation and evaluation of horses.

5. And this, too, should not be forgotten

I do not wish to speak of the division and classification that was undertaken in the land of my birth for the purpose of oppression and extermination of individuals and entire ethnic groups. To this day, there are uncounted attempts, particularly from certain esoteric camps, to classify and arrange human beings, their qualities, traits, and characteristics. That, which in its most sensitive form is possible with animals and very helpful for getting on with them, is always a violation when carried over and applied to human beings in any conceivable way.

Not infrequently horses of a particular strain and within breeds appear as similar to each other as two peas in a pod. Nevertheless, with respect to their characters, they are often very different. I have realized that character-group traits reveal similarities and differences much more practically and meaningfully than breed affiliation. As similar as the two horses in the foreground may look, they are very dissimilar in their natures. The mare on the right is finer, more sensitive and intelligent. The mare on the left is more grounded, more maternal and of higher rank. The mare on the right reacts more sensitively to psychic tension and changes, is very particular about her companions – be they equine or human – and can occasionally be very moody. The mare on the left is more patient, consistent, and persistent, has more stamina, but is also more susceptible to stomach problems and colic.

An Explanation of How the Following Chapters are Arranged

First we will take our time looking at and describing the 26 character groups. Where it seemed appropriate I included two or even more photos of horses that fit the particular description. It is important to get a good strong first impression of the character group in question and the photos, unless otherwise stated, always portray particularly good representatives of the particular type. You will quickly grasp how true to type this character group model is, and how greatly it simplifies the otherwise difficult task of better and more thoroughly recognizing and knowing your own and other horses. It was also most important to me that the descriptions of the individual character groups were given in such a way that, with their help, the overall nature of that creature, horse, would in time become ever more clear, and his secrets would be unlocked.

In the fifth chapter of this book I devote myself purely and simply to the first minutes of being together with a horse. Because, once you have recognized the nature of a horse, then this other previously unknown gate opens itself, and it is the step that shapes the foundation of my work: the first encounter from which comes the maturing process that leads to connection and friendship. Only when I first recognized beyond all doubt the Breton, Campeon 13, and Naranjero, could I then effect the transformation that formed the basis for a gradual, nearly unconscious development.

Finally we come to the section in which I dedicate myself to the question of how horses in specific character groups behave

All horses in the individual character groups are related to one another, and so, to truly recognize a horse of a particular character group, it is important to know what distinguishes the individual character groups Thus the overview is so significant. All the character groups together result in a complex picture of the universal 'horse nature'.

when working with humans. Here we go into great detail in order to get a broad overview at the end. These descriptions overlap with, and are relevant to, other character groups. The chapter explains, step by step, not only the individual qualities of a particular horse but also the general ones.

From the inter-relationship of all the chapters there arises a broad archway which begins in the primal world of horses and leads to the very practical steps of being together with them on the ground and in the saddle.

Finally, I have once more assembled the most important core points of all the character groups into short skeletal overviews, which act as an aide-mémoire, after you have absorbed the details of the large, broad arch.

A filigree of interconnectedness, or, how do you work with the system of character groups?

The complete system is like a body where everything is interconnected and part of the overall texture. Even the arrangement of the presentation of the 26 character groups and the sequence itself is meaningful in the most diverse respects. This means that you will not only get important information about a particular character group in the one section devoted to that group, but also I frequently compare certain behaviours with those of other character groups and discuss them. Thus, in the end, there emerges the complete interwoven picture which shows all the horse types of the world in relation to one another and sees them all as one whole. The Dancer, the Dove, the Child, and the North Wind are in relationship with one another as are the Friend, the Pilgrim, the Guardian of the Fire, and the Modest One. How is the Gypsy different from the

Dandy and why are they nevertheless similar? Why are the Minister and the King next to each other in the sequence, and how are they so different despite certain external similarities? Why does the listing begin with the Unicorn and end with Pegasus? And, again, what is it about those two types that is so alike and yet also so different?

Every single character group is there for itself as well as in relationship to all the others, and it is only in their interconnectedness that the individual characters truly reveal themselves.

The universal aid

My character group system is first of all a universal aid to getting to know and understand horses in general, and so you will be guided in the general as well as the specific world of horses. You will get an overview of the nature of all horses at the same time that you learn the meaning of even the minutest detail. From the comprehensive overview comes the certainty that is needed to recognize the nature of a particular horse in order to finally care for him in a way that is appropriate to his nature and type. That is the reason for, and the goal of, this new approach.

Here horse and human are together in a way that many only dream of. Morning fog lies over the scene. The sun is sending its first rays into the plains of the Pyrenean valley. Person and horse are as one and together they have learned and experienced. They have walked a good stretch of their life's path with one another. Yet on this common path there was always one very rare 'glue' that made their experiences possible: emotion!

In Order to Learn as Much as Possible, Take Heed of the Following

1. Read the descriptions all the way through without any thought to retaining what you have read. Relaxed and at ease simply look at the pictures and then let the complete image quietly have its effect on you. Please do that with all the character groups.

2. Under no circumstances should you try to assign horses known to you to a particular character group during this first perusal. Do not yield to the temptation to evaluate your own horse at the first attempt. Stay consistent and leave your horses out of the game during the first round.

3. Then direct your attention to other chapters or to other things altogether. Do not try to memorize anything. Rather, try to absorb the information and priorities intuitively and holistically. That way you can browse through the character groups and always discover something new, perceive something important. This sort of 'game' will slowly but fundamentally broaden your understanding. Take days, or even weeks to do this. That which spontaneously occurs to you, you should record in a separate notebook. Now your subconscious is working for you. Without your willing it, what you see becomes a profound part of you. Now you will approach horses very differently.

4. With the judgement of your own horse in particular, you should proceed very cautiously, because the being-together with your own horse, as with every person, is marked by images and preconceptions. Believe me, if you proceed as instructed without any conscious effort on your part, the kind of 'child' your horse really is will manifest itself. One morning you will awaken and you will know the truth.

5. Naturally it is now tempting to quickly characterize any horse that crosses your path – but be careful! Before you begin to do this, test yourself on photographs and postpone the real life premiere until you again awaken one morning with the certainty that this system has thoroughly become part of you.

How learning functions

Every person's potential is far greater than even they believe. Learning works quite differently from that which, as a rule, we have experienced in school. On the contrary, the forms of learning that we commonly know are more likely to hinder real learning, maturing, and development. Here are some words on that theme from my perspective.

1. **That 'superglue' emotion**

   You must know that any information that is not connected with feelings and emotions will only 'stick' for a moment. Imagine the learning process as a net, into which a piece of information flows. If it is without 'glue', that is, without a connection to your own experience which is always emotional and feeling-based, then it will certainly lie quivering a moment in the net, but at the slightest movement it will fall out through the bottom and be lost. That is 'school knowledge' that was taught without enthusiasm for the material and without any relationship to reality. That knowledge lasted just long enough for the next class assignment and even cramming until then was torture. If acquiring lasting knowledge is what you want, for yourself or for a child, then cover it with the thick 'glue' of feelings and emotion. Make it a part of real life. Then it will always stay in the net of experience and become part of a many layered and iridescent personality.

2. **Gather knowledge as spiders gather flies**

   My abilities in the area of horses can only be explained because I try to establish as many connections as possible which then lead to particular perceptions. It is like building the biggest spider web possible. The bigger it is the more likely that 'glue-covered flies of knowledge' will get trapped in the web. There is so much that is so very interesting and that you should therefore do. Today so many people complain that they no longer make music, have an interest in all the other things that formerly rounded out their lives. In the end, there remain only a couple of 'threads' and the spirit withers. In our world of horses the opposite is the case.

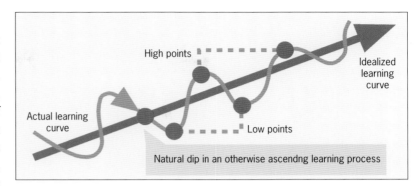

3. **The skyward slide**

   Nothing in nature functions linearly, not even learning. The illustration (above) shows how learning occurs in reality. You will again and again arrive at a point where you have the feeling that you know less about a particular subject than you did days or weeks previously. From a certain perspective that is correct, but this moment is only the preparation for the next dash upward.

4. **The creative pause**

   And what happens if you find yourself in such a trough and you simply pause for a while? Or you do something altogether different from that which you were doing before? Then you will already be quite a bit further along in your perception of true learning.

5. **The fountain of youth**

   Woe to him who believes he knows it all. Woe to him who stops truly learning, stops changing, developing, growing, and maturing. He is old and dead. Intellectual agility is simply liveliness. It is the fountain of youth, of life. Always simply begin at the beginning like a child then you will be on the best path to becoming truly mature. And now, I wish you much pleasure and much 'glue' in experiencing the new.

What Horses Reveal

21. The Prince

1. The Unicorn

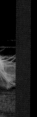

It may surprise some horse lovers to learn that it is not the breed that is the decisive factor in determining the nature of a horse. Irrespective of ancestry, I was able to assign all the horses of the world to 26 character groups, and what you find is nearly a never-ending story: nature and manner, likes and dislikes, and mental, physical and spiritual characteristics.

22. The Victor

3. The Sergeant

4. The Sceptic

5. The Friend

23. The Minister

9. The Guardian of the Fire

10. The Origin

11. The Pilgrim

15. The Lonely One

16. The Used One

17. The Gipsy

The Game of the 26 Cards

The individual character groups give information about carriage, and ways of working together. They describe how horses react in normal and in stressful situations, give information about which type of person fits with which type of horse, and much more. If you are ready to begin to recognize horses, here is the key.

2. The Dove

24. The King

6. The Fat One

7. The Peasant

8. The Dancer

25. The Tough One

12. The Child

13. The Half-born

14. The North Wind

18. The Dandy

19. The Modest One

20. The Frog

26. Pegasus

The Unicorn

It is not without reason that we begin with the Unicorn and end with Pegasus. These two character types are, in certain respects, very similar to one another, and yet, they are very different.

The nature

The Unicorn is a wise horse and therefore is not suitable for just anyone. He is a creature for whom you must clarify things and explain exactly why they must go a certain way. This horse wants to be persuaded and, once he is, he becomes an outstanding friend. The Unicorn is most certainly not a beginner's horse, he needs an experienced and very patient horseman.

It is only with great effort that such a horse, even a stallion, is driven to aggression, but if he is truly provoked he will attack without much warning and absolutely ruthlessly. Therefore, when a horse of this type stands before me in one of my clinics and shows even the slightest signs of pushiness toward his owner, my way of proceeding, peacefully from a distance and in just a few minutes, is to impress upon the horse my power and my absolute inner equanimity. With this distance between us and this inner attitude, everything proceeds very quickly, and our parting, after a few moments, is difficult.

Spontaneous associations with the Unicorn

The Unicorn is clever, wise, noble, aloof and ambitious. He wants to persuade and does persuade. He wants to be recognized and properly cherished. He places less value on a close relationship to people than on an honest, open one. This is a pertinent factor, particularly to the more 'romantically oriented' female riders to whom the Unicorn is hugely fascinating. Sentimental closeness, however, usually causes this horse to beat a quick retreat. He seeks a clear path for development and, therefore, a clear, self-possessed person who can support him and help him to mature. The Unicorn is easy to injure through injustice and most of all, through lack of clarity.

When the Unicorn suffers, he holds his feelings in, mostly unbeknown to the people around him. He seldom suffers from small minor illnesses, but will then suddenly fall prey to a major illness. The Unicorn will negate his suffering and fight against it, and then, suddenly break down completely. It is, therefore, important to take even the first small signs of discontent very seriously.

Physical characteristics in detail

High set, well-formed, clear eyes that are not too far apart. A relatively small brow and large nose, the slightly convex profile, and the finely-shaped nostrils and their high, well-forward placement create the noble, aristocratic impression.

The ears are set close together. Their size and the slightly inward-pointing shape speak of quiet diligence and a balanced disposition.

The lower lip is pulled back slightly – on the horse in these photos, slightly too much, which indicates momentary excitement that would dissipate immediately with a few moments of good work. The upper lip is shapely and well formed, which indicates capability and sensitivity.

The jaws of this horse seem to me to be a bit small and somewhat narrow. This indicates that occasional brow-knitting discussions are to be expected, but these can be worked through with quiet coaxing. As soon as you have once again explained to the horse, in a manner in accordance with his nature, how things stand, his friendly goodwill will immediately reappear.

The shoulder, elbow placement, and set of the neck are usually beautiful, yet, at the same time, have a tendency toward slight heaviness. This can become a real problem for the less-experienced horseman. It indicates that this horse must be worked below his capacity, particularly at the beginning of his education, otherwise he can become sour and totally refuse to cooperate. He should be given long breaks; even his conformation indicates this. This horse is not a high-powered athlete, he is a sensitive Unicorn.

Which person suits the Unicorn

As has already been said, this is a horse for an experienced, open, honest, and calm person, and is most certainly not a child's horse. In contrast to his many good points, the

Unicorn also displays some bodily weaknesses. We will come back to these once again in Chapter 6, On the Path to Becoming a Riding Horse. As a rule this horse can be taken to High School level but only with many years of comparatively careful schooling, because of the relative weakness of his back and hindquarters, particularly in the area of the hocks. With a person who is a match for this horse with all his strengths and weaknesses, the heights he can ascend are nearly boundless.

The Dove

Here we show a grey Arabian looking as many believe he should appear. But, be careful, many singularities and details hide themselves behind the mask of breed 'typiness'.

The nature

Beneath the concave profile so typical of the Arabian we see in this case the low set cheekbones which are so typical of the Dove. The whole head seems to follow the downward curve of the profile, which, for this horse is a sort of fundamental weakness, a kind of self-confidence deficiency. With the help of his owner the Dove can overcome this deficiency, and with his fearfulness transformed to attentiveness, a lovely lightness, sensitivity and agility will surface.

The foremost characteristic of the Dove is always his fearfulness, which is grounded in his alertness and his fragility, and which shows itself in his not necessarily bad tendency to simply worry. The Dove is very easy to overface but, at the same time, this horse has a good forward urge, and a strong desire for movement, which is indicated particularly by the placement and inward curving shape of the ears. These two qualities (easily overfaced versus urge to move) create a rare constellation of conflicts in the inner life of the horse which sometimes leads to his being emotionally torn apart. You must acknowledge that and always keep it in mind when you deal with such a horse. Only when this fundamental trait has been recognized can the positive potential of working with people properly develop.

The fearful mare that we met on page 18 was such a Dove and her anxiety is, therefore, normal for this horse. If I can, within a very few moments, successfully tie together character, fearfulness and overcoming fearfulness into a normal cycle for the horse, then I will have already opened the gate to the inner world of this horse's trust. The success in this encounter and the self-discovery of the horse lies, to a very large extent, in the recognition of his character type and knowledge of the nature of this character type.

Let us look again at the photo of the grey Arabian: it shows clearly that, at this time, the positive qualities of the Dove are not coming fully into play. The anxiety of the horse creates a simmering wariness, which, with poor handling, could lead to a not-to-be-underestimated aggressiveness. In these horses, aggressiveness born of anxiety, paired with a certain weakness, frequently leads to explosive reactions in stressful situations. With horses of the Dove type, this must always be taken into consideration.

Over the years this Arabian has walked his own ways in order to compensate for his own fearfulness and also the varied behaviours of human beings. So here we have a good situation in which you can see both: the inborn, genetically determined characteristics plus those that have developed in a way typical of the Dove over the course of time.

The latter characteristics include: the wide-open eyes, the wrinkling of the eyelid, and the contraction in the rear area of the lower lip. The inborn fearfulness of the horse was apparently not given sufficient consideration. In Chapter 6 we will learn how, in principle, you work with such a horse. For now, we will continue with the general description.

Spontaneous associations with the Dove

Fearfulness, nervousness, spookiness, a good desire to move, alertness, sensitivity, intelligence, and a lack of self-trust. The Dove therefore seeks support and the confidently leading, very patient and empathetic human touch. The Dove requires certain additional steps in his education, which very specifically address his nature and conformation.

Physical characteristics in detail

In the concave form of the entire head — even more than the typical standard for the Arabian horse — and broad, high-set nostrils that lie close together, the sensitivity and the lack of self-confidence are in evidence, as well as a good portion of inner uncertainty. On a brow of average breadth, the eyes seem relatively wide apart. With regard to the proportions of the head, here, yet again, the uncertainty in the behaviour of the horse is indicated. The jaws often seem comparatively small and narrow, which denotes uncertainty and fearfulness in this character type. The shape of the ears and the sharply-defined head indicate the horse's strong urge for movement and to develop his clarity, strength, and natural aptitude. All of this means that this animal already has within himself keen, brilliant inborn tendencies which can and must be drawn out through sensitive handling suited to the horse's love of freedom, which, at the same time, offers inner and outer security (see Chapter 6). At this point I would like to refer to the discussions in my book *Dancing with Horses* on the subject of The Concave Horse. To develop a Dove into a good and sound riding horse you need broad experience and background knowledge. The Dove moves quickly from one point to the next, but preferably alone. If you want to sit on a Dove in order to direct him, to limit his freedom, the required preparatory work is very different from that needed for the Friend or the Unicorn. Not without reason are Doves the horses that shine at horse shows, particularly in the in-hand classes. You should make yourself clearly conscious of these attributes if you own such a horse or are thinking about acquiring one.

Which person suits the Dove?

Basically it is possible for even a person with little experience to keep and care for a horse like the Dove. The special experience and knowledge is needed for the preparatory work, the breaking-in, and the riding. It is most important that this horse, which seeks closeness and support, feels understood in his nature and, because of that, can build up a counterbalance to the inborn inner tensions. The Dove seeks a quiet, empathetic, and not very ambitious person who, from the beginning, handles him carefully and with sensitivity. With supervision and control, even children can get along with this horse, although he is not the most suitable children's horse. You should spend a lot of time with this horse, in a peaceful atmosphere, going for long walks and quiet hacks. He should, working together with his owner, be able to broaden and increase his self-confidence. Then the deep-seated fundamental inner fear, which is not always clearly perceivable on the outside, will abate, and the horse becomes an affectionate and unbelievably loyal friend. The flightiness and fearfulness of the Dove will transform themselves into a wonderful elegance, which, like the display flight of this symbolic animal, finally expresses itself in contentment and elated pride.

The Sergeant

We must look very closely at this horse too. As we get to know his nature, we can learn much of a general nature that will fundamentally help us in determining horses' characters through external appearance.

The nature

First we come to the phenomenon of the chestnut; the Sergeant is very frequently of chestnut colouring. For a long time, Spanish breeding practice forbade the breeding of chestnut horses although, here and there, that prohibition has eased a bit. Many masters of classical horsemanship were of the opinion that chestnuts are basically not meant for riding. In fact, chestnuts, as a rule, have a very headstrong temperament. They often have minds of their own, just like the representative of the colour pictured here. Chestnuts suffer more heart and circulatory problems, have more genital problems and eye ailments than other horses, and they do not particularly like heat, but with good care and handling none of that is an issue. What is more important is the presence and alertness of so many chestnuts, and the horse in this photo demonstrates that too.

Spontaneous associations with the Sergeant

The Sergeant is a razor sharp, fiery, independent, fast, hardy, generally healthy, fairness-loving, exceptional horse, still wild in his nature, and mostly fixated on one particular person.

Physical characteristics in detail

Note the profile from the nostrils to where the ears are set on; it seems similar to that of the horse in the following character group, but actually means something very different for this horse's nature and behaviour. Also characteristic are the eyes and the triangular shape of the head when viewed from the side. This horse is a fighter, but he is neither a high-ranking officer nor a common soldier. He needs a clear order from a herd leader or a superior person so that, once he has understood the order, he can act independently and with total reliability.

The pinched lips of this chestnut horse and the tensions we can see there are easily released through good work. Once the horse has relaxed, snorting, for a couple of minutes then the softness and calmness that are also part of his nature will very clearly be expressed.

The relatively small eyes indicate that he is not possessed of the highest level of wisdom – which is why he is not a General or a Minister – but his whole nature is marked by a joyful clever competence and practical common sense.

That bony protrusion above the eyes, so pronounced in this horse, indicates strength and assertiveness. Whenever I run into this feature at one of my clinics I am definitely more careful with the horse than usual. Within other configurations this feature can be a harbinger of unpleasant surprises. The Sergeant can become very unpleasant when he is with people he feels are indecisive and cannot communicate the sense of their actions without confusion. Then he becomes the commander, the boss, and with full force.

The straight line of the lower jaw also indicates a creature that senses great abilities in himself, and does possess them, but is thoroughly content with a secondary or subordinate position. The nostrils are sensitive and relatively fine. The ears indicate a middling work ethic which in an otherwise 'hot' chestnut is quite good enough.

As with so many chestnuts, the head is relatively short, an indication that you can do anything you like with the horse, and this type of horse will go through thick and thin with his owner. Furthermore, the short head is a sign of severity and inner robustness.

The set of the neck on this chestnut is attractive, although the top line of the neck indicates a certain weakness that can be offset by good work.

Which person suits the Sergeant

This horse can be both simple and complex depending on which person approaches him and in what manner they do so. The Sergeant is definitely not a horse for a beginner or for children (normally the Sergeant has no use for children); he needs a General. As already mentioned, if the Sergeant does not have a clear relationship with a person then he can sometimes become aggressive. He will soon feel lonely and abandoned and then develop a rebellious nature, finally retreating further and further into himself in sadness.

If this horse finds the right human counterpart – a strong, self-confident horseperson who strives for fairness, order, and proportion, who wants to school him, can show him the world, and will give him a lot of time – the Sergeant can give this person a wonderful insight into the freedom that horses carry within themselves. For the right person there is much joy to be found on the back of this horse.

The Sceptic

The nature

Here, as with the chestnut in the previous section, we see again a bump in the profile on the level of the eyes. But take a look at the inter-relationship of eyes, lower jaw, ears, profile, and nostrils altogether. As has been said, it is not about randomly using isolated characteristics to draw conclusions about the inner nature of a horse. Only the interaction of all possible, even barely perceptible, singularities opens the gates and allows a true glimpse into the depths of our charges' natures. Scepticism dominates every facet of the nature of the horse shown in the large photo above. A horse like this one can quickly be made ill-natured with the wrong handling. Why is that so?

Physical characteristics in detail

The relatively small eyes, the flat and relatively coarse shape of the bones of the eye socket, the placement of the eyes close to the centre of the face, the relatively small, fleshy nostrils, the coarse, pursed, contracted upper lip, the almost shapeless jowls, the slightly hanging lower lip – all indicate a horse of little intelligence that is not very mobile but nevertheless wilful; a thoroughly strong character that is powerful and serviceable.

This horse is just difficult to win over to new things, to change. He must be given the details of your work together in small portions, frequently repeated, so that, in the end, it all becomes tasty and digestible for him.

Which person suits the Sceptic?

It is easy to be unfair to this horse because he is often expected to do things of which he is physically and mentally incapable, and then we have a vicious circle that results from the increasing impatience of the owner and the ever harsher reactions of this vigorous horse. In the worst case, this horse can pose a truly grave danger to a person, therefore the owner of a Sceptic should know exactly what he is dealing with, and he should demand and expect very little of his horse. If the horse has patiently been taught, and learnt, small steps and the dominance-trust relationship between him and his owner is correct, then a nice, loyal, 'buddy' relationship can develop. This horse is neither a beginner's nor a child's horse, although you often encounter these horses with beginners

and children; this is totally irresponsible but most likely occurs because the experienced horseperson does not want to be bothered with this type of horse.

The owner must know that everything about his horse seems to say, 'What you are telling me just cannot be true'. This horse's lessons should, therefore, be conducted with other horses present as often as possible. Basically, the Sceptic will believe other horses before he believes human beings and must first see anything new performed by other horses, in order to see that it not only does not harm the others but also actually brings them joy. Then, over time, even this horse will occasionally participate and happily learn his lessons, if only in small steps.

It is very important that the owner knows that his horse is one that does not hesitate long before he expresses his ill humour. Bucking, biting, striking – these are the weapons at a horse's disposal – and it does not take much for this horse to employ them, without much warning. The horse in the first photo is one that exemplifies this description. The horse in the second photo is altogether more flexible, more intelligent and more sensitive but, nevertheless, has the same fundamental characteristics. Above all, the muzzle is much softer and therefore this Sceptic is more open and ready to work. With the right well-grounded and patient owner, the unpleasant behaviour we have mentioned may never be seen, and then, even this horse, will, over the years, become a good friend and be grateful to his owner because he feels acknowledged and supported.

At this point I want to emphatically state one more time that, for me, it is not about a value judgement, good or bad, or whether or not you like a horse. Even the trace of such a thought and perception would pull the rug out from under the feet of my work. However, clear recognition and identification are prerequisites to respect and a loving approach.

The Friend

The individual horse types seem so similar, and yet they conceal enormous differences. This horse, similarly to the two previously described horses, also has a clearly recognizable bump in the area of the eyes, and yet, overall, this is a completely different type. Common to all three types are strength and assertiveness. However, the way and manner in which they demonstrate these characteristics are very different.

The nature

The person who owns such a horse cannot really be a bad person since this horse is the Friend.

Every horse can be a good friend, but those of this character group embody what we understand by the word 'friend' in the purest and most beautiful way. That does not mean all the qualities they possess are good – but we do not require that of a friend, do we?

Spontaneous associations with the Friend

Grounded, loyal, reliable, uncomplicated, of average intelligence and talent, healthy, good stamina, mentally stable and easy to deal with, positive, forms strong bonds, understanding, quite easily satisfied, physically solid and coarsely built, friendly, usually brave, modest and open.

Physical characteristics in detail

In the pinto, the straight, symmetrical shape of the head is very noticeable. The eye is small and placed high and close to the front of the face, which does not indicate great intelligence, but rather, occasional stubbornness. Above all, it indicates reliability and the ability to bond unconditionally. Once this horse develops trust, then you will not easily get rid of him. This kind of friendship is not to be confused with clinging. Despite his loyalty, this horse does *not* have a tendency towards clinginess; and it is that which is, basically, a sign of devotion and friendship.

Characteristically, nowhere in the profile of this horse is there a dip. This means that this horse is reflective and thoroughly courageous, although not as markedly so as the King or the Minister. He is confident, but at the same time modest and reserved. He has tact and average sensitivity, and can occasionally be a little stubborn. The nostrils are comparatively small, as well as coarse, and set high and forward; that indicates an uncomplicated nature and simplicity. The silhouette of the head is angular and that too is indicative of simplicity and an uncomplicated nature. The jowls of this horse seem small and narrow, which makes him unsuitable for High School work. The neck is set on well, although the upper neck is a bit too compact and stiff.

Which person suits the Friend?

When working with this horse, you must be careful not to overface him. He is not the type that is always looking for new challenges; he would like to slide quickly through his schooling in two to three years and then be able to stand loyally at his owner's side, where he will be a practically bombproof comrade for twenty or thirty years. Physically, these horses are, on the whole, very fit. They seldom become ill as long as you are careful not to let them give in completely to their urge to eat. These horses, as a rule, are from 140 cm to 150 cm (13.3 hh to 14.3 hh) in height. It is easy to determine from all this information just what qualities a person should possess to be happy with such a horse.

Unfortunately this horse is rarely considered by beginners because he is not especially attractive or very elegant; the newcomer to horses often turns to a more beautiful horse. The Friend is a good and reliable partner, even for children.

With this horse you can explore the world without fearing anything. He will not be difficult to train because the inexperienced owner will always be able to get advice about training a Friend. What is important is the good-natured and completely non-ambitious behaviour of the person toward the horse. Anyone who wants to show off, brag or scale the heights is definitely not the right person for this horse. Friends seek friends, and so the person should have attributes similar to those of the horse, or seek to learn them from the horse.

The Black Forest chestnut, a southern German coldblood, is surely a very uncommon representative of this group. Such a horse is, mostly, not recognized. He is not particularly intelligent and not as sensitive as others, but he is fundamentally a hunk of gold covered with a hairy coat. The Black Forest chestnut is nobler than the pinto. In his well-modulated nostrils and mouth you can perceive a greater sensitivity and higher rank, despite his massive size. The shape of the head is not quite so geometric, indicating that the owner will occasionally find himself in some critical situations. This horse will continually question people and demand strong leadership.

With the Friend at your side, you can confidently venture on your life's path in good spirits.

The Fat One

When I speak of the Fat One, I do not necessarily mean actual body-weight. The pinto on this page, for example, is not a physically fat horse nevertheless he definitely falls into the character group of the Fat One.

The nature

The Fat One is very similar to the Friend in outer appearance, but displays completely different character traits. To begin with, the Fat One is a horse that lives in his own world. He would be happy without human beings. At my demonstrations, where the aim is to show my audience as many horses and their transformations as possible, I always put this type at the end. I explain that with such a horse we must reckon with a much more protracted response. This type of horse actually demands quite a lot from me. Neither the extremely jumpy horse, nor the aggressive one, nor the very shy one requires as much patience as a Fat One.

In distinguishing between the Fat One and the Friend, for example, the student must recognize and understand how closely these two types of horses resemble one another and yet how very different their natures are. Only one group requires more patience than the Fat One and that is that of the Peasant, to which we will come next.

To begin with, let us firmly grasp the fact that we are dealing here with an extraordinarily good-natured type of horse; it is not easy to disturb his peace. Neither is he easy to spoil, although once he is spoiled it is not so easy to correct. In our previous example we had a horse that was actually fat, a coldblood. But he did not have any of the traits we are describing here. Let me emphasize that there are a lot of fat horses that are extraordinarily quick, speedy, alert, and react promptly to every sort of communication.

Spontaneous associations with the Fat One

On the whole, this type is easy-going, careful and slow but not very forward-going, assertive, brave and unflappable, has an average to low intelligence, good endurance, and can also be stubborn. If this horse is driven to aggression, he will want to solve his problems with the least possible expenditure of energy, and that is when he becomes most dangerous.

Physical characteristics in detail

Here too the eye is small, set high, and close to the front of the face. However, the area directly above and behind the eyes is very bony and well defined. Not infrequently, the eyes are placed like those of a human; that is they are not placed at the side of the head but seem to have been placed at the front. You can see this more clearly in the pinto. On the whole, the head seems coarse and not in proportion. The nostrils are fleshy – again, you can see that particularly well in the pinto. The mouth is not 'communicative' and not playful. The ears are short and fleshy, the neck is massive, compact, and seems inflexible. The jaw and jowls are not very pronounced and are also fleshy.

The pinto's conformation is more typical of the character group than that of the bay. Particularly noticeable is the muzzle angle: just above and behind the mouth the upper and lower jaws drift far apart and, again, reinforce the impression of coarseness and a lack of 'final details'. The lips are particularly simply shaped and the overall impression is one of immobility.

Which person suits the Fat One

The Fat One displays a very special and very important peculiarity, which the pinto in the photo possesses in great measure. Because these horses have an enormous power of self-assertion, but at the same time show very little inclination to movement, they can be very dangerous for beginners. Unfortunately, beginners, especially those training at a riding school, are often left with Fat Ones because no one else really has the desire to work with them for any length of time. These horses come across as totally quiet and easy-going and therefore are not infrequently thought of as bombproof in pleasure-riding circles. But they are that only so long as no one really demands anything of them. If their peace is disturbed, and a beginner could easily do that, then, for the Fat One, the person becomes an annoying fly. As a rule, that is correct because only a very experienced rider can persuade a horse like this to move and work (see Chapter 6). Unfortunately, in most cases that occurs only with much pressure. These horses are certainly not beginners' horses and under no circumstances are they children's horses. The person for this horse should be completely patient and calm, and not be possessed of the least bit of ambition. In fact, he should have the same nature as the horse and find in him a soul mate. He should be familiar with the fundamentals of educating a horse, and, above all, take note of the guidelines I give in Chapter 6 regarding this matter. In short, he should be one of those people everyone calls a 'jolly good fellow'. All others will despair of this character group. An apple tree is simply not an oak!

The Breton that we met in the early pages of this book was not only physically massive, he was a classic example of this character type, and he behaved accordingly. Without the knowledge that I have presented here, it would have been impossible for me to have had an effect on that horse. I knew that there was only one thing I always had to give him between his attacks: peace; his aggressiveness was only the expression of his wish to be left in peace. That did not make the encounter with him as easy and delightful as a springtime stroll, but nevertheless it was a controllable adventure.

The Peasant

With this horse we finish with those character groups in which a convex head shape on a problematical body signals a nature that is not always very simple. Our journey has led us from the Sergeant, who is not so easily recognizable, to the Sceptic, a type of horse to enjoy with caution, to the good-natured Friend, to the Fat One, and now, finally, to the Peasant. We will return again to the trait of the ram's head when, later in this section we describe the Hard One and the King, but we will see that their type of ram-headedness signifies completely different qualities.

The nature

The Peasant is the only type that I cannot identify with certainty from a photograph. The reason for that lies in the character group itself, because in this type of horse there are actually two extremes. It comes down to polarities and surprises. Naturally, the basic foundation of this character group can be determined without doubt, as with any other horse. But the remaining identification determines whether the horse becomes a jolly, playful fellow or a test of patience. The latter is by far the most frequent case.

First though, we want to establish that, contrary to the previous character group, this horse only very infrequently becomes aggressive through being overfaced and treated unjustly. This type of horse is more likely to let everything just bounce off him. However, if he is continually driven to defensiveness, or pressured in some other way, then uncompromising aggression can result.

Spontaneous associations with the Peasant

This horse is ignoble, narrow-chested, of low intelligence, either extremely stubborn and inflexible or jolly and joyful in a self-willed way. As a rule, he is of small stature, natural, simple, robust, of good health, has very flat gaits, and, usually, only educable as a riding horse with much expenditure of time, effort and patience. If you expect nothing, or nearly nothing, of him, this is a wonderful and loveable primal being.

Physical characteristics in detail

This horse has by far the most defined convex face line of all the groups that have this trait. It is obvious that this curve begins between the ears and continues in a big arc with virtually no dip to end at the upper lip. As is shown by our example horse, the eyes are often extremely small, which denotes low intelligence and inferior inner flexibility. The ears are small, set to the outside and have little animation. The mouth opening is set very low, is short, not expressive and gives a contracted impression. The lower lip is small, easily pulled back and of firm structure. The jowls are small and narrow and not expressively shaped but, overall, the lower jaw is massive and heavy. The overall impression of the head is ignoble and coarse. The neck seems short and stiff and is set on low. The top line of the neck is straight and normally runs down to a so-called axe-cut (a V-shaped dip just above the withers). The horse is usually built downhill, meaning that his croup is higher than the highest point of the withers, which influences how you should work with the horse (see Chapter 6).

Which person suits the Peasant

Horses of this type not infrequently find glowing admirers in pleasure-riding circles. But, to develop such a horse into a good-natured riding horse requires a great deal of patience and much experience.

In my opinion these horses come from locally occurring breeds, which in the past were used as riding horses purely and simply because there were no other horses available. To put such a horse into serious training is to do him an injustice. This is not a riding horse!

In the vast majority of cases, this type of horse is extremely self-willed and inflexible but, as previously mentioned, now and then you get a surprise and encounter a horse of this character type who is playful and of a childlike nature throughout his life. Even if a horse does seem more interested and willing to work, however, nevertheless the total conformation defies any serious training as a riding horse.

The person who suits a Peasant will most likely have come to such a horse accidentally. He is certainly not the horse anyone with riding ambition would choose. In fact, a horse like the Peasant suits a good-natured, down-to-earth person who feels drawn to the nature of this animal, primarily because he is an animal, and not so much because he is a horse that needs training. In my view, the Peasant should get good basic training so that you can lead him perfectly, and so that he can be in the world of human beings without any problems. The unambitious and patient person will then find in the Peasant a sympathetic and primal farmyard companion.

The Dancer

The greatest weakness of this beautiful and charming horse is his back. The horse in the first photo seems to be hanging from two threads, namely one at the croup and the other between the ears and it is for this reason that the horse has his lightness, the expression of a dancer. Altogether, though, this horse has a weak constitution. In conformity with the line of his back, he tends to trail the hindquarters out behind, make himself 'long' and lets the delicate back sink down. Training this type of horse to become a riding horse presents a great challenge to the ability and experience of a person.

The nature

As a rule this type of horse is highly intelligent and very creative, which means that he is not a beginner's horse. This horse has a very friendly and sensitive nature. He is clinging, uncomplicated and lovable in his approach to human beings. Generally the Dancer is curious, loves to move, and is very willing to work. Despite his appearance and the name I have given him, this horse often has problems with his gaits because of the weakness of his back. Naturally his gaits are far more expressive than those of the representatives of the last four character groups. However, the truly relaxed, rhythmic, powerful, graceful expressions in movement, which you associate with a dancer, are usually lacking.

Spontaneous associations with the Dancer

The Dancer has a pleasant nature and outer appearance, is light-footed, lofty but of inferior stamina. The gaits are normally weaker and flatter than you would expect. The horse has a fine nature, back and carriage problems, is intelligent, sensitive, occasionally built downhill, and is very dependent on attention and recognition from humans.

Physical characteristics in detail

The head of this horse is finely chiselled and usually sharply defined. Note the wide, full-of-character brow and the large set-forward eyes. The overall appearance of the head is similar to the final horse in this section, Pegasus, but the Dancer is lacking that last tiny amount of depth, earnestness and toughness.

The profile is straight and has a 'hard' appearance. The nostrils are wide, finely chiselled and set on very low. All this indicates a lightness of spirit, sensitivity, and inner flexibility. In comparison to the relative solidity of the body, the head seems a bit too delicate and too small, and that is an indication that this horse sometimes has difficulty getting along well in the herd, often getting along better with humans than with his own kind. It is especially with the tougher characters that this fine and thoughtful horse has problems, since, because of his body weakness and his thereby undermined self-confidence, he does not assert himself as he should. The other horses, particularly the tougher ones, do not take this type too seriously, and that can cause a Dancer to break down. With this equine type it is therefore very important to pay attention to the correct composition of the herd. This horse gets along best with smaller representatives of his type, and would bond very closely with a pretty pony, and protect him in a tender, motherly way.

The croup of the Dancer is most often high, the neck is set on high, and the entire bearing is therefore upright and proud. On the whole, however, the neck is another weak point and, therefore, part of the overall inferior carrying power.

The ears are fine, mobile and nobly set inward, and of expressive appearance in proportion to his nature.

A fine-spirited person with an inwardly sensitive and flexible nature, and an artistic talent and interest, would make a good partner for the Dancer. This horse does not need a consistent, continuous training schedule; as long as he feels understood and approved of, and feels the inner connection to people, he will have a happy and easy life's path.

The palomino is a somewhat tougher representative of this character group and, because of that, there is the imminent danger that his abilities will be overestimated by his owner. His nature indicates some tendency toward the character group of the King. The horse has good musculature and the top line shows better carrying capacity than that of the bay horse. Nevertheless, the overall weakness remains the determining factor. I strongly urge those of my students who intend to work with horses professionally and act as advisors to people, to clearly impress on themselves the top line of this type of horse. It is only with great difficulty that the inexperienced person can be convinced that this seemingly powerful and thoroughly representative horse is, in truth, easily overfaced. So, be careful! In Chapter 6 we will discuss this further.

Which person suits the Dancer?

The owner of a Dancer should never imagine that he can take the horse to High School level. Beginners may easily make this mistake because the horse's appearance indicates that he has a greater ability and potential than is, in fact, there. The weak back and the weakness of the entire top line will prove to be a real problem. The horse will become stiff and tense up, he will withdraw into himself and lose all of his charming playfulness, and only with great effort will he be drawn out of, and freed from, his not necessarily visible suffering.

This horse is a beautiful one with which you should enjoy nature and life, without making particular demands of him. He is spectacular in his appearance and will meet with great approval from non-horsepeople and inexperienced observers.

The Guardian of the Fire

The nature

Be it mare, gelding, or stallion, this is the most motherly of all horses.

Being with this horse is very pleasant; he is plain, uncomplicated, very easily satisfied, steady, persevering, and reliable.

He is a wonderful beginner's horse, probably the best animal for an inexperienced horseperson. He usually has soft gaits. Because of his strength and size he forgives the occasional insecurity of the beginner's seat, and because of his good nature he forgives at least the less serious incidents of lack of control in the inexperienced human soul. The experienced horseperson and the mature human soul will, however, receive this animal's gratitude and devotion.

Owing to his unlikely appearance this horse is all too often undervalued! Who seeks the qualities of this horse where they are hidden, buried in the simplicity of his appearance?

Spontaneous association with the Guardian of the Fire

This horse does not demonstrate spectacular gaits and he is not meant to be taken to the greatest heights of the art of riding. The Guardian of the Fire is even simpler in his nature than the Friend: he is more constant and steady, more devoted and warmer in his feelings, and is therefore the ideal daily companion. The Guardian of the Fire is centred, down to earth and knows himself. He can repeatedly remind a person of the middle point, of the simplicity of his origins and of life, that is, of the fire in the centre and that is why this horse is the Guardian of the Fire.

Mares of this type are outstanding mothers, and since they have no ambition to engage in adversarial encounters, they are particularly sensible lead mares.

Physical characteristics in detail

The total appearance is plain and leans in the direction of coarseness, but this horse is in no way coarse. When considering the Guardian of the Fire, we must pay particular attention to the interplay of the individual characteristics. Despite the relative shortness of his head, smallness of the eyes, fleshiness of appearance, the shortness of the neck and the coarseness of the ears, the overall appearance is symmetrical and harmonious. Everything simply fits together and is harmonious in its own unique way, so simple and yet so sensitive and tender that a truly experienced and deeply empathic observer cannot fail to see the true nature of the horse.

Look at the gentleness of the eyes, the finely curved lids. Admire the simplicity of the brow, the matter-of-factness it brings to expression. Look at the sensitive play of the actually quite fleshy nostrils and the expressive though, again, quite fleshy mouth. This horse has a great inner beauty that he only barely senses, upon which he never depends, and which he would never thrust forward in his association with other horses or human beings. Arrogance in any form is alien to this horse, and so other horses hold him in the highest regard. Mares with these characteristics do, therefore, have a great talent to be lead mares, even if they are of small stature.

Stallions of this type are uncomplicated companions. They are seldom overly 'studdish' and despite a thoroughly masculine appearance nevertheless have something motherly, something of feminine caring in their nature.

The black horse is a more serious representative of this character group. His profile is not so even, his nature not so straightforward. The eye indicates the

sadness that befalls these horses when they must share too much of the burden of human suffering through contests, competition, being overchallenged and vanity. The Guardian of the Fire weeps for his children.

Which person suits the Guardian of the Fire?

Actually everything about this horse has already been said. The spectrum of people who suit this horse is nearly as great as this horse's connection to the earth. And just as the earth nourishes all and shelters all, so this horse approaches every person with high regard and humility. Those of goodwill will easily find themselves in this horse while those of a baser nature will inevitably soften. Only the ambitious do not as a rule turn to this horse, for he hides his treasure beneath the cloak of plainness.

The Origin

In certain ways the Origin is related to the Guardian of the Fire as well as to the next character group, the Wanderer. Although two similar breeds, the Icelandic horse and the Fjord, are pictured here, remember not to be misled into directly connecting certain breeds with character groups.

The nature

In studying these photographs one thing immediately meets the eye: both horses are of very similar natures and therefore cannot be assigned to any other character group. Yet their physical appearance is very different.

The black Icelandic horse's facial structure is convex, the Fjord's concave! The nostrils could hardly be more different, and even the eyes have very few similarities. Nevertheless their inner natures are as alike as two peas in a pod. Once again it comes down to an overall impression, very particularly in this character group!

This description shows you why I have no use for stereotype and cut-out templates when assessing character. But everyone must decide for himself and find his own way.

Spontaneous associations with the Origin

He is freedom-loving, independent, unyielding, difficult to influence, living deeply in his world, a stranger to civilization. That which appears to be stubbornness is in truth the expression of independent existence. The Origin is very much of the earth and bound to his region, therefore he reacts with sensitivity to climate and feed and above all to change. The

Origin is much nobler in his nature than he appears to be. He is mostly very intelligent, assertive, agile and nimble, talented, and honest. Before physical symptoms resulting from errors in understanding and management appear, this horse will withdraw into himself.

Physical characteristics in detail

Let us very slowly feel our way into the similarities of these two horses and thus into the parameters of this character group. At the very least the ears are very similar. The shape and position of the jaws are very much alike, and the mouth of both horses shows exactly the same expression. But there is something unusual here: the interplay of nostrils, profile and eyes of the two horses is nearly identical, and they both have a carefree attitude that no other character group can demonstrate, not even that of the Child to which we will come very soon. This carefree aspect of their nature, the aboriginal appearance, makes the horses pictured here, seemingly so different, members of one and the same character group.

Which person suits the Origin?

Horses of this type are often set aside for children, which is a gross error with possibly grave consequences. The most suitable horse for children is the Minister. Origin horses like these are by nature much too uncompromising. There is an 'inevitability' about these horses. You will most likely have observed that in the combination of children and Origin horses a certain kind of love-hate relationship can quickly develop. Only inexperienced non-horsepeople make that sort of mistake and bring such pairs together. Not only can such an undertaking become dangerous for the child, but the very nature of horse as such also becomes anathema to him. This is not because there is something inherently negative about this character group, the child becomes disgusted because he simply cannot lead and trust this basically very refined and independently reacting horse. This is something that is very difficult even for most adults! In opposition to all common practice I can only say over and over again: if a Shetland, an Icelandic, a Fjord (even though less common), belong to this character group they are definitely not beginners' or 'childrens' horses.

Just look around to see all the problems horse owners have with these animals. Here we find one of the biggest errors in the horse world and the one most rife with consequences. Not everything that is small is also cute, simple, and right for children. Also Haflinger and Camargue horses, for example, can be quite complicated in their inner nature, and not at all suited to beginners or inexperienced horsepeople. I will go into this in great detail in Chapter 6.

The Origin's nature is rarely understood by people. The gulf between the two is a bit like the difference between a 'modern' and an aboriginal human being.

The Origin has remained untouched by the passage of time, despite centuries of continuous domestication. Of all horses, the Origin dies inwardly most radically after an angry outburst. He breaks down, he disintegrates. Unfortunately, in the world of leisure riders, many such examples can be found. The horses' small body size often prevents the worst catastrophe, namely death for the person due to truly dangerous attacks.

The Icelandic horse in particular is of such a complicated and rich inner structure, which, according to my observations, is truly understood and interpreted by only very few owners. Strictly speaking this horse is not a prey, a flight, animal anymore. He has had to take on completely different behaviours in the last thousand years due to changes in his environment. Many of these very important characteristics remain unknown to the owners and even professional trainers.

The person for the Origin should be very wise, very open and thoroughly mature. He should neither be under any illusions about the horse, nor let himself be guided by sentimentality. He should be stable, sensitive, very fair and striving for righteousness. It is not so important that he understands a lot about horses as it is that he is mature and centred as a human being. The Origin belongs to the high-ranking character types that demand and expect the most from mankind. Who would have thought that? We will cover this subject more in Chapter 6.

The Pilgrim

Here we come to another very special and very interesting type of horse. The intensity of his expression approaches that of the Minister, his good nature is comparable to the Guardian of the Fire or the Friend. And yet, here is a manifestation of the spirit that brings its very own qualities into being.

The nature

First of all, this horse is very independent. As we can well see in the black horse pictured here, the eye is focused on the distance, like a wise man's, it seems to want to penetrate the farthest reaches, and that is how this horse behaves. The Pilgrim only rarely feels the urge to go back home to the stable. He is ready for anything if he can explore new and unfamiliar territory. His independence makes him at once exalted and a good pilgrim since he does not distract himself with the irrelevancies at the side of the road. It is as though this horse wants to take seriously only that which is valid in the distance, the course of the path, and the goal. This animal does, therefore, seem a little arrogant, but that is an erroneous conclusion. From his exalted position, he can let certain restrictions bounce off him, but he cannot tolerate lack of freedom.

Spontaneous associations with the Pilgrim

This horse is uncomplicated, good-natured and, in the main, enjoys good health. His body is likewise very balanced, powerful, and of a good carrying constitution. His back is usually pleasantly short, the hindquarters are well angled and the hind legs have a pronounced capacity to step under the body. With a wise horseperson the entire education of this horse proceeds without any setbacks. Even here the horse follows a straight path. He is freedom loving, calm, wise, pleasant in his nature, noble, loyal, and very people oriented. The Pilgrim is, all in all, a wonderful horse.

Physical characteristics in detail

Here coarse and very fine characteristics combine into a kind of sensitive power. The head is short – if you are following accepted breeding standards it is actually too short. It is not exactly sharply defined and fine. The nostrils on the other hand are very beautifully formed, and the upper lip is very powerful and highly expressive. Characteristic of this horse is the interplay of profile, eyes and, above all, the position of the eyes. The profile shows a downward dip in the middle. In other types, this signifies a particular fearfulness. In the Pilgrim this tendency is thoroughly possible, but with this horse it would be more accurate to speak of caution, foresight, watchfulness and far-sightedness.

A hand's breadth above the nostrils the line of the profile rises again to flow straight and well formed into the nostrils and mouth.

The beautiful interplay of the muzzle and the eyes creates the thoughtful expression of this horse. The eyes are beautifully proportioned and placed in a markedly balanced way. They are set a moderate distance from the front of the face.

There is a fine balance to the structure of the head, which indicates that it is easy for the horse to look to the future and trust himself to new experiences.

Which person suits the Pilgrim?

This horse needs a horseman who understands him, who can give him direction in the most uncomplicated fashion, in order to then, as far as possible, leave the horse to himself.

This horse can be a beginner's horse, or a children's horse, as long as the beginner is prepared to learn from the horse. It is very difficult to irritate the Pilgrim, and he almost never reacts aggressively. It is almost as though the horse simply ignores whatever does not quite suit him or his nature. He picks out for himself that which seems appropriate for his development and the course of his life. Only strong force will break this horse.

The beginner who gets a horse of this type that was previously in good hands can consider himself very fortunate. This new horseman will have found his teacher. The person for the Pilgrim should be modest and reserved, of a noble and fine disposition. He should, like the Pilgrim, love to look and move forward, and to travel towards a goal. He should have enough time to explore the world, or at least the immediate surroundings, in the company of his horse. With the Pilgrim such a person will have a quiet, contented, but also a varied and adventuresome time ahead of him. Good luck!

The Child

You can see immediately how this horse got his name. I do not know the age of the first horse pictured here, but he might still retain some childlike traits because of his actual youth. However, the nature of the Child within this character group goes far beyond this temporary appearance.

The nature

This horse is a relatively open, simple and, in a certain way, jolly creature. Contrary to the previous character type, this animal lacks nearly every trace of seriousness. You must keep this in mind when you are with such a horse. He is neither suited for High School work, nor for continuous, or long, concentrated sequences, of work. He is, and remains, a child! If you keep that fact firmly in mind, then you can have a lot of happiness and fun with this friend. Long rides requiring stamina – in fact any kind of challenging tasks – should not be undertaken with this type of horse under any circumstances. It would be like entrusting a child with a difficult professional task. Corresponding to his childlike mental state, his physical appearance is also very delicate. Throughout the whole of his life this horse's body will retain something childlike and undeveloped. Even in old age this horse does not seem truly mature. Like the Prince, this type occurs relatively infrequently.

Spontaneous associations with the Child

Unsurprisingly he is childlike, childishly playful, of delicate constitution and health, he is not suited for demanding or difficult work, loses concentration easily, and has a charming and captivating nature.

Physical characteristics in detail

Everything about the head of this horse seems pretty, but in contrast to the Minister, the King, the Tough One, or many other character groups, it is also decidedly 'flat': there is barely a hook or handle to which character could fasten. This horse gives the impression that he comes from the world of Barbie dolls. Everything seems to be a little artificial, a little too perfect, like the results of a certain kind of cosmetic surgery procedure, when, on the whole, the part that is cut away is that which could have revealed a tiny bit of character and uniqueness.

The nose is absolutely straight, the nostrils beautiful, the eyes well formed, the mouth delicate and loosely held. Everything is markedly symmetrical and therefore sometimes has the effect of being boring. The light bay horse possesses a well-set-on neck, a relatively good back, and a beautifully proportioned elbow and shoulder. Here too the measurements are symmetrical and harmonious, which gives the horse light and free gaits and a good temperament.

Which person suits the Child?

This very loveable horse will pose hardly any problems for a person as long as you cater to his childlike nature and offer him every conceivable opportunity to satisfy his momentary inclinations. Now and again the Child can be steered into structured activity but, as mentioned, you must be very careful.

The Child needs a mature person, or one who is on the way to maturity, who will be patient and tolerant and totally unambitious with respect to competition. If two children come together, they will only reinforce each other's immaturity.

The Child continually challenges his owner to progress from a subjective observation of the world to an objective view. That naïve, self-centred side of a person, and the tendency to act without immediately taking into account the consequences of that action, will cause intense chaos in a relationship with this horse. This horse needs an example to follow.

The following photo shows a representative of this group that exhibits clear traits of the Minister. This Child is altogether more serious and mature in his nature.

The Half-born One

The nature

You frequently come across horses of this character group. These are creatures that leave the impression that they are only partially in this world. They often seem to be absent, and they even run into difficulties with other horses because they are often rejected by them.

The bay horse with the blaze is a typical representative of this character group. In this connection even the blaze speaks for itself – it nearly halves the lower half of the horse's face.

Horses of this character group always seem to be suffering. It is as though they do not understand themselves, and are not understood by others, whether horse or human. Their nature is therefore either rather introverted, or thoroughly aggressive.

Their overall nature is interesting. If you recognize the cause of their suffering, if you take them seriously and approach them in a manner appropriate to them, then a unique friendship can develop, and then these horses can teach you about 'other worlds'.

In their outer appearance these horses are similar to the Frog and the North Wind. Nevertheless, their natures are very different.

In my experience, more female than male animals belong to this character group.

Spontaneous associations with the Half-born One

Altogether the effect is one of a frightened and startled horse. Generally, the animal is of a concave basic structure, a poor-doer and of unstable health. He can easily seem undernourished, with weight gain usually confining itself solely to the underbelly which then seems to hang in a pot-bellied way from the otherwise bony horse. The Half-born One is often 'absent', unfocused, but at the same time tries very hard and is very obliging in his way to human beings. He wants to work for human beings, but often cannot. The horse of this character group possesses a deep inner nature that appears to be concealed, heavily veiled and sleeping. You can easily wrong such a horse and, ultimately, break him, if you judge him by criteria that are far too high.

Physical characteristics in detail

The head usually seems long and narrow and shows little modulation. The eyes are prominent and, not infrequently, as with the bay horse, you can see the whites of the eyes. The upper lid appears to have been pulled back, and that too strengthens the impression of the wide-open eyes. The forehead is flat, small, and expressionless. The muzzle is narrow and also without expression. The nostrils, like the eyelids, appear to be pulled backward and upward and therefore look narrow and slanted. The back is usually very weak, and the neck is long, set on low and has a very weak top line.

The little chestnut also belongs to this character group, but in his case I am not certain whether he was born with this appearance or whether he went into 'inner withdrawal'

because of longstanding mishandling. The overall head shape and the current expression totally correspond with the character group of the Half-born One but the great sadness in the horse's eyes and his acute 'absence' lead to the conclusion that his predisposition was intensified through incorrect handling.

The grey horse is a mixture of the character group the Half-born One and the next group, the North Wind. These character groups are very similar to one another, but the horse of the North Wind type is more amenable to the various positive developmental possibilities available in the company of human beings.

Which person suits the Half-born One?

This horse is not a riding horse! Only with the greatest effort, with an enormous level of knowledge and experience, and with much patience and empathy can, over the years, this horse be brought to the point where he can carry a lightweight rider at least halfway in balance, and most importantly, without pain.

Far too often, however, you see such horses with their heads pulled up, completely hollowed backs, and a pain-distorted expression, trudging along under an inconsiderate rider. That is probably one of the most lamentable images the riding world has to offer.

Both the Half-Born One and the North Wind groups are definitely not beginners' or children's horses. These horses suffer terribly, even after only a short time with an inexperienced horseperson.

The person who feels himself drawn to the Half-born One should be very clear about the background of his own existence. He is also probably of a fine, dreamy, 'absent' nature. Through realization and understanding he can, together with this horse, clear new paths for himself and the horse. The person for the Half-born One should be extremely understanding and should get very good advice from experienced people about working with this horse. This will be expanded upon in Chapter 6.

The North Wind

The nature

Horses of this character group have something 'metallic' something 'sharp' about them –
just like the north wind. Outwardly they are very similar to the previous character group.
They are also poor-doers with a concave body form and weak backs and necks. They are,
unlike the Half-born One, completely part of this world although they follow the wind that
gusts from on high and moves between heaven and earth.

They seem to be very spiritual, and for this reason often seem to be 'absent'. If a person
does not find the right key to the soul of this horse then he will always remain distanced
from people. Even though this horse has a high measure of spirituality – the facial
expression makes this very clear – the North Wind is very dissimilar to horses in the
character group Pegasus, whose spirituality has an entirely different dimension because it
is accompanied by incomparably greater power and expression.

Spontaneous association with the North Wind

This horse is 'absent', distanced, a poor-doer, of fragile form and inner nature, but also thoroughly capable of assertiveness with respect to human beings, even to the point of heightened aggression. Not generally suitable as a riding horse, the North Wind is completely independent and detached, and his nature is difficult to read and predict. If he finds a human counterpart by whom he feels understood, then he arrives at his own form of attachment and even loyalty.

Physical characteristics in detail

In contrast to his uniform facial expression, this dark grey horse's ears are remarkably full of character, which indicates this animal's forwardness and urge to move. Movement suits the North Wind, a fact that differentiates him from the Half-born One. The eye is of medium size, but open and clear, it is harmoniously placed and indicates a fundamental readiness for an uncomplicated relationship. The profile is straight and not very striking; the nostrils are relatively small and have little expression. This horse displays an unusual tightness in the area between the jowls and the mouth.

The ears and the arrangement of the features on the head in an otherwise simple, childlike, and relatively characterless expression, are the stamp of this horse's nature. It is here that energy and wilfulness show themselves, and the complexity which estranges this horse from human beings expresses itself.

The overall appearance of this horse is lean, although not as lean as the Half-born One. With the North Wind too, we have an overall concave form, with an inferior carrying power of the neck and back.

Which person suits the North Wind?

It is a long and difficult undertaking to develop such a horse into a riding horse. Horses of this type are frequently seen in leisure-riding circles. Unfortunately I have had to acknowledge the fact that it is leisure riders who are gripped by a sort of sentimental liberalism and want to develop horses of any and every type into riding horses, and they do not mind if the horses are off the racetrack, come from the transporter who takes horses to slaughter, are of lesser breeding, or have arrived in some overseas shipment. Their intentions may be admirable but real life demands discernment and mastery, and creation has magically put innumerable differences into this vast and colourful world. Whether we want to or not, we must come to terms with these differences.

The person considering the North Wind should, therefore, ask himself why he feels drawn to such a horse. There is nothing negative in this horse but a great deal that is very specific to his nature which needs to be heeded and thoroughly examined. The wind from the north is simply a very particular occurrence and not an everyday one. Its positive qualities are power, freshness, independence, clarity and mystical presence. All of those qualities can be discovered and developed in the company of this horse if you abstain completely from pursuit of superficial performance and achievement.

How and when a horse of this character group can be developed is something I will address in more detail in Chapter 6.

The Lonely One

Warmbloods can have representatives in various character groups and, again, we do not want to equate breed with character group. However, it is noteworthy that many warmbloods are to be found in this character group.

The nature

Horses in this character group have been bred for a very particular purpose for generations. This horse is a specialist within clearly delineated categories of use, in which it is all about top-level performance. That is not questioned. Breeding goals are oriented around this. I am of the opinion that animals should, under no circumstances, be pulled into those competitive and performance vortices that even human beings cannot endure for long periods, but that is not the topic under discussion. Here we are concerned with the fact that, together with certain external breeding goals, certain inner qualities and characteristics have insinuated themselves. The character group of the Lonely One is formed and influenced most strongly by the horses resulting from this type of breeding. I may approach these horses with certain preconceptions, and have to make an effort to be as neutral as it is possible for me to be. My possible bias relates to the fact that the very sight of such horses fills me with a kind of sad powerlessness, because these animals actually live in a withdrawn and lonely world and, for me, the tragedy is that the fact that they live that way is determined by breeding. These horses are the product of decades of 'work' on the part of breeders. Certainly there are major differences among the warmblood breeds, but the most successful breeding areas just happen to be those that produce horses of the type described here because horses of this character group are particularly useable, no matter what the specific function.

This horse tends to be mentally slow, not because he is fundamentally mentally rigid, but because he has, over the generations, given up expressing himself creatively and flexibly. This horse has learned to function, and breeding has concentrated on those individuals that do function, whose performance fits a certain model, and that can reproduce it at any time. When I come into contact with a Lonely One at a clinic or demonstration, my way of proceeding is different from that used with nearly all the other character groups. How can I, in a very short time, make clear to a horse with traits celebrated for centuries for their suitability to sporting uses and competition, that life outside his withdrawn state is much more exciting?

This bay horse still displays a great willingness to be with human beings, compared to many horses of this character group that do not. Nevertheless, he seems designed for those movements and tasks that are diametrically opposed to a more brisk, spontaneous, agile, fast, creative, continually changing and varied way of working and spending leisure time. These horses excel in the work for which they were bred. The Germans breed the most successful horses in the world for a type of work that naturally suits them better than any other in this world.

Spontaneous association with the Lonely One

His movements are determined and standardized by breeding, and he tends to be mentally inflexible, introverted, isolated, not understood, resigned, mostly insensitive to every form of stimulation. Seen objectively, the Lonely One has a moderate to low versatility relative to the whole spectrum of horse character types. Performance is tied in to the continual giving of aids. If you bring this horse into a completely peaceful and totally stress-free situation, he can easily break down and become very slow and clumsy, and can barely be motivated at all. The class and temperament that seem to be present are in fact often built upon tension and fear. If that driving element is missing, there is total absence of motivation.

Other than that, this horse is patient, calm, quiet, moderately – sometimes highly – intelligent and, with dignified treatment, loyal and much attached to human beings. Through breeding he is 'culture oriented' and adapts easily to humans and his world. If you break through the horse's experience of withdrawal and loneliness, then he becomes a quiet and balanced partner.

Physical characteristics in detail

First of all it is noticeable that this horse is in fairly good proportion. Warmbloods are differently proportioned from other types of horses intended for other speciality pursuits, or those that are closer in type to archetypal or primitive horses. The horse pictured here has a slightly 'held together' forehand, i.e. a forehand that is not free: the upright shoulder; the neck set somewhat too low; the too-solid appearance of the lower part of the neck, particularly visible when looking at the horse head-on; the too-flat top line of the neck; the weakness of the back directly behind the withers; and a head that, in proportion to the body, seems too short. All these points result in a total picture of a horse that shuts down in response to internal pressure. It is as though this horse cannot react or move freely.

The eye is small. The accenting bone structure above and behind the eye is massive and coarse, which is a particularly typical feature of this character group. The profile is uncomplicated and clear, the nostrils are fleshy and immobile. The muzzle is firm, coarse, and also immobile. The entire lower jaw is not particularly well developed, and comparatively small and narrow.

Which person suits the Lonely One?

In the sporting world, different criteria count when pairing horse and rider. With our criteria, the person for the Lonely One should be without ambition. He should know that outside the patterned movement of horse sports these horses are not capable of nimble action. Conformation, size, and predisposition make this impossible from the outset. Because of that, this horse is useful only within limits for work or leisure riding.

The person, through his restraint, should be able to find a new way to reach this horse, appropriate to the psyche of this type. Simplicity, peace, patience, as well as clarity, form and proportion in the schooling will open this horse and allow him to mature into a dependable and even somewhat joyful partner.

The Used One

In this type too, one breeding line is particularly strongly represented, and in that breeding are contained the causes for a very particular behaviour over many generations.

The nature

In his basic nature this horse is, to a greater or lesser degree, sad. Out of what were once classical archetypal Spanish horses, 'marionettes' were deliberately carved that document with apathy and sorrow the evisceration of primal equine existence.

Horse whispering and imprinting also fit into the basic system of use at the expense of individuality. Along with the warmblood and the Thoroughbred, the Quarter Horse is a particular specialist and he, like these other breeds, was designed by humans for his usefulness.

Let me reiterate that we must not equate a particular breed with a character type, and, therefore, not every Quarter Horse is a representative of this character group. Certainly there are horses among them that are marked by their openness and sensitivity and have nothing in common with the Used One. Nevertheless, truth is that we must recognize and acknowledge that certain breeds put their stamp strongly on certain character groups. I must keep that fact in mind in my daily work because only then can it yield good fruit. I want to repeat that I have the same esteem and affection for every horse. For this reason I am also duty bound to look at and recognize every horse without sentimentality. Only then can I help in individual cases.

Communication is a two-way thing: joy that is accepted and given back, interest that inspires and is exchanged, that is communication. We all know people with whom our efforts at communication seem in vain. Being with them remains uninspiring no matter how much we try to 'grease the wheels' of communication. I often have this problem with this horse type because he is so inward looking, so resigned.

Spontaneous association with the Used One

When such a horse encounters me during a clinic, then, as with warmbloods, I must employ special and thoroughly different standards from those used with other horse types. This horse is surprisingly easy to manipulate. He is either functioning completely or is absolutely not centred, and hysterical. The latter seldom happens, but it seems to be the final form of expressing anger. It is generally not easy to establish a genuine contact with this horse type since he lives behind a protective cloak of apathy, as you can clearly see in the expression of the chestnut horse.

Inherently this horse is good natured, simple and has an uncomplicated disposition. He is persevering and enjoys good health. Owing to his breeding, he could never achieve High School standards. Only with considerable effort can sensitive communication be established with this horse. However, if you do succeed in establishing communication then the Used One demonstrates a moving, enduringly active attentiveness to human beings, and he becomes a steady friend.

Physical characteristics in detail

Through breeding, the head is short compared to the physical mass of the body, the neck is set on low, the elbows are too far forward, the croup is overbuilt, and the shoulder seems narrow compared to the massive hindquarters. Also massive are the jaws, the brow and the connection between head and neck. Compared to that, the head looks narrow as it runs down to the nostrils and muzzle. The eyes are wide apart and often appear to have a pitiable sadness in them.

Which person suits the Used One?

This horse is associated with sentimental and cliché-like images of riding and being with nature or with the desire to profit in betting circles. But that is exactly what this horse needs the least. He needs an unindocrinated person who is not shackled by these preconceptions and who can, therefore, awaken the horse's primal source, self-trust, individuality, joy in communicating, trust in others and renewed devotion. Then he will, with gratitude and attentiveness, build a solid bridge to his owner. Under these circumstances he will be of a cheerful, simple nature and become a reliable and enduring partner. The person for the Used One should definitely not be a 'horse expert'. Beginners and even children get along surprisingly well with this horse once they have recognized his nature and made the effort to find a new and different approach to him. Indeed, this task is often best suited to children and beginners rather than to experienced riders who sometimes are inclined to be blinded by the urge to compete.

The Gypsy

The nature

This is a very exciting and interesting equine character. He is intense and wild and will always remain so. The Gypsy is not a beginner's horse; he suits very special people with very particular ambitions. The run-of-the-mill, but capable horseperson will easily be driven to despair by this horse, and probably the horse will as well.

The legendary black stallion of countless novels, stories and tales, that always runs away from everyone and only lets himself be caught and ridden by one particular person: that is a Gypsy.

Spontaneous associations with the Gypsy

The Gypsy carries within himself the complete gamut of the many possible ways a horse can express himself. He is as charming as he is stubborn, as gentle as he is unrestrained, as insightful as he is unreachable, as loyal as he is unattached and free. He is the adventurer who is unfit for almost every adventure. He is like the lover who in reality never truly makes a commitment.

When I have such a horse before me, then the game, the dance, the exchange, begins. It is like a fiery tango in which giving and taking melt into a harmonious chaos, where no one cares about the beginning or the end, or even the purpose of the dance. Time seems not to exist for this horse; every despairing thought of the future is alien to him, and he wants to experience only the here and now.

Physical characteristics in detail

In the first photo we have a narrow 'catlike' horse. The overall appearance is sharply defined, sinewy, but not haggard. The horse has a very compact, strong bone structure, but the effect is nevertheless delicate. This delicate effect deceives some people as to the toughness of this horse. In confrontations over herd rank, this horse has the advantage over, and is superior to, even much more massive opponents.

Horses of this character group are mostly of small or medium height in comparison to their bloodline average. In the black horse we see lovely primal horse proportions. The neck is well set on, although a little tight in the upper part. The forehand is well formed and the angle of the shoulder is good. The hindquarters are too weak, but the right work could correct that to a great extent. The back is relatively short and, on the whole, of good carrying ability, although currently it is too weakly muscled; but that too is just a question of correct work.

If we look at individual characteristics of the head, like the eyes, profile, nostrils, muzzle and jaw, there is nothing particularly noteworthy there. However, the expression formed by the combined characteristics is very indicative of the Gypsy. The eye is relatively small but very aware and alert. The powerful, long upper jaw flows into a delicate yet powerful muzzle. The lower line, from mouth to jowls, curves noticeably downward, and it is this, in interplay with the other details, which indicates the self-willed energy. The ears are relatively small, playful, and thin walled. The slight convex curve of the forehead, coupled with the line of the lower jaw, is also characteristic of this horse.

Within a particular breed, a horse of this type always seems a little out of place. As a rule, he does not fill the breed standards as purely and fully as might be desired. In my view, that is often an advantage since such a horse seems to me to be a throwback to the primal source. The wilfulness also seems to lie deeply hidden in his genes – free play in the ocean of creation.

The pinto is a coarser representative of this equine type; his nature is not quite so clear. Here the Gypsy is paired with a certain cunning that, with his natural tendency to unpredictability, makes him even more unpredictable.

With this horse it is important to curb all attempts at pushiness even in early youth. For, if a horse like this matures without restraint and guidance from a correct hand, then it will be very difficult to accustom him to an acceptable framework of behaviour (see Chapter 6).

Which person suits the Gypsy

A Gypsy requires a lot of time and attention, despite his urge for freedom, which will then help him form a thorough and good attachment to other horses and to human beings. In the Gypsy, loyalty and the desire for freedom are not necessarily antagonistic forces; in certain circumstances they are two sides of the same coin. If this horse is provoked into aggression, his attacks are always predictable. They are telegraphed well in advance through warning signals and, even in the deepest despair this horse remembers to defend himself only to the required degree, not to truly harm.

The person for the Gypsy should not be a beginner or a child. He should, like the horse, be possessed of a free and playful nature, be calm and, above all, tolerant. The person can bring temperament to the relationship – quite a lot in fact – but he should under no circumstances be choleric or inclined to anger, because that would quickly lead to vehement confrontations between him and his horse and to the horse's inner breakdown. This horse belongs to the spirit of the south as does the sun. He who loves the temperament of the south, its lightness and also its lack of earnestness, will find in this horse a wonderful soul mate and much stuff of which dreams are made.

The Dandy

The nature

In certain ways the Dandy is related to the Gypsy. He is usually not quite so rough and forceful in his manner and his whole appearance, but he is similarly playful and broad in the spectrum of his behaviour. He is mentally, emotionally and physically a bit more vulnerable than the Gypsy. He also has traits in common with the Dove and, in certain respects, with the Child. In his appearance the Dandy is often the most attractive of all these groups, and in his nature he is superficial but uncomplicated. He is always a horse, no matter what the breed, to which even people unfamiliar with horses easily give their hearts because he is so very open and charming. The Dandy is usually aware of his effect on people; he plays and flirts with it.

Spontaneous associations with the Dandy

The Dandy is thoroughly compact, agile and solid but, in general, less sturdy than the Gypsy. He is not a workhorse, and has little inner stamina. He learns quickly, but does not always have the sharpness to apply what he has learned to a lasting behaviour. Because of that, this horse is not equipped for certain tasks and uses. Nevertheless, his education can proceed in a quite uncomplicated way if you take his inherent weakness into consideration. Within the framework of his abilities, the Dandy is a thoroughly fascinating, enormously impressive horse. He is playful, happy, full of humour, of a superficial, sensible disposition, tolerant, thoughtful within limits, attentive and focussed, and relatively easy to lead and persuade.

Physical characteristics in detail

The Dandy is quite simply a beautiful horse, and particularly when possessed of masculine traits, he easily ensnares hearts. His expression is always friendly and a bit childlike. The head of this black horse is short, sharply defined, and relatively expressive. Note the eyes; they have the look of those of a human child, and the whole expression is almost human. The eye is large, open, and normally very clear. The eye of the black horse pictured here is slightly closed because of a momentary mood shift. The ears are relatively simple and not very spectacular; they denote an uncomplicated creature with an average forward urge and only average endurance. In comparison to the overall look of the head the jaws are massive and shapely. The interplay of jaws, brow and eyes in combination with the expressive play of the nostrils and the delicate muzzle with its small mouth create the impression of this horse. This interplay of various characteristics gives the Dandy his noble and attractive demeanour – particularly to women, I am told.

The Dandy's profile is almost always concave. A profile like that of our black horse could, in other horses or in a different sort of overall look, be construed as indicative of fear or failing self-confidence. The small dip directly above the nostrils could be particularly critical but, in this case, this element of the profile is more likely to indicate playfulness and imagination, although fearfulness has much to do with imagination and creativity.

The pinto is a tougher example of this character group. His disposition is closer to that of the Gypsy. His brow is more pronounced, the eyes are smaller and less prominent, and he has the combination of brow, eyes, and the powerful jaws in relation to an otherwise rather short head, that is typical of the Dandy.

The bay horse shows the distinctive traits of this character group, although his spirit is much more serious. He is more persevering than the black horse and so he can undertake more demanding tasks in his life. He shows some similarity to the Minister, although his fundamental character type remains recognizable.

When judging a horse, this inherent nature plays a profound role; it provides the musical key so to speak. Although various melodies can be played in this key, the basic character of the horses remains the determining factor. Dealing with a Minister who has certain features in common with a Dandy is, however, different from dealing, as in this case, with a Dandy who shares some qualities of the Minister.

What sort of person suits the Dandy?

This horse is uncomplicated and very pleasant to work with. He is cooperative, joyful and friendly. Even beginners can own a Dandy if they approach work carefully and with a gentle hand. This horse is a pleasant and loveable companion, and he will keep his charm and enthusiasm his whole life if he is not overfaced and not locked into stamina-demanding tasks unsuited to his type. The person for the Dandy should himself be playful and rather unambitious. He should be in touch with refined childlike playful strains in himself, enjoy interaction, and be curious and open to the world and its magic. In fact, he should be of a light, charming and, shall we say, dancer-like nature.

The Modest One

The nature

Now we turn to another extreme of possible equine character. The Modest One is, in a certain sense, the opposite of the Dandy. This equine type is simple but, is inwardly much richer than it appears on the surface. The Modest One has a certain similarity to the Guardian of the Fire, but he is not so motherly, and his overall appearance is simpler, coarser, and fleshier. A horse of this type is very frequently underestimated. In riding circles, this horse is frequently regarded with contempt but carriage drivers value, recognize, and acknowledge this horse type more readily.

We actually always find the Modest One in one form: horses in this character group look very much alike. If this horse becomes discontented in human hands he will first withdraw into himself but the moment will come when an outbreak of forceful aggression can ensue.

At that point, these horses become unexpectedly dangerous.

I repeatedly discuss the aggressive behaviour of horses not least because I must confront it again and again. The horses I deal with in clinics, for example, are, more often than not, those that have left a trail of suffering, often of considerable dimensions. I must evaluate every horse very quickly in order to establish how he behaves given his fundamental potential for aggression, and in what circumstances he finds himself at the moment. I found out that the predisposition of an equine character to behave a certain way in extreme situations also gives a great deal of information about the true nature of the horse in a normal, quiet situation. Again, that is why I repeatedly refer to the aggressive behaviour of a particular equine character in these descriptions.

Spontaneous associations with the Modest One

In our world modesty is unfortunately far too often confused with weakness and a lack of energy. A modest primal human being is very aware of himself, including his abilities and strengths; he is absolutely ready to assert his self-interests and when necessary to attend to them with power and energy.

The word 'modest' when applied to this horse should be understood in the original sense. The Modest One is of robust good health, good natured, simple and uncomplicated. He has many more qualities than would initially appear to be the case, is of average to high intelligence, and is willing to learn and attentive. Horses of this type are quiet, grounded, good mothers and lead mares. Their physical abilities are quite limited but, within their limits, they are agile, nimble, powerful and of a good carrying constitution.

Physical characteristics in detail

The shape of the head is very geometrical. The upper half of the head, the upper jaw, the eyes and the nostrils are harmonious and well-proportioned. Here depth, sensitivity, simplicity of nature, and willingness to communicate and cooperate reveal themselves. The profiles of the horses in this character group are always straight.

It is a different picture with the lower jaw and the ears.

The entire lower jaw is coarse and fleshy, which gives the horse his somewhat clumsy impression. In these areas, aggression, power, self-will and assertiveness reveal themselves and here too the propensity to fall into light to moderately severe depressions under long, continuous unwholesome situations is revealed.

The eye of this grey horse already shows the typical sadness that remains hidden from some owners for long periods of time because the horse continues to loyally fulfil his obligations. But, internally, under the still 'protective layer' of modesty, things are brewing. Caution is recommended here.

Which person suits the Modest One?

This horse is a good all-rounder. Of course, we cannot take this horse to the highest levels of training, even though some representatives from the world of leisure riders aver that we can. A horse like this is neither physically nor mentally able to do that but, in general, he is suitable for many jobs, even coping with more than one; the Modest One can go very nicely under a rider, and also happily pull a carriage. He is very sociable with other horses and is a good companion to human beings. He is relatively uncomplicated to train – but now and then leans towards unwillingness and shows displeasure. In such cases, the person must respond with much patience and empathy. He can in fact deflect these phases in a very elegant way by every now and then yielding to the horse because with this animal there is no danger of a dominance problem evolving. For the raw beginner however this horse will always pose problems because his basic disposition does not permit him to immediately let it be known when something is wrong. The inexperienced person is then perplexed when suddenly 'nothing works anymore' even though up until that point everything seemed to be going so well.

The person for the Modest One will himself be of a down-to-earth, solid and simple nature. He will not demand too much of his horse and he will recognize and treasure the depth of his protégé, which will lead to an uncomplicated, peaceful, not spectacular but very harmonious, relationship.

The Frog

The nature

The Frog is anything but a fighter and he expresses that in his entire bearing. The similarity of the pictures that we see here is no coincidence; you usually find the horses of this type in this carriage.

The Frog is a good-natured, closeness-seeking, straightforward horse. He allows himself to be used and exploited very easily. In southern Europe you always find Frogs among the rental horses at the cheaper tourist spots. Although they are not rugged or suited for hard work, they have given up themselves and all fight at birth and thus let themselves be oppressed so easily – without protest.

Spontaneous associations with the Frog

Weakness and sadness are written in the faces of these horses from the first day of life. The Frog is patient, simple, good-natured, modest, unassuming, and of a weak nature in every way. The back is too long, weak and does not have good carrying ability. His nature is marked by a certain submissiveness and tendency to injury. The horse is, in general, likely to be defensive, reserved and fearful. If a person can set aside the notion of advancing his horse in order to strengthen and fortify his nature and constitution instead, he will have a very grateful and loyal friend at his side.

Physical characteristics in detail

First let us take a look at the degree to which, with all three horses, the face tapers towards the nostrils and mouth. On the bay horse this configuration is particularly characteristic;

the head almost seems to end in a point, resulting in an expression that is oddly weak and indecisive. With the chestnut, this configuration is not delineated quite as clearly, and therefore he is stronger in his nature than the bay; we also see the hint of a form that we will find again later, in much clearer delineation, when we come to the King. This characteristically long, downward tapering

simply not created for, and is not fit for, riding.

Of the three horses illustrated here, the chestnut, though affected by many problem zones, has a higher energetic level. His body structure is of a stronger type. When I discuss this character group in the section on developing a riding horse, I use this particular horse as an example. With a great deal of effort, a great knowledge of the subject, care

muzzle is easily recognizable in the pinto, as is the pulled-upward upper lip.

That is the typical picture of the Frog, and this look carries over in a figurative sense into the way the horse behaves; he always sees the world from the bottom, and generally resigns himself to whatever happens with the attitude of 'nothing can be done about it'.

The head is comparatively long and narrow and, as just mentioned, tapers to a point at the muzzle. The eye is relatively small with an upper lid that always seems on the verge of closing. That feature can be seen well in the pinto. The profile between the eyes and nostrils is always absolutely straight. Just below the level of the eyes there is a 'step up' and then the brow runs straight again to the base of the forelock. The jaws have a pitiable expression, and this is where the overall weakness of the Frog is clearly recognizable. The entire lower jaw has an underdeveloped shape. The mouth is unspecific and indicates nothing, and it is carried mutely and stiffly. The body structure of this horse is weak with a long and concave back. The thin neck is set on low and is without any carrying power whatsoever in its top line. The shoulders and croup are narrow and the hindquarters trail out behind. Frequently these horses tend to be overbent, and all the gaits are flat and concentrated on the forehand. As a rule the Frog was

and patience, certain representatives of this character group can be brought to the point of being able to perform some ridden exercises.

Which person suits the Frog?

The picture of the person who can, should, and might dedicate himself to such a horse has already become clear through a description of the character group itself: anything coarse, rough, unjust, forceful, sharp and exploitive should be kept as far as possible from this horse. The person for the Frog, therefore, should be able to act accordingly. However, too much misdirected tenderness is also inappropriate here because the horse needs someone at his side who understands how to lead definitely and clearly. This horse wants to be able to depend on someone who is gentle but acts with clarity and certainty. The Frog is through and through a beginner's horse, but not a child's horse, and the beginner should certainly obtain good advice as to what the work with, and development of, the Frog entails, because absolute caution is in order here. Otherwise the Frog will too easily break down and be lastingly damaged.

The Prince

The nature

This horse has a conflicting nature in some respects. He is: attached to human beings, but also concerned about maintaining his distance; cooperative, but also critical, second-guessing, doubting, and only to be won over by conviction; reserved and careful but, when it comes down to it, also thoroughly courageous and ready for action. The Prince is just like a not yet fully mature monarch and he remains that way even at an advanced age – he does not become a King. With, or despite, his conflicted nature, he is an interesting character.

Spontaneous association with the Prince

Horses of this character group are rare. If you take their basic disposition into account, they are by and large simple and pleasant to associate with. They sometimes come across as somewhat immature, but are also extremely correct, fair, and righteous.

It actually takes quite a lot to bring these horses to the point of aggression. They are much too distanced to immediately deal with minor injustices. It is more likely that such a horse will tend to simply switch off and become sour. Despite their sensitivity these horses have a sort of 'security armour' that protects them inwardly from the encroachment of human beings in a different way from that which is the case with many other equine characters. The Prince is reserved, of moderate temperament, occasionally a bit absent and unfocussed, good-natured, patient, has an average to high intelligence, a powerful body structure and good carrying ability, and is willing to learn, modest and diligent. The Prince is a pleasure to have around.

Physical characteristics in detail

The head of the chestnut horse in the main picture is rather small relative to his body. He is also, in my opinion, atypical of his breed – he is a Quarter Horse. Note the massiveness of the jowls and forehead in relation to the nearly delicate tapering of the muzzle. But, most noteworthy are the eyes: they are almond shaped, elongated, of a strange sharp presence and, at the same time, as though veiled.

The Prince's profile is always a bit concave and, usually, evenly curved. On this chestnut we see a slight 'bump' a hand's breadth above the nostrils, which indicates occasional fearfulness and that this horse can sometimes be a bit obstinate. The nostrils are fine, wide, sensitive and open and have a typical placement and shape for this type: they are elongated downward and strongly define the head of the animal. The upper lip is sensitive and fine and indicates an uncomplicated clarity. The chestnut holds it a bit tightly, but with correct work this could be resolved in a short time. The bottom lip is likewise fine and plain: it is held in a slightly pulled-back position, which indicates quite a good willingness to work and also a not-too-wild temperament. The ears are well delineated and here too a quiet, moderate temperament reveals itself. The fact that the ears also are a bit fleshy indicates that the horse is fundamentally grounded and reliable.

A Prince's body is usually powerful and compact. The animal is seldom ill and capable of resisting disease. Depending on the particular conformation, horses of this type can in certain circumstances be brought fairly readily to High School level, for which they are mentally and emotionally equipped. This horse can master even difficult exercises without signs of stress if worked quietly.

Which person suits the Prince?

The Prince is an independent horse for an independent person. If horse and person fit together in such a constellation then you encounter a very interesting pair.

This horse is ideal for beginners and will easily and magnanimously ignore the mistakes of a generally succinct owner; indeed he finds it is a pleasure to occasionally show human beings the 'right way'. The Prince is a very good schoolmaster for new riders because he is patient and of a quiet and thoughtful nature. He avoids everything coarse. The person for the Prince should, therefore, also possess a certain aristocratic radiance and should have a fine nature and pleasant form. From the very beginning the communication with this horse can be fine and sensitive, and so the Prince's owner should be as aware, and as in control, of his own body and movements as possible.

The Victor

There are only five more character groups and they are certainly very special. Let us begin the final section with the Victor.

The nature

Everyone, whether or not he knows horses, can without difficulty find the connection between the horses pictured here and the character group described. With these horses it is easy, at least with regard to what suits their needs. For their owners these horses nevertheless often pose some difficulties. Hot-blooded, very, very specially bred, and equipped with special abilities, these horses can very easily tip over the edge temperamentally and exhibit behaviour that ultimately is barely controllable. For generations they have had to adapt themselves to a 'business' that actually in some small way suits them; it offers them the opportunity to win. This is something these horses really want when it can be offered to them in a way that is, in my opinion, more ethical. I am happy to start clinics with horses like these because I can easily make general explanations and concentrate on the onlookers, while what takes place in the arena seems to occur of its own accord. Horses of this type are extremely sensitive, fine, and alert, and despite, in many cases, countless negative experiences with humans they are still wonderfully cooperative. They want to understand and to be understood, and once that understanding can be transmitted to them, within seconds a closeness ensues that is nearly mystical in its power.

Physical characteristics in detail

The profile of this character type is nearly always straight. If you encounter a convex profile with the following features then you are usually dealing with a Minister or a mixture of these two types. Then the behaviour of the horse changes greatly and it is sensible to be very cautious. If a Minister is forced into a riding 'business' he will present the owner with completely different problems, even though many of these wonderful horses are locked into competitive sports.

The head shape of the Victor is in general placed between harmonious and square. The palomino shows a harmonious head shape, the Thoroughbred a squarer one. Let us stay with the Thoroughbred. His round, large, fine nostrils show strength, character, will and sensitivity all at once. The rounded upper lip furthers this impression: it is powerful and expressive. The head overall is sharply defined, slender, and of inner robust strength. The forehead is fine but massive. The eye is clear and well placed. The jaws are small and narrow but with this configuration do not imply weakness and inner powerlessness. In this head all of the power has been concentrated in the area of the eyes and the forehead. Here the energy and expression gather. It is almost as though the animal thinks and acts with forehead and eyes. The ears are fine and well formed. They do not indicate the very greatest strength and intensity, but define an affinity with the earth. There is something crocodilian about this horse type: the observation, seeing everything around it as spoils, the lightening-speed attack and then resubmergence.

Physically these horses strongly exhibit the shape and form which has been bred into them for generations. They are generally not much, if any, use as riding horses because the structure of the back and the neck is not intended for carrying but running and pulling. These horses find favour with pleasure riders because they can often be picked up cheaply from racing and sport-horse circles. These horses can, with a lot of effort and love, make good hacks that can usually be ridden in walk and occassionally in trot or, better, a slow canter uphill. Victors can then establish strong close ties to people, which they need to aid their recovery from an existence than can barely be called humane. Even if the burden on a relatively weak back occasionally seems too heavy, it is certainly paradise compared to what they have often endured.

The palomino is a strong, noble representative of this character group. He can not only react quietly and thoughtfully if he is with a quiet and thoughtful person, but he can also get extraordinarily wound up. In the latter situation he can be uncontrollable and rather dangerous to the people around him. The eyes, forehead and the small fleshy nostrils are indicative of this; the tension of their configuration shows the variability of his possible reactions. The ears are more defined and stronger than those of the thoroughbred and, when everything is considered, this horse has a greater strength.

The chestnut horse demonstrates well how unsuited horses of this type are for riding. The neck and back speak volumes. Generally the head corresponds to this character group, but the eyes, ears and large forehead reveal that we are dealing with a weak representative of this type.

Which person suits the Victor

Victors are suitable for beginners provided they are handled and cared for very quietly and respectfully, then they will be alert and, usually, uncomplicated companions. I emphasize that anyone wishing to undertake the development of a Victor into a general riding horse, requires a very experienced hand. This subject will be covered further in

Chapter 6. The Victor is, all in all, a very human-friendly horse that also gets along well with children, but it is important to make sure that children do not overstep the horse's boundaries because that could quickly lead to a defensive reaction.

The Minister

Here we come to a very special type of horse that is frequently met, but just as frequently unrecognized.

The nature

Of all horses the Minister is probably the most mentally agile, the cleverest. He is very superior in his nature. He is a wise horse, and one that you would gladly 'turn to for advice'.

As a rule the owners of such an animal do not, by a long stretch, measure up to the inner abilities of the horse in terms of awareness, directness, honesty, clarity, thoughtfulness, peace and purpose. The horse then knows only too well that, with regard to these qualities, he is a long way ahead of his human, which can lead to difficult situations. The Minister is a horse that always wants to challenge and be challenged. He learns extraordinarily quickly and is only too ready to take on and master these new challenges. A child's genuine down-to-earth attitude and agility make it surprisingly easy for him to approach this horse. The Minister loves children because they are so much more like him than the adults. The

Minister does, therefore, make the most wonderful children's horse; it would be hard to find a better schoolmaster.

Physical characteristics in detail

I have chosen eight examples of the Minister to illustrate in just how broad a spectrum of breeds this character type appears.

First let us look at the bay horse (1). He is a very typical representative of this character group. The head is sharply defined. Sharply-defined heads in this shape are actually only found in the Minister, the King, Pegasus, and the Victor.

Particularly characteristic is the downward sloping line of the muzzle. We find something somewhat similar in the King but in combination with other characteristics. Minister and King are relatively similar to one another in appearance although their behaviour clearly differs.

The head is always long and narrow but never weak. The contours of the head are hard and firm as is the whole body. The horse is sinewy and solid, and in no way tends to corpulence.

The nostrils are fine and not very large, a feature that only adds to this equine type's noble exterior. The mouth is very expressive, but also comparatively small. The upper lip is powerful and sensitive, and the noble lower lip is held correctly.

The characteristic downward slope of the muzzle actually begins about a hand's breadth above the nostrils. Above this

point, the profile runs straight all the way to the forehead, which is small but powerful. The eyes, set relatively far up the face, are encircled by very expressive, prominent bony sockets. The eye, too, is not particularly large, but always very alert and receptive.

The neck is usually slender and mobile, as it is on this bay horse, well set on, and its top and bottom lines are convex. In general, the neck is not very strong and can in some cases, therefore, be of inferior carrying power. This is something that must be taken into particular consideration during the development of the horse.

The ears are normally narrow and finely formed. On the Paso Fino (4) on the following page you can see the typical Minister ear shape particularly clearly. I have included eight different photos of the Minister to make clear in how broad a spectrum of breeds this character type appears.

The black Lusitano (2) is also a wonderful example of this type, even though he is comparatively long-backed and his croup is underdeveloped. The hindquarters and

development of the upper leg and stifle are also weak; a fault that, as with Spanish horses, is unfortunately often rooted in the breeding of the Lusitanos. Aside from this weakness, to which you would have to give appropriate attention during training, this horse is very strong and noble.

The Friesian (3) too is a beautiful representative of this type. On him we see the unique Ministerial head – although in this breed head and body do not quite seem to fit together. Nevertheless, this too is a good, clear, strong horse.

The Paso Fino (4) clearly shows the faults that occasionally come with this character group. The upright

neck that is set on too low is a bit too long and, on the whole, weak, will make the development of this horse more of a challenge. An inexperienced horseperson, or a horseperson with the wrong kind of experience, would ruin such a horse

in a very short time. The head still belongs to this character group even though the nostrils seem a little broad and the muzzle as a whole seems a bit coarse. This trait makes this horse more susceptible to mood fluctuations, which usually are virtually unknown to the Minister. This horse too is inherently a very strong animal.

The Arabian (5) also has that Ministerial dignity. The wide nostrils, the very fine upper lip, and the overall narrow shape of the head combined with clearly sharply-defined delineation make this horse appear to be a bit more sceptical and complicated than other horses of this character group. Nevertheless, this is another horse of upstanding character and a noble nature.

The next two horses of this character group (6 and 7), particularly the grey, show an expression in the eyes that I unfortunately find so frequently in these horses: it is the expression of wise and gentle sorrow but, in spite of that, the horse still makes an effort to forgive. These two horses are also marked by a wonderful character and have a

dignity that no other character group can surpass.

Which person suits the Minister?

If the Minister feels that he can encounter a person on the same plane then he will be the first to tear down every barrier between human and horse. Overall, he is the most open type of all horses but he is also the one who can quickly hide himself, or even entrench himself behind a wall of feigned ignorance; he will pretend not to understand. The Minister is a wise horse and he seeks wisdom in human beings and, ultimately, the Minister can only accept a fine, high-ranking person of strong character. In fact, he is the most exacting when it comes to the selection of a suitable person. For that reason the Minister often feels very ill at ease in the world of human beings since this world, particularly these days, and particularly the riding world, is not exactly liberally sprinkled with wisdom and nobility.

The Minister is a good beginner's horse for the person who approaches him modestly and is prepared to learn. This horse knows instinctively who and what a person is. He literally learns more quickly than most two-legged beings. The Minister, as already mentioned, is an outstanding children's horse (8), and I know how strange that seems even to most horse experts. He is extremely considerate and careful and can, in a horse's sense, easily sympathize with the particular situation of a human being, even a child, and act accordingly. With the Minister a great equine character is always in our midst.

7

8

The King

At first glance the King looks very similar to the Minister, but you must be careful about this because the two character groups differ in their behaviour and, above all, in their bodily structure and suitability for High School work. The horses of Spanish breeding in the first two photos are examples of the King type in its pure form. Overall the head is often more solid and heavy than that of the Minister, the forehead is flatter, and the eyes are set even closer to the front of the face, but the head is sharply defined like that of the Minister.

The nature

The King is uncomplicated in his nature. Hardly anything unnerves him. He is tougher than the Minister and not quite as sensitive. He is one of the three types of horses that as a rule are very well suited to High School levels of training. If you look at old prints you repeatedly find one of these three character types, often in exaggerated form: the King, the Tough One, or Pegasus, all of which display the character and conformation most suited to classical High School.

Spontaneous associations with the King

An exceedingly interesting classical equine character that can be found even in the most diverse breeds, the King is an outstandingly good horse, often a sort of icon. He is uncomplicated, clear, powerful, honest, practical, loyal, noble, and 'discreet' in his nature. This horse enjoys good health, he is quiet because of inner strength, grounded, spirited, and very alert in character, and he usually has a solid compact conformation. This horse demands to be guided into High School work. In his training it is not necessary to delay for very long doing preparatory exercises. The King is through and through a late developer but, when he has developed, he brings almost everything with him in fully ripened form.

Physical characteristics in detail

Particularly characteristic is the kingly expression of the head, and especially the eyes. These lie close to the front of the face and seem to be almost 'placed' on the head, which indicates great joy in making decisions and the desire to take responsibility. The King is therefore a horse that is pre-destined to sense the rider's aids in advance. He does not need many repeated requests but, instead, pays constant attention to ensure he understands something and can then translate it into action as quickly as possible.

The King is occasionally not as intelligent and mentally agile as the Minister but he is more consistent and less reflective. Because of that his nature seems even more cooperative than that of the Minister. His neck tends to be short and massive, which is not a problem with this horse. The neck is set on high and its structure is strong and has good carrying power.

The nostrils are relatively small, slender, and almond shaped lying in the tapering, very fine but also extremely expressive downward curving muzzle that is typical of the King.

The mouth is sensitive yet firm and indicative of a powerful will. The entire lower jaw generally appears relatively small in relation to the expression of the eyes and forehead.

That bay Andalusian tends a bit toward the Minister, but he is tougher and his conformation is considerably more suited to High School work. I think this is a riding horse par excellence. The chest is powerful and broad, and the neck might appear to some to be too short and solid. However, in my eyes, nothing about this horse could be bettered. With his seeking, expectant expression this is a kingly horse from the character group of The King, ready for anything.

The chestnut is also a representative of this group, but is physically weaker than the bay. In this horse, too, we see the comparatively small lower jaw, the high-set-on eyes, the almond-shaped nostrils, the nobly held mouth, and the very open, clear forehead. This horse has very great inner qualities. He is wise, very intelligent, and of a fine noble nature.

Which person suits the King?

This is no beginner's horse; he must and will scale the highest heights, and so he is a horse for an experienced horseperson who wants to achieve mastery, of himself and with his horse. If this is not offered to the King then depression, sorrow, and grieving for unused and dormant talent will ensue.

The King is a horse for mature human beings. And if such a horse and a mature, experienced, enlightened horseperson meet, few words and aids are needed, and there is no fuss. They are as one from the very beginning, full of respect and modest self-awareness.

In bad or unpractised hands this horse will quickly become brutal. He does not become sad but merely atrophies, which results in a sort of unemotional and unmerciful aggression. Then a horse of this type, particularly a stallion, can become a killer; he reacts without any pity, and the consistency that this horse offers his humans in a positive way is then employed in battle against them. This is merely the other side of the same coin. In work and in the daily relationship these horses are open and honest. You must always be able to give them answers to their questions. This horse is not a child's horse, on the contrary, children are burdensome to the King, and he quickly becomes impatient and harsh with them.

The Tough One

The nature

What a horse! Again, this is a very high-ranking riding horse, but of an entirely different nature from the King. Sadly, I must mention that nearly all Spanish breeding has diverged from this type of horse and moved in the direction of a type that appears more streamlined and is more suitable to, and preferred by, the 'new market'; this old type does not adapt itself to the kind of dressage, for example, that competitive riders like so much.

This is a 'rock hard' though not large animal. He is a 'war-horse' that has the collection to canter around the edge of a dinner plate, only to then charge forward with enormous force at the next instant.

This animal belongs among the least complicated of all, if he finds himself in the proper hands. In his nature he is free of doubt; he never questions himself, the world, or human beings. He is a happy, always good-natured horse that is almost completely free of any sort of mood swings. The Tough One is a horse that needs an assignment and a path, so that he may then ruthlessly walk that path and fulfil the assignment that was given him. Like Pegasus the Tough One stands between heaven and earth, only he is turned to earth, and not, like Pegasus, to heaven.

Spontaneous associations with the Tough One

This horse is basically the original type of Spanish horse. He is an animal for very experienced people. He is not particularly intelligent but very canny, and is an outward-looking horse, but without being frivolous. He knows his own worth but is without a trace of arrogance. He possesses the type of pride that is at the same time down-to-earth and modest.

The Tough One is powerful and uncompromising, and at the same time, gentle and compassionate. He is sensible, practical, creative, enduring, healthy, does not complain, and he is a good-doer, robust, and very adaptable.

Physical characteristics in detail

The whole horse appears to be 'carved from one block' (there are very few 'inlets and dents') and to be taut and full of power. The forehead that looks very strong when seen from the side but when viewed from the front seems rather narrow and delicate, is very typical of this character group. Typical too is the small but alert, gentle and fine eye, as are the profile which runs straight down from beneath the eyes and the very sensitive, narrow, and sensual muzzle. The face as a whole seems smooth and taut and, at the same time, massive and clear. Despite all this power, surprisingly the head overall seems slender and fine.

This horse is in a class by himself. Although the ears are a bit fleshy, they are beautiful and vigorously curved inward. The horse is massive and short and you forgive the somewhat low set of the neck and disadvantageous line of the lower neck that goes with that, because it can eventually be erased with correct work. As with almost all Spanish horses, this horse's croup could be a little stronger, although it is much better than those of many other Spanish-breed types.

The head on the whole seems relatively small, particularly because the neck is so massive and powerful. In fact, the entire top line has incredible carrying power and compactness, which means that the horse can carry heavy weight and is also manoeuvrable; qualities for the ideal work and 'war-horse'.

person who is inwardly weak and, because of that, outwardly uncertain as well as tough, I would not bet a penny on the long-term health of that person. This horse does not get aggressive because he simply does not need to. In the worst circumstance he will simply bring about a 'work-related accident'. Without notice and without a recognizable cause but also without ascertainable blame, he will shortly 'explode' and the horse will have rid himself of his 'problem' without prior warning and without regret.

The Tough One is neither a beginner's nor a child's horse. The Tough One seeks a person who has already learnt a great deal about life. This horse does not need much training. The person who truly suits the Tough One will simply spend several years with him in a gentle and friendly manner, devotedly care for and feed him, and then one morning they will suddenly disappear. At this time no one knows for sure whether they will be seen again.

Which person suits the Tough One?

The person for the Tough One should under no circumstances be tough himself; quite the contrary. He should be filled with great inner strength, and outwardly be able to react flexibly and yieldingly. If this horse meets a

Pegasus

Our circle closes. Here Pegasus and the Unicorn meet, two horses that in a certain way are kindred spirits, and yet are also very different. Both animals belong to the spiritual among horses.

The nature

Pegasus is the horse that soars to the highest heights. He is the connector between the worlds, and plainly embodies the mythological horse: just look at the expression of the grey horse. Consequently, horses of this type are not among the toughest and most resistant. Although this horse is also very well suited for High School work, he must be accompanied on his path in an entirely different way from, for example, the Rugged One. Pegasus is extraordinarily sensitive, and is greatly prepared to absorb the sorrow of others.

Pegasus is like the eternal power that seems to physically manifest itself anew in every moment. This horse is like the primal force of original creation, that has just revealed itself for the first time, and which you fear will disappear into other spheres at any moment. Pegasus is like self-empowering matter and the most sensitive spirit all in one, and you can never be certain which part will prevail.

Pegasus is manifest and timeless mythology. In him the battles between the light and dark powers of all eras appear to be constantly present. In him is the heartbeat of the original source which unceasingly seeks to remind us of the beginnings of all existence. Not without reason is Pegasus the figure of light of sagas and myths, the discoverer of the spring that nourishes poets and philosophers – here we have that symbol real before us.

Physical characteristics in detail

The small head is very noticeable. It almost seems to be composed only of eyes and nostrils. The profile is practically always absolutely straight. The eye socket and the eye as a whole seem to be nearly too large for the head. A noteworthy feature of this character group is the relationship between the relatively delicate head and the massive body; Pegasus is a strong, muscular, short horse. In his way this horse is the most sensitive of all. He is the archetypal classic horse, the classic knight's horse. Compared to the body the ears seem small, solid and compact, yet they are noble and very sensitively shaped. The symmetry of the head and the relationship of all the individual parts to one another indicate clarity and power. The mouth is soft and very sensitive. The mouth opening is relatively long and the upper lip is shapely and very expressive. The nostrils are full and of a delicate contour.

The jowls of the grey horse are comparatively small — horses of this type can have much more shapely jowls.

As mentioned, this horse is a being that, because of his particularly superior spiritual orientation, can fulfil the archetypal purpose of equine existence. But these days, horses are no longer asked to accompany a seeking human being on his spiritual and true path. Those times are gone — we will see what my modest efforts ultimately bring about. In the world of pure exploitation, however, this horse is like a grain of wheat beneath the millstones: he will be ground away. Horses of this type are hardly bred anymore. They fight, they rebel against exploitation by human beings, and then they die.

Which person suits Pegasus?

The King and the Tough One are both horses that represent the power on earth and absolute stability. Pegasus, on the other hand, is a light, ethereal creature. He needs a very empathetic person at his side otherwise he can quickly break down, and then he will not live long.

Pegasus chooses death rather than a long life of suffering. Faced with an unwholesome environment, Pegasus quickly escapes into incurable illness or into such a severe acute episode that he seems to die in the person's hands.

People who suffer from mood swings, or other psychic ailments and problems are not suitable for this horse. Pegasus needs a sensible, considerate and just person who wants to undertake the journey to truth with this horse.

Pegasus behaves very sympathetically with children, although this horse should never be put into children's hands alone, and under no circumstances should he be considered a beginner's horse. Even the most good-natured and understanding character would find it heavy going with this horse at the beginning.

This horse always requires a very special partner. Unlike the Minister, for example, this horse cannot simply ignore even small mistakes. Everything is judged on a minute scale. A person's smallest mood swings are reflected back to him by this horse as though enlarged by a magnifying glass. That is why this horse is so worthwhile for a spiritual seeker: nothing is excused and nothing is unobserved.

However, our loud world echoes deafeningly in the infinitely fine natures of these horses that can still be found from time to time. And maybe all the disruptions in our world are what push some individuals, who perhaps seek each other but because of ignorance and inexperience cannot find one another, towards the quest for a greater understanding of each other. How fortunate is the person who, being meant to find such a horse does find him, truly recognizes him, and who then lets himself be taken along on his journey.

Our journey through the world of equine characters has, with Pegasus, arrived at its high point, its end and its starting point to continuously begin anew from here on. Whoever has carefully looked into this theme perceives that this is not a circle, in fact, but rather a spiral that ascends without end.

Here the stallion, Paco, shows a very typical reaction. After a deep intensive encounter he displays complete relaxation. The gesture and expression of the horse reflect inner liberation. Nothing more stands between person and horse. Space and time are lost in the moment of the experience. Therein lies the art of the first encounter. Often, only minutes pass between the first eye contact and healing. Here I describe for the first time how you can walk this path.

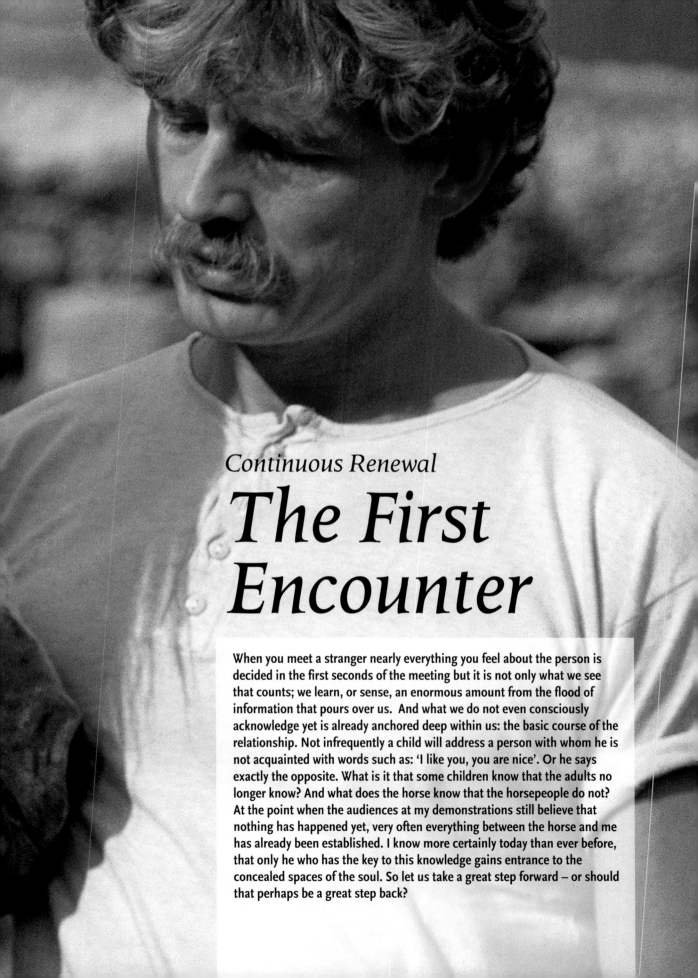

Continuous Renewal
The First Encounter

When you meet a stranger nearly everything you feel about the person is decided in the first seconds of the meeting but it is not only what we see that counts; we learn, or sense, an enormous amount from the flood of information that pours over us. And what we do not even consciously acknowledge yet is already anchored deep within us: the basic course of the relationship. Not infrequently a child will address a person with whom he is not acquainted with words such as: 'I like you, you are nice'. Or he says exactly the opposite. What is it that some children know that the adults no longer know? And what does the horse know that the horsepeople do not? At the point when the audiences at my demonstrations still believe that nothing has happened yet, very often everything between the horse and me has already been established. I know more certainly today than ever before, that only he who has the key to this knowledge gains entrance to the concealed spaces of the soul. So let us take a great step forward – or should that perhaps be a great step back?

Magic or Sorcery?
The Truth of the Detail

The following example is just one of countless examples that I could give: this picture sequence captures a few minutes during which a great deal happens. To the observer a horse seems to fundamentally transform himself very quickly. But, what actually happens?

For your first experience of how much sensitivity is required in these encounters, look at the following seven photos. What you see there is an everyday situation for me and it is photographed from an angle that shows my gestures and body language extremely clearly, which allows you to really study

All of that happened in about thirty seconds! What the observer does not see in that short time, and does not even suspect, are the **wealth of details** that only become clear in the sequence of photos. For the horse, however, these details are like a loudspeaker announcement.

1. Why is the person not looking at the horse? Why is he pushing the whip ahead of him along the ground? Why is he approaching the horse sideways?

2. Together with the clarity of my entire demeanour I have to 'make myself small'. I push myself between the horse and the boundary of the horse's area, but to what purpose? In this picture you can see my basic posture very well: my shoulders are always low and totally relaxed, and my body never shows even the least sign of excitement, fear, or aggression.

Please study the pictures in this book repeatedly with regard to the basic posture, because there you will discover a very large

what transpires picture by picture. For the onlookers, everything appears to happen with lightening speed.

What does the onlooker see?

He sees a horse that purposefully resists working with human beings and creates certain problems for his owner. The horse repeatedly places himself threateningly in a corner with his hindquarters towards his owner, as he also does here with me, and that is not a safe situation. Now the onlooker sees how, in a very short time, the horse is moved **without effort** out of the corner, how he makes a circle, and how he is then stopped with a small signal from me and turns towards me open and curious. The onlooker also sees that, from this moment on, the horse's relationship with me is transformed.

What really happened?

I enter the space as an open and assured human being. The horse takes seriously a creature whose behaviour is as decisive as it is **non-aggressive** and, most importantly, is not even *unconsciously* aggressive, which is something the horse would pick up on instantaneously. I do not look at the horse, I push the whip ahead of me on the ground, and nothing seems able to stop my **sideways** movement toward the horse.

In the second photo you see clearly how I 'gather myself up' and make myself small in order to demonstrate my friendly disposition, how I keep his gaze directed downward and away to the side, but at the same time leave **no doubt** about who can claim which space and who cannot. Any other posture at this moment would prove very dangerous and could put my wellbeing, and possibly even my life, in danger, and at best my efforts would simply be unsuccessful.

In the third picture you see that the horse now yields to me, although, or, more correctly, because, I have not lifted the whip at any time in this situation; had I done so the horse would probably have unequivocally shown his disapproval. My different approach caused the horse to yield, not the aids, not force, and not some sort of pressure. It is particularly important at this moment that I do not show even the tiniest hint of triumph. My gaze remains deliberately directed downward and to the side and I consciously refrain from looking at the horse as he moves away.

The importance of a few centimetres

The distance between human and horse is immensely important. In my experience just a few centimetres will determine how a horse reacts, whether the result is a quick connection, a greater gap between person and horse or perhaps even a battle. We will discuss this at greater length later. The photo shows clearly that the horse is very respectful but still a bit disturbed. He is still very withdrawn and aware of his past experiences with human beings. I therefore remain in my passive posture with my gaze still averted. I follow my

part of the secret of my way of being with horses.

3. The whip is still trailing on the ground, the gaze is still averted, but the horse yields!
Now nearly everything has already been established, which the subsequent behaviour of the horse will confirm.

4. Here the horse still seems a bit withdrawn, and so my gaze is still deliberately averted.

5. After a few more steps the picture is completely different: the horse has turned towards the person and he looks at the animal in a friendly way. Does that which seemed senseless before make sense now?

6. I have halted the horse and, again, he is standing in a corner. But after only one circuit of the arena he seems completely transformed, and is no longer hiding himself. Obstinate peculiarities that had been part of him for years seem to no longer exist.

that these points must also be seen as parts of a greater whole.

In addition, we will try to analyse what is going on because, as already mentioned, even though it all happens very quickly, we can separate the various pieces of the action very precisely from one another and shed light on them. Here is the overview of the following more detailed steps.

path, not the horse. Any turn toward the horse, any gesture with the whip that still trails along the ground, any change in my gaze, and any shortening of the distance between us, would greatly hinder a quick connection.

The horse sees everything as though it is occurring in slow motion. He has barely turned one more corner, and already behaves completely differently. Now, after only about twenty seconds, nearly everything required from the first encounter has already happened. The horse is open; one ear is turned towards me, his face shows clarity, he has understood and, because of that, I can now lift the whip and direct my gaze toward the horse.

After the horse has moved through two more corners of the arena, I stop him. He looks at me (in the way shown in photo 6) and waits for a signal to come. He is standing contentedly and no longer budges from my side. The first encounter has come to an end. In an unimaginably short space of time, segments clearly differentiated from one another, with flowing transitions, were passed through in such a way that many observers found themselves in urgent need of explanations. But neither magic nor sorcery is at work here; it is something much more exciting. Note the individual points but remember

The sequence of a first encounter is always the same

1. We must **recognize** the horse's character and his individual way of experiencing and behaving.
2. Before the first step, the **approach**, we must already be moving totally and completely in accord with this recognition. That requires two things: firstly, we must be aware of the importance of our own clear outward appearance; secondly we must be able to adapt very quickly to what the recognized horse tells us about his nature.
3. Then we must **open the door**. This should happen within seconds; I emphasize that because it is precisely this quick move into trust that is our only confirmation that we have found the **right key!**

4. Now I can carefully step into the 'house', which requires great care because it is not my own house. I am a guest in a fantastic, filigreed, and unknown realm. Wounds and injuries are now visible and can be **healed** relatively quickly.

5. Only then can I get more and more acquainted with this 'house', which develops through the groundwork, through the horse-oriented riding, and simply through being at one with the horse.

7. Quiet and with no physical ties to me, the horse remains with me. A deep inner relationship has been established. What happened in that short time? Once again I want to draw your attention to my posture: it is always quiet and extremely relaxed. Even at this point every movement has to be valid.

The individual segments of this path are:

— Recognition, as well as the right moment for the first step
— Approach
— Appropriate distance
— The first touch

— Zone of healing and becoming conscious
— Dissolving anger, aggression, and fear. The active leap of forgetting
— Following and leading

— The daily first encounter
— Groundwork, riding, and being as one

The Gordian Knot
The Alpha and Omega of the First Encounter

The following is very important but it may also be, for some, even a shocking revelation.

The first encounter with a horse is like trying to enter a house: if you have the key you can open the door and enter quickly in order to then take your time to familiarize yourself with the individual rooms. Desire, conception and reality are then virtually one and the same thing. No matter how often you leave the house you will always choose the same entrance or one of the other possible doorways in order to enter again. This example might seem banal but the background of this story is in fact anything but banal. In my opinion it defines the sorrow or the joy of the horse and his togetherness with the human **and yet hardly anyone has a key for direct access to, i.e. communication with, a horse**, indeed hardly anyone is even aware of the existence of such a key.

Stepping in or breaking in?

'Immediate communication' is a very important concept for us. It is the alpha and omega of the first encounter. For, if you do not have a 'key' to the 'house', i.e. you cannot immediately communicate with the horse, then, to stay with our analogy, you are an intruder breaking in, particularly if you are forcibly entering the house, and, as a rule, anyone who enters forcibly violates and steals.

This is so immensely important for our relationships with horses because, **if we cannot successfully enter actively into the nature of the horse, and make him intimately familiar with us, within minutes, then we will probably never be successful. And, with every minute that passes it becomes more difficult.**

This example will clarify this matter. A woman came with her Icelandic horse to a clinic in northern Denmark. She led the horse into the picadero, and, in tears, told us that for three years she had been unable to saddle him or touch him in certain places, that he would run away from everyone, and that, above all, he had a great fear of men. Even while the woman was still speaking, the horse came to me, lowered his head, and from then on would not leave my side. No matter what item I put on the horse, or what I did with it – all of which was impossible for the woman – the horse was completely quiet and wanted just one thing: to stay with me. Whatever the key to this horse was, I had apparently found it. What was the fundamental difference between this woman's behaviour and actions and mine?

I know without doubt that **if I cannot establish a clear contact to a horse in a few minutes then he will not come around even after days, months, or years – no matter what I do!** A kind of habituated lack of understanding sets in. Sadness and distance or, even worse, oppression and violence take the place of connection and understanding. But, as yet, nothing is lost, because this state of affairs only means that our traditional conceptions of a fundamentally positive closeness must be thrown to the wind. Many people who come to me have tried everything possible for years without success. The idea that a person can spend years removing a horse's fear millimetre by millimetre is plainly and simply false! That will not lead to the goal; on the contrary, it will only block future possibilities. The endless patience should be put to use in learning and developing the understanding necessary **to find the key, to sever the Gordian Knot with one precise healing stroke**. That knot cannot be untied and, as in the legend, thousands before you have tried.

Let us go back to the Icelandic horse and his owner. What happened between the two of them? The horse always associated this woman with the negative things that she related to me and all the participants in the clinic. Day after day the horse associated all the described problems with his owner. This negative image became solidified over the years into an impenetrable lump. If I had approached this horse and had not immediately succeeded in altering the circumstances, then the horse would make the same mental bridge to me. He would think, 'the saddle is negative so you are negative, leave me alone'. **And that, obviously, is the very opposite of what I would have wanted.**

The grey horse in the previous seven photos was also hardened in his behaviour.

Over months and years behavioural traits had established themselves so firmly that they were not going to be undone by someone working for a long time trying to cultivate the desert; endurance of this kind simply means that the key has not been found and the house can not be entered. Such a person is acting like a fisherman on a fishless sea. In the end he whines: 'But I was so patient'.

This is how you find the key to your horse

I have just given you the raw material for this key in the descriptions of the individual character groups and in the new thought structure for recognition of a horse. Later in Chapter 6 you will learn more about that.

To help you find the key I will give you an assortment of tools. But you must work the raw material yourself! This key will not be handed to you ready-cut and set to go.

During your search, consider the following:

1. Most of those who come to me have basically given up. They cover the same ground day after day and no longer believe in a true solution. They need to go further forward in order to be in the sun, but to walk new paths if the old ones only lead further into shadow.

2. You carry the solution within yourself – believe me. But influence and wrong advice, habit and dulled perceptions make you blind to the simplest things that lie before you. It is not the bucking, for example, that is the problem but rather the wrong perception of it. Look for a sea with fish in it.

3. It is often not easy to fight a trend which tells you that this is the way to do things 'because this is the way they have always been done'. But things do not always have to be done a certain way, and it is also simple to act without fighting.

4. Many people find themselves in a paper cage and feel as though they are trapped for life and they do not want to believe that one single movement would be sufficient to burst through the bars of the cage. But this is possible; you only have to act!

Killing a lion with bare hands

A young male Masai must kill a lion bare-handed in order to be accepted as a man in that aboriginal community. Is it possible to do that? And is it possible for me, to put myself between a stallion and a mare in season – a stallion that has injured many people when a mare was merely within earshot? Both are possible with the right key (see photos on pages 46 and 47). The Masai youth and I would injure ourselves or die if we were to depend upon force or apparent might to achieve these ends.

Finding the key to these problems means being in the right place at the right time and recognizing the right approach to take; then even the most massive doors open for you. It will then become apparent that you are less aware of exactly why something happened you will only notice that something is happening. Does that have anything to do with luck?

From Exploiting to Understanding! My Way to Enlightenment

Now we can see the entire path. The illustration shows how the important factors have been displaced from the top of the triangle to the base.

Only riding is featured at the top in Zone I. In this zone the preparatory work is given no or very little importance. The initial backing process is too often only a way of 'breaking' or frightening a horse into the work. In Zone II the groundwork is added as preparation. However, my way of working and being as one with horses begins much earlier.

The base of my red/orange triangle shows other areas that are established before riding, one arising out of another. It begins with an **increased awareness**, including, not least, bodily awareness (consciousness). Discovering the nature of the horse through, for example, the character groups is also a part of this.

The area of recognition is next and only after that is a person prepared for the first contact with the horse. After all this preparation, a person has such **inner potential**, a marvellous tool, with which to encounter his protégé for the first time.

Now we come to that first encounter. It begins with the **approach** and leads to **healing**. This **'healing strike'** as I call it comes **before** the groundwork and **long before** riding. The whole of Zone III is of only a few minutes duration in fact, which means that the healing occurs in a few moments and is for the most part already accomplished when the actual 'work'

begins! This can be seen very clearly in the illustration: the solid yellow area in the yellow oblong beneath the triangle marks this time span, and that is what onlookers at the clinics perceive as 'magic'.

My videos also show this often unbelievable and unexpected transformation. The expression and appearance of the horse seems completely changed, but he has only been healed; I have simply led the horse back to himself. That is the power of healing, the precise 'healing strike'.

The horse will quickly slide back into his old condition if the owner does not take these measures to have this healing effect. Yet for the horse the experience remains for his whole life. Even after years I can pick up in the same place I left off.

My book, *Dancing with Horses*, was revolutionary because it presented an 'old' method of groundwork and preparation for riding in a new way.

Now it must be clear that before a horse can truly reveal himself to a person it is important to uncover the hidden complex world within the horse. If the foundation of the relationship is well built then everything else happens very quickly and with great ease.

Now the (almost) complete picture of my way of being as one with horses lies before you. I put 'almost' in parenthesis because there is something more that I will explain at a later time; it is too soon for that now, and it requires a book of its own.

my path to enlightenment: the path from rider to knight, from exploitation to recognition

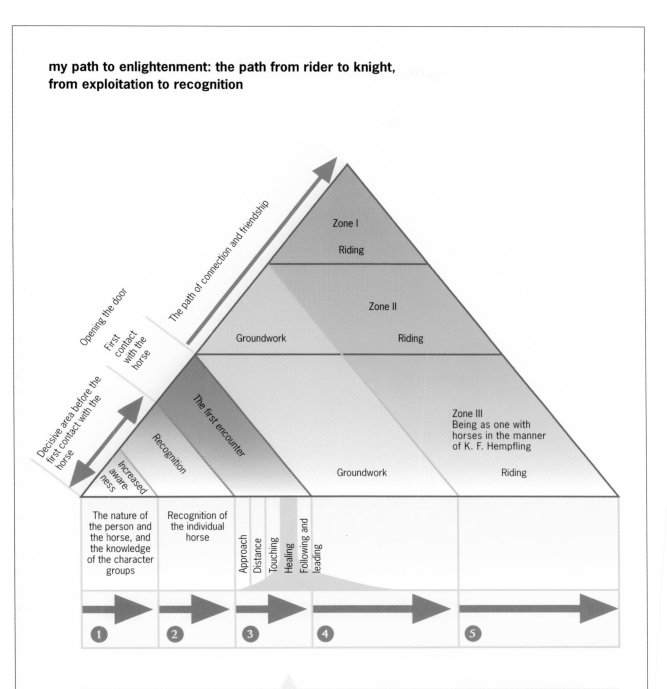

The path of connection and friendship

Opening the door

First contact with the horse

Decisive area before the first contact with the horse

The path of connection and friendship

The first encounter

Recognition

Increased awareness

Zone I
Riding

Zone II
Riding

Groundwork

Zone III
Being as one with horses in the manner of K. F. Hempfling

Groundwork   Riding

| The nature of the person and the horse, and the knowledge of the character groups | Recognition of the individual horse | Approach | Distance | Touching | Healing | Following and leading | | |

1   2   3   4   5

Note: The greatest part of 'healing' takes place in that minute phase of the first encounter

Always an Open Door
The First Pillar: the Approach

Clarification

1. If we must speak of healing as part of the first encounter, does this mean that all horses are ill? Obviously, not all horses are ill in the common use of the word but, with only a few exceptions, most of them do, in fact, have a disturbed equilibrium. The world of human beings, made by human hands, is not only frequently a hard nut to crack for us, but also for all the other creatures that live within its confines.

2. Does the principle of 'quick transformation', the 'opening of the door'

great humility, we are serving another creature's needs. It is a purposeful, patient form of approach, and that brings us back to our subject.

The tools for the job: the thirteen qualities of the approach

First of all, my task is to give you a good idea as to how a person should fundamentally approach a horse, particularly at the moment of the first encounter. That may seem unimportant to some, but that is precisely why there are so few people who

A young, jumpy and fearful stallion at a clinic in Namibia. The pictures show what happened within the space of a few minutes, and they only seem to be similar because the behaviour of the horse does, in fact, change all the time and I, therefore, have to change my approach. This photo sequence shows step by step how many ramifications even the smallest nuances of the approach have on the nature of the horse.

1. In the first photo the horse is not yet totally with me. There is scepticism in his eyes and in the overall bodily expression. At this moment I am making a great effort to reach this animal. Look at the horse's expression in the second photo; there he has been completely won over. But to achieve this I have to 'ask' the horse, whilst keeping a dignified distance, whether he wants to accompany me in an experience of peace and trust, and so my energy and awareness are totally with the horse. In such a situation I would never speak to the onlookers.

mean renouncing our patience? No, quite the contrary. The time when patience is required has simply been moved to the period before the first encounter. There the invisible and the very smallest visible details are patiently assembled to form a veritable mountain. The moment of the first encounter is a moment of the most concentrated patience, because, with

are truly successful with horses. At the same time, the pictures I have provided will give depth and dimension to my words.

It is difficult to explain in words things that actually can only be felt but I will try to transmit 'feel' to you as succinctly as possible. I have listed the thirteen qualities required for the first encounter, which, accompanied by the photo sequence of the young stallion, may set in motion something probably already long known to a sensitive person; for him this is only a reminder.

So, what is this approach?

1. It is consciousness of self, you must be aware of your every expression and particularly their effects on the horse.

2. It is always conducted with a clear, upright posture that is at the same time open and supple. If your head moves down or to the side it is never an arbitrary or accidental move, but rather the correct sequential gesture in a greater flowing communication. I always observe myself from within as though from the outside. Nothing can be left to chance. Everything is under a sort of natural (conscious)-unconscious control.

3. It is an expression suited to an immensely important and unique event. That is very important, and it is something I unequivocally demand of my students. Very many people have become accustomed to living life on a 'trial' basis. But life and death are not for 'trying out' they are always final and unique.

4. It is an expression that reflects the deepest peace, sincerity and heartfelt cordiality, not mere superficial 'friendliness'. We live in a world in which that superficial 'friendliness' can sell vacuum cleaners, land a job, or even win an election, but it will not win the true friendship of a horse. I make clear to the horse by the manner of my approach that I never want anything from him. Nothing happens without his invitation. I am never permitted to overstep my boundaries; at most I can defend my boundaries for my immediate protection.

5. The greatest alertness begets the greatest possible perception and clarity. Nothing, not the tiniest detail about the reactions of the horse can escape me. Clarity begets security; security begets peace; peace begets a state of no resistance, which in turn begets creativity; creativity begets a lust for life and serenity; and together they beget naturalness. (And the horse is little accustomed to naturalness from us human beings.) Already we are on the path to healing.

6. This approach remains free of attachments. It exists without making promises and without demanding any. Therefore it is boundless and free.

7. This approach will not allow itself to be deceived. Even horses have frequently learned from human beings how to manipulate; it has helped them to survive.

8. This approach is extremely careful and 'timid'. It expects harsh reactions from even the mildest horse. When the bullfighter thinks himself to be safe, then he is most likely to be gored. Therefore this approach can never be completely safe.

2. The horse is totally with me and will remain so even if I turn to the spectators. Matter-of-fact closeness and gentle, firm clarity serve to bind the horse to me more and more. Note the gentle look on the horse's face and the deep affection radiating from his expression.

12. This approach is so modest it almost seems pitiful. If success were not always immediately visible, you would simply overlook it. This approach is rooted in modesty and expresses only modesty, and that is the only thing that is allowed to be exaggerated.

13. This approach brings everything to a conclusion. This approach always arrives at a goal. This shocks people who do not want to move in the spiritual world because they seek power, but to their amazement 'power' is to be found here.

3. Now something important happens. Look at photos 3 and 7. In both of them I interrupt the harmony that has been achieved. In photo 2 the horse is very close to me. The closeness is sufficient to keep the horse in place when I touch him with the frightening saddle pad. Look at my body. If at this point I do not proceed with absolute clarity, gentleness, and razor-sharp precision all at the same time then the situation is spoiled, and that should not be allowed to happen.

4. The horse's expression is still pinched, but he trusts me and remains standing still. I always stand as though ready to leap away. My openness conveys security to the horse, although every action of the horse is followed by a reaction on my part.

9. This approach has the potential to be 'played out' very powerfully at any time. It is like inhaling and exhaling. The situation can change with lightening speed.

10. This approach is continually renewed from second to second. Nothing is rigidly determined in advance; everything is dependent upon the communication and reactions of the moment.

11. There are no expectations with this approach because expectations beget images and images want to be fulfilled. But what role does my counterpart actually play? Having no expectations he deals with the issues in one healing stroke.

The following pictures illustrate the art of the first encounter, and for further background material, look at the other pictures in this book and in *Dancing with Horses*. If you discover something special in them, a particularly rich, deep kind of trust and encounter, it is that which we are seeking here.

I would like to make one more important point. Bit by bit we are making our way into the practice of the first encounter. I am hiding nothing from you; I am revealing the deepest secrets and I do so with the knowledge that misuse is a possibility, but I do this also in the knowledge that over the years these explanations will be helpful many times over.

Try always to comprehend the whole; without preconceptions, let everything just flow by you. Let what you have read have its effect on you for several days, and then return to the material again. The space in a book like this is always limited, but he who does not perceive that which is essential after thirty pages will not perceive it after 300. Even though my knowledge and experiences are crowded into a compact book form, everything is in there. Do not underestimate the subtleties, and above all, do not underestimate the force and power that lies in what follows. It is the heart of my work!

5. The horse's eyes are already a little softer. As in photo 1, I am again completely focused on the horse in order to impress upon him the significance of the moment. I demand much of horses; they must overcome their fear, and I can only accompany them on that journey. In a situation like this I actually speak to the animal as I would to a person and they always understand me.

6. Once again the horse has made a choice and, as in photo 2, I can now give my attention to the spectators. The situation is stable and although the horse is still not totally relaxed he is certainly on the way to being so.

7. Deciding just how much the healing screw can be turned is always a particularly delicate decision. Here I want to push the little stallion just a bit further because he is still not quite quiet enough, and that is the reason for using the blanket. With caution, as though I am dealing with a raw egg, but with unshakeable steadfastness I convince the horse. Observe the approach in this moment.

8. Now the horse is completely at ease. I am even able to touch him everywhere. Blanket and saddle pad are no longer frightening to the little stallion. The first encounter is over. Were we to remain together we would build the foundation of our friendship on these few minutes. My approach is now one of a quiet matter-of-fact manner.

The Approach in Pictures

1 and 2. I chose these photos because they show how clarity, dominance and gentleness unite in the span of a single moment. The aroused stallion is standing near a mare in season. That is a part of stallion training. In this approach, my yielding strength is having its effect and the stallion gives me power over him. Please note the clarity and straightness of my bearing, and the intensity of my inner attentiveness toward the horse. Power, clarity and the gentlest attentiveness unite into trust of the horse and he, therefore, responds to me in the same way.

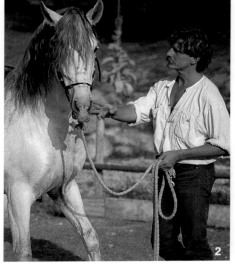

4. Another picture of stallion training. The stallion is bridled with only a light headcollar. It is the person's approach that keeps the stallion in place. Clarity and precision stamp the situation as much as understanding, friendship and attachment do. The rider's seat is a part of the total approach.

5. Here again the stallion is being trained. With the reins dropped to the ground only the person's approach keeps the stallion in place. There is no outward trace of harshness; instead the scene is filled with clarity and watchful energy. My way of interacting with horses can thrive only on the foundation of such an approach. For me that is not only the most important, but also the most difficult, thing to teach.

3. The outer bearing of the person is only one part of the approach, although an important one. In my school, body awareness is learned over the years of a course. Here we can see that the course participant is not yet straight and equally balanced in the upper part of her spine.

6 and 7. In this encounter with my stallion Almendro our concentration nearly jumps off the page. However, it is the person who must determine the form and quality of the approach, which will then carry over to the horse. Relaxed watchfulness, playful precision, and animated composure connect the seemingly apparent extremes into a communicative dance with one another.

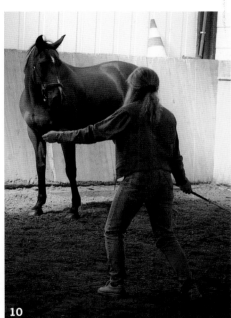

8–12. This course participant is still in the very early stages of her training. In each of the individual pictures it is clear how much the horse still distrusts her. Even the reward is at best an enticement; the horse takes it with great doubt and a contracted muzzle. Nothing is gained by that. In photo 9 it can be seen clearly how the student's gesture makes the horse uncertain; he does not know what she means. Here we see the fisherman on a fishless sea. It does not matter how long a person deals with a horse, or with life itself, this equivocal way will lead to nothing, and, indeed, often to the opposite of what was hoped for. But what is the path? First of all, the person must have extensive practice in the two areas of my triangle that come right at the very beginning before the first encounter with a horse.

From Teddy Bears to Monsters

1-4. Can you see that the cause of these dramatic situations lies in the approach of the girl? An approach that does not possess the majority of the described thirteen qualities will quickly become dangerous when dealing with horses. In addition, you must know that although horses are flight animals, they know how to defend themselves extraordinarily well. Striking, kicking and biting are fearsome offensive reactions. In this sense the horse is a thoroughly defensive fighter and this primal behaviour is rooted deeply even within our closest equine companions.

Being around horses is a dangerous activity that comes at the top of all accident statistics. I know, for example, of a 28-year-old riding instructor from a local stable who lost her life when she broke her neck as a result of a fall. Whenever I refer to incidents like this, I am criticized by the glossy magazines, particularly those of my

homeland. But is it not better to look at riding honestly than to hide the facts?

Expression and behaviour determine what transpires

Study these six photos. In the first four pictures it becomes clear that it is the girl herself who undoubtedly unleashes the aggression. Her posture and behaviour, the overall expression of her body, gestures, and facial expressions determine what transpires. In the fifth picture everything seems all right, but upon close observation warning lights should go on here as well, because uncertainty and fear in the person's approach allow the stallion to direct things to his advantage, and it is written all over him! His complete domination of the situation can be expected at any time.

In photo 6 I show you a special situation. This stallion's problem must be cleared up now. Look at his expression; here he is

pressed into the corner and seems insecure and doubtful. **This is something that should be done only by very experienced professionals, specialists,** such as those I have decided to train in my Akedah School. Please do not attempt something like this yourself. If a situation has reached this point, things get very dangerous. Nevertheless I will describe what takes place over the course of just a few seconds. At the precise moment shown in the photo I am

5. My movement has already stopped. I am satisfied with the stallion's peace offering, expressed in his gesture and his look. What the observer of the event does not know, what he cannot perceive in the rapidity of the event, is made very clear in this picture. The horse can now only wait quietly in the corner until I slowly retreat for the appropriate distance and give him the opportunity to move. The decisive thing, however, was the first short

5. If you look more clearly at what is happening here then you will see the girl's uncertainty and, resulting from that, the stallion's latent desire to dominate. An overstepping of bounds with severe consequences can be expected at any time in such a situation.

6. Here my assignment is to take the wind out of the stallion's sails through a clear

entering into the nature of the horse very deeply.

1. With the whip drawn back, I can strike forward with lightening speed if need be. In 99 out of 100 cases it does not come to that.
2. With the rope in my left hand I can, with equal speed, ward off the hindquarters. In these situations stallions fight with the front and back ends at the same time.
3. My approach is both certain and unassuming. That becomes clear even in a frozen image. I am consciously looking at the stallion and thereby signalling him not to attack.
4. Very consciously I enter the stallion's 'security circle' (see the next section on the subject of appropriate distance). That means I approach him a bit too closely. By doing that I am showing him right from the start that I want to clear up this situation once and for all.

moment of the approach. I repeat: **under no circumstances try something like this in such a situation; get professional, specialist help instead.**

and unassuming approach. Now he seems thoughtful and has backed off, and after only a few seconds, everything has been cleared up. Caution: leave something like this to the specialists.

An Eternity in Space and Time
The Second Pillar: Distance

In the heart of the African bush at the home of a farmer with whom I had become friends, I found this horse (photos 1-3). For years he had not allowed himself to be touched. Even the patience of the farmer's son and his months-long efforts met with no success. The horse did not respond in any way to human beings. After two or three leaps at a somewhat greater distance, the horse started to show great interest in me. Can you detect, even from the dust-clouded photographs, the relationship that already exists between man and horse? To further the work on our key to the house, we must become familiar with this subject of **distance**. I could easily write an entire book on this subject because this area is so complex, extensive and important, but for now I must just hope that several of the suggestions about distance in this book will become catalysts that will send you in the right direction.

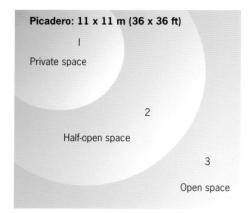

Picadero: 11 x 11 m (36 x 36 ft)

1
Private space

2
Half-open space

3
Open space

1–3 An encounter in Africa at the farm of a friend whose horses are half wild. Only through the phenomenon of the appropriate distance between person and horse and through the game of movements within the allotted space can a first connection at a distance quickly come about. The distance and the change between the zones are of the greatest significance.

areas and the zones of the encounter into open space, half-open space, and private space. Anyone may linger in **open space**; here intermingling is accepted and desired. Open space is then the greatest possible working distance from the horse. I can make the distance even greater if I do not directly look at the animal, and even more if I go into a crouch. The **half-open space** is somewhat like a front garden. I only enter here if I have

The zones of the encounter

After recognition, after becoming conscious of the approach, then you have to understand how to maintain the appropriate distance. This is always dependent on the situation, the horse, and the horse's condition at the time.

Just as with humans I differentiate the

something specific in mind: a visit for example, or a conversation with the neighbours. I am not yet in the most intimate private space, but nevertheless I need a legitimate reason to be there. To enter into the intimate circle of the **private space** I need a clear and credible reason. I should be known to the residents and invited in by them.

Too many human beings do not recognize

the meaning of these spaces, either in the world of animals or the world of human beings. They crowd uninvited into the personal space of others and by doing that allow others in turn to crowd into their own areas unchallenged. Both are offensive and not infrequently very painful. Since so many people are already not able to respect these zones when they are with other people, how can they manage to do it with animals and nature?

At the first encounter however it is precisely this element that is important. Asking for the correct distance, choosing the correct distance, and changing it according to circumstances, is most decisive for the success of the first encounter.

fundamental meaning of the appropriate distance, give the direction for the path to success, for the way to healing and connection at the first encounter.

Reassurance

In my school the aspiring professionals learn all of this over many effort-filled years. Ultimately they should be able, within only a few minutes, to attain clarity with any horse they meet.

You, however, probably do not want to go this far but only want to have a better relationship with your own horse. You do not need to work with all the horses of the world in order to heal them. My purpose, therefore,

4-7 Here one sees the gentle progression from Zone 3 to Zone 1. To increase the distance at the beginning, I often go into a crouch. This horse is very afraid of being touched. Very gently the preparations for the first touch are made by playing with the distance.

There are no further hard and fast rules for individual cases. Within the basic foundation I have described, the character of the horse and his circumstances at the time will determine subsequent procedure and action.

My method of determining a horse's character, the phenomenon of the approach, judging the circumstances of the horse at a specific time, and the knowledge of the

is not to develop you into a specialist but to give you enough knowledge so that you **with your own inner knowledge, with your own primal self, can find a new direction.**

It is important to use that inner knowledge to truly listen and hear, and to understand with your heart. Everything that you absorb in this way will always be yours, will always be understood. Believe in this and have confidence.

In the moment of recognition, the following, among other things, should be considered:

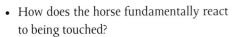

8-10 When dealing with stallions, the significance of the correct distance becomes even greater. This stallion is responding so peaceably and quietly in proximity to the mares only because he was first worked at the appropriate distance.

- How does the horse fundamentally react to being touched?
- Is he a horse that basically seeks closeness to, or distance from, human beings?
- How disrespectfully handled was the horse by human beings up to now and to what degree did these people violate his private space?
- Is the horse lonely, and does he therefore require quick close contact from a confidently approaching person?
- Is there any danger connected to increasing closeness?
- How long must I remain in each zone in order to then quickly get to the process of healing?
- Which 'rhythm within the zones' shall I set?

The rhythm and the game of the encounter zones

In my video *Body Language* you can see this game performed excellently in the last example on the video. With the shy white stallion I play very obviously with the phenomenon of distance and above all with the 'rhythm of the zones'. This means that

in a soft and steady way I purposefully change from one zone to another (you must develop a feel for that); only very rarely do I remain in a single zone. Again and again, and also later in the work on the ground, a sequential change in zones is required. At this point I want to open your eyes to the fact that this procedure is so immensely important to the relationship between a person and a horse. Even the best of friends becomes a burden when he does not respect my space. And the friendship is in danger when, uncontrolled, distance becomes too great.

Important notes regarding the encounter zones

Zone 1

As a rule Zone 1 is entered late in the encounter. The horse must have sent out good, clear signals and invited me to enter this zone. Only with extremely oppressed or lazy horses can spontaneous intimate contact be initiated in order to bring empathy and understanding into being. For mares and stallions this zone is larger than for geldings. Entering this zone can be an encroachment and signify aggression. That can then lead to a thoroughly justified defensive reaction which some unjustly label escalation of aggression.

Being in this zone must always be justified, particularly with stallions. Do not become a burden, like a guest overstaying his welcome. Particularly awful is the endless patting of horses by strangers, the eternal encroachment into the horses' dignity. Forbid anyone to do this. Petting, stroking and showing affection are fine as long as it is only as much as the horse wants – but not one whit more! (See the next section.)

Zone 2

An intimate first encounter is possible here. In the first phase of this initial encounter I seek out this zone whether I want closeness or distance. Depending on the intention and the approach, I signal the horse either to come or to yield. This is, so to speak, the neutral zone.

Zone 3

Right at the very beginning I like to deliberately remain a long time in this zone. Here I can steer the proceedings from afar. I can observe, and through subtle movements and signals I can communicate with the horse. The horse determines when I leave this zone but under no circumstances should that be too soon. I repeatedly return to this zone to give the horse time to reflect and to

give him the opportunity to turn to me of his own free will.

It is always the beginning

The first encounter determines the quality of our relationship with our horses at each new encounter. Each time, the same sequence of events occurs albeit of always shorter duration. Yet every single time we must try to perceive if anything has changed, if anything has happened, if everything is okay with the way the horse is being kept – the feed, the herd, the circumstances – and if things are good between us.

You cannot go to your horse in the morning thinking that because everything was okay yesterday, it will still be that way today. Everything must always start at the beginning and must always begin with the subtlest connections. Every time the slightest deviation from the ideal happens in the first encounter it must be balanced out and healed.

And this should not only be the case in our relationship with our horse. How would life be if every morning were like a new gentle birth? Everything is open; everything is fresh. Yesterday I lived in the south; today I live in the north. What a pleasure!

11

11. This is exactly what should not happen. If the horse is worked at liberty and from the correct distance, then such scenes will belong to the past. After the phenomenon of distance comes correct leading. When everything blends it brings peace and trust, connection and understanding.

12-14. Simply look at the pictures and try to feel how space, distance and time melt into one very special occurrence. Look, and feel, how the horse responds to me, precisely because of the correct distance.

12

13

14

The Third Pillar: Communication through Touch

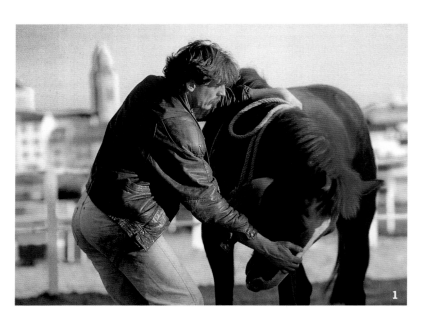

1. What is it about touch? What happens in such a situation, and how did it come to be? Why does a horse that I have known for only a few minutes give himself over, visibly without resistance, to such a situation.

2. This horse actually seems to be smiling, his head is turned to me, and the touch is tender and truly of a devoted intensity as well as reserved and modest.

3. Even when a horse is trusting, I do not smother it with touches. What is important is that no encroachment on the horse's part arises from this situation, and that the horse truly accepts the closeness of the person.

4. The extremely shy and fearful stallion here suddenly turns to me with unbelievable openness. Here too the horse determines what happens so of course everything is just fine.

How to touch a horse, particularly at the first encounter, is of much greater significance than you would ordinarily suppose. But we should all understand this. Who cannot feel the difference between the sort of touch that truly creates connection, intimacy and understanding and that touch, no matter how tender and well-intentioned, from which we, at least inwardly, quickly distance ourselves?

In the first picture on this page you see a way of touching that comes across as intimate as it is unusual. My attitude towards the horse contains much information about this subject that I would also like to explain in words, if there truly were words for it. How do you respond to a touch that is very gentle but which has no strength? My little son Karsten chortles with such joy when I hold him firmly round the chest and then gently but very definitely swing him through the air. The firmness becomes loving through the gentleness by which it is bounded, led, and maybe also transcended. In a true touch **everything is always present**, the whole spectrum of the whole person is there. Gentleness without strength is like a beautiful package with nothing inside. And power without gentleness will only disrupt.

Soft as a feather, yet visibly so strong

The chestnut in photo 1, like all horses, is many times stronger than I am. He could easily extricate his head from my embrace, and then the first encounter would be destroyed straight away.

I frequently hold horses on the spot for several minutes in this way. Observe my face, the left hand, and the attitude of my posture. Everything is as soft as a feather. My left hand lies very loosely on the crest of the neck. The right hand is lying very carefully on the bridge of the chestnut's nose. Understanding, tenderness, and devotion are part of this posture at this moment. But, at the same time, my entire bearing leaves no doubt that I mean exactly what my handling indicates.

The horse could escape, but he does not. Even powerful stallions submit to this situation from which they could easily extricate themselves. It seems as though I could literally knead and bend the horse and yet I have only known him for a few minutes. It is worth noting about my bearing that I appear powerful even though I am not using any strength. Horses love this, and by doing this I can lead them back to themselves.

Recognition, approach, distance, and now the unconditional, devoted, selfless, powerful and precise form of touch, lead to healing and to the point at which the horse will follow us, indeed, must follow us.

5. In this photo there is great scepticism about touching on both sides, but mainly on the part of the horse. The time for touching has not yet arrived; initially a first encounter as described in this chapter should take place. Through that, the horse would open himself and easily allow touching.

6. In this photo you see a very devoted person but a horse that is more sceptical. This touch is more an expression of the person's wish than an expression of true understanding. Here too several preparatory steps should be taken to make the relationship truly a trusting one, and then you should wait until the horse approaches the person of his own accord.

7. The 'distanced closeness' in this picture has something very fine about it. In this moment at least everything seems perfectly all right.

8. Here the horse has a cheeky and jolly look, but the person less so, and she has good reason because such nibbling can quickly lead to greater acts of disrespect.

9. Here the horse is apparently quite pleased, but, again, the person is a bit sceptical. In this case too, this sort of behaviour can easily lead to acts of disrespect on the horse's part, and they are anything but tender touches. Be very careful about this kind of closeness.

10. In this encounter and touch too there is more distrust and estrangement than trust and closeness. If both could participate in a correct first encounter in order to definitely establish trust through distance, and if the person would try to recognize the nature of this horse, which is a very fine, sensitive Minister of upstanding character, then a new and better form of intimacy would occur. The person would then know that the Minister only very occasionally likes being touched.

11 and 12. This horse is anything but happy. He perceives the touch as bothersome and inappropriate. The eyes are all in all very sad. Here the touch is an expression of the person's desire, a desire that is certainly not shared by the horse. This sort of 'closeness' only creates distance.

13. In this picture the horse shows great mistrust. The person touches the horse very uncertainly and almost threateningly, which is something I observe very often. Horses react very negatively to this.

Pictures say so much more...

The thirteen pictures on this and the previous pages all show touches and encounters between people and horses. The people all look good and loving, but do they, in fact, give this impression to the horses? What can be gleaned from the pictures when you look a bit deeper, when you truly feel the

quality of the encounter? In the captions, I have given you my impressions.

The last pictures of this section show me in the first encounter with a little stallion. The photo on page 164 is also from this series. Please look at each picture with the caption to see what I mean by a touch which apparently seems to make the horse 'melt'.

No matter what I put on the horse, as long as I do it in this way, wounds will heal themselves. In most of the chapter title pages of this book you will see such 'touching' including the title page of this chapter.

What is there still buried in the heart of this secret that is portrayed so clearly in the photos themselves? The following points contain information about something that is actually beyond words.

- Anyone can touch; it is one of the simplest things in the world. But a spectrum can only express itself when in fact there is a spectrum there to begin with! And power, energy and true empathy are part and parcel of the spectrum of touch.

- It is not easy to admit honestly to yourself that you have very narrowly defined limits when it comes to such fundamental issues as those dealt with here. But taking the first step to deal with this covers practically the entire distance. Look at pictures of yourself touching horses. What do you see; what impression do you get?

- It is precisely this close connection that nearly everyone wants with their horse. With this connection we have arrived at the first true goal. At this point the horse opens his soul or he does not; either the walls tumble down or they remain insurmountable obstacles. If you have reached the goal successfully, the horse's devotion shows itself most clearly, the revelation of a mystical nature: that devotion which is neither disrespectful, nor an encroachment, nor simply the result of the urge to eat. It pays to stick with this quest. Many people tell me that they have wanted to give up over and over again, but I hope my books show that it is worthwhile continuing further along the path.

- The difficulties with being close to a horse are often very great, so great that sometimes it seems as though the horse

has sworn to set itself against you. It is sensitive people in particular who suffer in this situation. But, if they master this step, together with the previous steps, I promise them a connection to their horse which they probably no longer even believe can exist. Simply toss the garbage overboard and focus on the essentials.

Look at these pictures that show me with a stallion I have known for just a few minutes. These pictures, like most of the others in this book, are defined by the horse's devoted closeness to me. Note my basic demeanor toward the horse, and how the horse turns towards me. Every single touch seems to be asked for by the horse, not the other way around. Horses are not surrogate stuffed animals and neither are they a substitute for a lack of human closeness and tenderness, but they are frequently misused for these purposes. And that results in misunderstanding instead of the closeness that was desired and sought. In the relationship between the stallion and me, the qualities of closeness and touching lead to trust, devotion and healing.

Leaping the Great Hurdle
The Fourth Pillar: Healing

These days it has become normal that 'professionals' dance, create theatre, make music, heal, paint, create works of art, etc. And everyone only does one thing, everyone is a specialist. That is not my conception of life. I believe much more in the unmitigated power of all these things and in their necessity, and that they can and ultimately should be practised by every individual. Everyone should sing, make music, paint, be creative, and also heal. That way even healing will resume its place in the life of a human being that it has always held in the master pattern of existence, namely as a way of **taking responsibility for the process of staying healthy**. Therefore, a responsible natural healer is always aware of this responsibility to self-heal, and, in this way, he supports those who seek help. Becoming healthy is something you can only do yourself.

That which transpires from this relationship has a healing effect on the horse, which can be seen particularly clearly here. At first the horse was frightened, particularly of the whip. What I call 'the healing stroke' involves binding the horse to me with trust right from the start of the first encounter so that he, totally calmly, can overcome his own fears. But this must be attempted with great caution. Try something like this only with your own horse or with animals you know very well. Assimilate everything that is written here and allow yourself plenty of time before and during every encounter.

I now want to explain where the basic principle of healing is to be found in my work. The aspect of healing is **an intrinsic part** of my relationship with horses, it is not an addendum. In order to be able to walk my path with horses it is fundamentally significant to recognize that healing constitutes an indispensable core, because only through healing in its broadest sense can my form of relationship with a horse happen. And only through this form of relationship can **the reflex of following** arise in the horse.

I am, therefore, not a horse whisperer, but the exact opposite, and everyone who wants this kind of closeness with horses must, quite unequivocally, be able to heal.

This kind of healing will not, like much else, be forced into the area of specialization.

Recognizing the hurdle

Let us look at the photo of the flea-bitten grey. His slightly open, totally relaxed, mouth, the direct and candidly tender attention to me, the half-closed eyes, and the thoroughly relaxed overall expression of the horse are all indicative of his willingness to give himself up to that which is transpiring. Thus something very dramatic is happening here! What is it?

As the first encounter continues to unfold we must keep something very much in mind: what is the tip of the iceberg and what is the underlying main problem of the horse in front of me? (I address this point again in Chapter 6 where I discuss the work with each of the individual character groups.) The principle is that each horse always shows a palette of very diverse symptoms. These are great or small, significant or insignificant. What is important to us is to find the original cause of the symptoms, and to determine which packet of symptoms indicates the most significant underlying causes. This is yet another reason why it is so important to truly recognize horses. All of that can be 'easily' determined when you are practised in the art of recognition. Just the descriptions of the character groups are an incalculably great aid in this.

The horse in the photograph displayed great fear, particularly of the whip. There are two things that are very important to solving this problem.

1. I have to know without a doubt where this fear originates. Is it something the horse was born with? Was there a traumatic experience? Is it human beings who are still responsible for the shock and fear this horse displays? In my work I always state openly what I think. At first that honesty often makes me enemies, but at some point even the most annoyed person realizes how important this moment was, for himself and for his horse, even if it sometimes takes quite some time to admit this.

2. Here comes the leap over the hurdle. The head of this horse, for example, says to us that this is a very fine, sensitive horse that is not fearful by nature, and was definitely not born fearful. The ears are in a certain opposition to the eyes and nostrils. The horse is sensitive, but not jumpy or overly nervous. He seeks contact with people and requires a fine sensitive hand. We have before us a rare mix of Child and Minister. He is a wise but also childlike horse: a mixture of delicacy and wisdom. From this alone I can immediately conclude that human beings and their incorrect handling of this horse are the direct cause of his fearfulness. Upon the exchange of two or three words with the horse's owner this theory is confirmed. This horse is terrified of the whip. And now the 'miracle' happens. Through all the steps that have been described here I am, in a very short time, successful in persuading the horse to 'take the leap over the hurdle' that troubles him most. The horse too has to heal himself. I simply show him great trust, set up the obstacle, and help him to jump. The unbelievably devoted expression, the look of extreme reverie, could only be achieved because I confronted the horse with the source of his fear in such a way that he could conquer it. The face shows the peace after the storm, the recovery after the liberation, the healing after the long illness. This process is different with animals from that with people and, particularly with horses, it happens extremely quickly – if you have found the key that fits. If you want to do this with all horses it requires either great experience or a particular gift. You should concern yourself only with your own horse – and that should be possible with the help of this book, good will, and genuine devotion.

This mare showed great fear of, for example, the saddle blanket. Look carefully at the details in the pictures, most importantly that the horse is always at liberty during the first encounter. Very soon the horse seems to seek out the saddle blanket of her own accord. A unique conflict develops between the horse's fear and her desire to overcome that fear together with a now very trusted person. I experience this in almost every case. The horse is at liberty and feels free; I am simply holding the saddle pad and demonstrating with my entire being how harmless it is. The horse now independently seeks out the avoidable danger in order to overcome it.

What the horse experiences

Through recognition, maintaining appropriate distance, and approach the person becomes a 'leader' for the horse. He becomes example, helper, trusted friend, and protector. If the 'leader' approaches the feared object, the whip for example, and shows no fear but only unwavering certainty and calmness, then the person becomes the **bridge to conquering fear,** because the horse still does not trust the whip but rather the person. The person can then approach the horse with the object of fear and transmit his own confidence to the horse. But the aspect that is even more important is: **once a bridge, always a bridge.**

Once the trust in the 'leader' has been secured, the person can lead the horse through every danger without first having to do a great deal to accustom him to something. The horse will follow the 'human bridge' into the trailer, through water, practically through fire, and simply everywhere. That, then, is the 'miracle of

3. Taking the horse in hand and, through healing, overcoming the greatest problem. That happens in minutes, and from then on the horse knows that he is being helped by this person.

4. The horse now follows the person revealing his true nature.

5. The horse has opened his soul to the person and he stands there before him, completely vulnerable. This vulnerability is what makes the horse so sensitive and so easily wounded. This greatest of all potential for trust must never be destroyed because of human inattentiveness. The horse must never experience anything negative from us. His soul would again be locked away from people, and this time forever.

following' and there will be more about that in the next section.

The steps of healing

1. Recognition
2. Achieving trust through approach, respect, clarity, distance and touch.

Let us go back to the frightened grey horse on page 154. In his case it is important that I do not hide the whip from him; instead I must lift my presence and power to a higher level and bring it into play so that, in the presence of the much-feared whip, the horse maintains his expression of deep affection and peace. I touch the horse all over his body with the whip and, eventually, I even crack it. But the horse will not now react to it.

Thousands of people have witnessed this healing experience at demonstrations and clinics and the German equestrian press in particular has expressed the sentiment: 'He can do that, but he cannot impart or teach it'. Until recently there was certainly some truth in this reproach, but now, with this book, I am attempting to teach this way of establishing true relationships with horses to those who are genuinely interested.

WARNING

If there are people who want to employ what I have described here for mere exploitation or to get on a fast track to a career, they must realize that they hold a very sharp 'knife' in their hands and can cause serious injuries. If they do not truly feel, and thoroughly assimilate, everything I have described then they will unleash unimaginable chaos. They will neither overcome a horse's fear nor heal his suffering. Instead, the horse will become more disturbed. They will create panic and a new trauma for the horse will only make everything worse. The proper key is required to enter the horse's 'house' to move freely within it. This is not a guide for 'wannabe professionals' or 'part-time horse whisperers'! This is a book for sensitive people who are carefully searching for a way to interact more sensitively with perhaps one, two, or three horses. If you need help, please turn to one of our partners who have trained for many years with us and not to plagiarists whose only 'expertise' is self-proclaimed. Unfortunately our address book is filled with the names of people who falsely use me as a reference and do not have the ability to even touch the tip of the iceberg, thus making things worse instead of better.

Observe the bearing of this horse. You can still see traces of the fear that was there at the start but that is being overlaid with increasing trust and self-confidence. The horse is being healed and begins to follow the person unconditionally – even when he has the fear-inducing object in his hands. Thus following is a natural consequence of healing.

The Fifth Pillar: Following and Trust; Turning to Me of his Own Free Will

The fact that the horses follow me is the result of everything that leads to this point: recognition, approach, help and healing. Because of the trust these qualities instil, a 1000 k (2205 lb) Breton horse follows me, Campeon 13 follows me, and all the horses with which you have become acquainted in this book follow me. Horses follow me in this spirit, in my spirit, because of a consequence of recognition and healing and not as a result of pressure in the way that horse whispering is so often practised these days. One should not be confused with the other.

1-3 The fact that the horses in these photos are following me is the consequence of recognition, a conscious and thoroughly clear approach, help and healing, and not the result of force. I have oriented myself in the most natural way to the primal feelings of the horse, and presented myself as the horse's helping, protecting and healing partner. The horses now follow me as they would a powerful lead animal in the wild. Very quickly the trust is so great that even outside the confined area a horse seeks closeness to me. Everything that has been established up to now will later carry over to riding when this great leap becomes a totally different experience for both human and horse.

When horses love!

Only helping and healing lead to free-willed following. Only when a child, or a horse, or any other being, perceives that it not only will not be exploited but that, in the proximity of a particular person, it will also experience protection, help and healing, will following result.

Only a first encounter, of the type I have described, leads to a genuine following by the horses, totally of their own free will. That is my path, and that is the path of true horsepeople as I see them. It is healing that gives us the connection we seek and desire, and healing in this spirit also means bringing a thoroughly healthy and open horse a bit further into the world of human beings, thereby offering new security, and better understanding.

Important points regarding following and trust

- If all the other stages were accepted peacefully then the horse will also follow! Do not try to instigate it, not even inwardly, because the horse senses that as pressure.
- Never give the horse the feeling that he has to come with you, because he really does not have to. But sooner or later he will come, and with such intensity that you will quickly have another problem: how do I get rid of him again? But I am sure you will be able to cope with this

4

5

4. Filio was one of the officers who attended the clinic at the Spanish breeding facility. He could not believe his eyes when, after just a very short time, one of his favourite stallions simply followed him with a trustingly lowered head. The stallion simply followed him as he would a high-ranking, very trusted lead horse.

5. In the first encounter, the connection that has been won through trust is the best foundation for everything that is to follow. In my opinion, this foundation is the only one that can last a lifetime.

Over and over again the horses come running to me in the centre of the arena, as the stallion Almendro is doing here. The change from coming to going, from leading and being at liberty becomes a game that lets a young horse become a riding horse in such a way that he barely notices the transition. Only fun, adventure, a continual fresh outlook, and clear, inwardly strong leadership and reliability accompany our protégé on our path of lifelong friendship.

pleasant problem on your own.

- In the first encounter move the horse as little as possible, and preferably not at all. He will follow nevertheless.
- When you sense that he wants to come to you then, depending on the situation, keep him at a distance a few moments longer. The coming together should and must be celebrated, and that is again a matter of distance and space.
- When the horse comes to you and stays with you and when he no longer wants to move away from you – out of genuine respect and not because of any force or because you are luring him with food – then you will have achieved something that comes high up the 'pyramid of human existence'. Accept this in a spirit of peaceful joy and great calmness – otherwise what you have just won will escape you.
- On the subject of following and leading, use my book *Dancing with Horses* as a guide to the basic body signals. Perhaps in this respect you will rediscover this book because you will now be more aware of all that is written between the lines, and the meaning will be clearer to you.

This extremely frightened mare was presented to me at a clinic and would let nothing and no one near her. I followed all the steps that were discussed in this chapter. Out of distance, through a clear and conscious approach came closeness and trust. Because of closeness and trust I could lead the mare to herself and help her overcome her fear. She then followed me, even over plastic sheeting and even when I placed the formerly frightening blanket on her back. Her trust and connection to me – this being that has no doubt about how right this whole situation is – were always stronger than all the former fears. The horse followed me through obstacles, relaxed and with a lowered head as though we had known each other for years. Is that not also a very good path for you and your horse?

The Significance of the First Encounter: Another Look at the Whole Process

This too is a 'first encounter'. Fighting and very seriously intended attacks precede the peace and devotion. I put these pictures at the end of the chapter to again document the significance of the person's inner presence and calmness. With practically nothing I parry the attacks of the horse and thereby let them fizzle out completely. As with the Breton stallion and Campeon 13, my movements seem to be a light dance. I never encroach and I never want anything more than to lead the horse to himself. Therefore I am never in any real danger. If I acted differently then this situation would be extraordinarily threatening and risky.

After all that has been said, it should now be clear just how significantly a true close relationship with horses impacts the fundamental qualities of human existence. And surely it is now easier to understand why I repeatedly insist that it is not primarily the horses that interest me but rather human beings and their transformation. I work with horses to understand this process better, against the background of the origins of this world, because horses are one of the most important symbols for the recognition of the primal connectedness of existence. But now, all that remains for us in this chapter is one last condensed look into the practice of the first encounter.

You are standing before a horse... then what?

- You must ask yourself whether or not you are inwardly and physically prepared to **lead** such a creature?
- If yes, you must then **recognize** the nature of the creature in front of you. Generally, that comes down to fine details. What is the **first impression?** To which character group does this horse belong? What are his **individual characteristics?** What is his **current condition?** How does he appear outwardly? How does he behave toward other horses? What is his relationship to human beings?
- You will then be able to recognize how to get close to this horse at that moment, how you must **approach** him. You will now decide if it is in fact the **right moment** to do something. You will recognize what the horse's **cardinal problem** is, at which you want to direct the **healing lever.**

- Then you will decide on the **first actual step**, which is particularly important. Often I begin my work not in, but already outside the picadero. **Before entering** I might give some signals, or walk a step here or there, or move the rope or the whip. Then the **first distance** is particularly important. Ask yourself these questions. Shall I act first from a long way away? Shall I move immediately and directly into the horse's Zone 1 to seek closeness for example or, the opposite, to suggest that the horse yield to me? Shall I be particularly gentle and tender in my approach, or at first even provocative and fierce? Which tool shall I choose for the first step? I do not always take the rope. Occasionally I use a short driving whip or a blanket or even a saddle or a piece of plastic.

- Then the **dialogue, the primal conversation**, begins. Now time and space melt away. Nothing intrudes on this encounter; nothing of any meaning takes place outside this event, everything is centred on the here and now. Now there are no more ideas, no more plans. The recognition must fulfil itself; the senses must form a picture that is no longer instigated by us. The person is nothing more and nothing less than an **instrument of creation**. Ultimately the horse is totally part of us and we are totally part of the horse. All gates have been opened and timelessness streams through a pair of beings that have melted into one experience.

- Then we decide how high we want to lift the horse and ourselves. It is the eternal struggle of the artist to perfect, or shape, a picture or a work of art, without taking it to the point of destruction. The issue therefore is to **stop at the decisive moment**. If we stop too soon, we risk an eventual uncontrolled backslide; if we wait too long, if we overstretch the bow, then the string snaps and the work is destroyed.

- Finally, **we bid farewell** to that creature with which we were able to experience oneness. We bid farewell to a creature that we know better than anyone else and that knows us better than anyone else does. As at the beginning when we ask the horse if we may work with him, we now gratefully ask him if we may bid farewell. Because in the process of creation, animals came before us human beings.

Finally this stallion too is totally quiet and peaceable; he did not fight, but he reacted to that which he had previously had to endure from others. I did not fight either, I simply reacted to the horse. We both acted in the spirit of a greater truth – the dragons of chaos and unconsciousness were slain. The circle closes again, and I hope I have succeeded in allowing the nature of this art, the nature of the 'first encounter' to become clear?

Again, power, harmony and intimate encounter are evident between person and horse. After only a few minutes the stallion allows himself to be 'kneaded and shaped', he gives himself over to the person's healing and beneficial attention, participating both inwardly and outwardly. But what is happening here can happen in exactly this way only with this horse. This chapter covers this 'made to order attention' in detail.

How to Shape Horses Correctly

From the first recognition of horses, our path leads to the enormously significant first encounter. What awaits us now is an insight into interacting with horses that is as practical as it is conducive to bonding; we now turn our attention to the question of how horses should, in principle, be worked when you make their individual natures the foundation of the work and, in doing that, we repeatedly move from specific details to more general ones. We now bring into play everything that has been learned and incorporate it into an even more precise picture.

Theory and Practice: How this Chapter Works

What happens when you hear some music, a symphony for example, that really gets under your skin? There is nothing solid, nothing that you can grasp and latch onto, and yet worlds of memories, associations and, above all, emotions well up in you. You are lost in the moment as you grasp and absorb every note. The emotions that arise are just as real as they are removed from your ordinary reality, and they distance you from your ordinary reality. But which reality is truer, is more genuine, more yours? At any rate, the one into which music leads you probably is moving, stirring, and arresting to a different degree. In the concert hall you forget space and time, the cares and greyness of the every day, and you are warmed – warmed around your heart and at your centre. And surely once during such an occasion tears have come that had no external cause, no purpose except simply to be – an expression of being deeply moved.

The cement that binds me

Can you imagine a life that always unfolds as though you were sitting in a concert hall? As though you were following the drama of a symphony with its tensions and frictions, its questions and finally its stirring and redeeming answers and

resolution? The primal sources describe a way of life for human beings exactly like that. Only that they say is true life, and only therein lies the true meaning, far from flight and frenzy, far from sentimentality and fragmentation.

I try to arrange my life according to those ancient principles. I remember a morning nearly twenty years ago. I woke up after a nightmare and for a moment I had the impression of 'feeling nothing'. My physical senses were awake and I was physically perfectly healthy, but within me was a coldness unknown to me until then. I could no longer feel the warmth in my belly that was always with me. Something I had always known, this fundamental vibration of life, a continual melody, was just not there. I was frightened but, since that moment, I have viewed this experience differently; was what I was experiencing possibly similar to the feeling that accompanies most people all their lives?

The warm feeling soon returned to my belly, and also the experience of a deep emotion, with which I could again look upon everything in my accustomed way. But from then on I was more conscious of my good fortune.

This fundamental feeling is the 'cement' that, among other things, binds me very personally to this world. It is the cement that binds the horses to me, and it is the cement that keeps me glued to my questions until the answers to them are forthcoming.

Shattered in the cold

This 'cement' also allows a book like this to come into existence, and is ultimately the beginning and ending of every encounter with a horse. What does a person, who knows nothing of this cement, do with all these hints? And what about the person who has stopped looking for it, or something like it? I fear he will take everything I say into his cold nature, in a shattered form, in the firm belief that he knows exactly what I am talking about. In other words, he keeps the packaging and throws the contents into the bin. However, I cannot give the cement to anyone – I can only tell them about it. I can also let it become visible in the encounter with a horse. And I can add the following to what I have already said.

- I know that this cement is carried like an invisible package by every human being. It is there. But as long as it remains unseen and unfelt, a person is not truly born.
- If you are in the company of a horse, then this deficiency is more pronounced than anywhere else. Everything that I teach in my books and clinics can only be understood and put to use with the background, the support, of this cement.
- The horse is symbolic of matter. This cement is spirit and wisdom, and when it is missing then matter meets matter, chaos meets chaos, and exponentially increases. However, the horse wants to be led by wisdom and spirit. Then matter meets spirit, and a complete entity comes into existence.
- In ancient China you spoke of a man who had lost his way in life as one who continually leans for support upon thorns and thistles and wonders why he falls to the ground bleeding. He does not see the splendour surrounding him and goes far away to find something better. In the end he returns home, only to find no one is there anymore. He has forever forfeited his life. I cannot emphasize enough how simple things really are, and particularly as pertains to horses; to them everything complicated is alien. When I see people with horses, this ancient image always comes to mind. If a person carries no rhythm within himself, a metronome will help him only conditionally or not at all. If a person carries no sense of 'feel' within himself, then sentimentality, insipid emotions, and 'being a good person' will not lead to understanding or success. And if someone has no inner sense of order and proportion, then an outer corset of morality is no replacement.

On the Path to Becoming a Riding Horse: Concepts, Definitions, and Classifications

Protecting yourself from the thorns

This background information leads us into the practice, on the understanding that this practice can only be successfully utilized by that person who at least makes an effort with all his heart and with all his will to protect himself from the 'thorns'.

In this chapter you will find an individual 'instruction manual' for the work, abbreviated to key words, for each character group. I put this term in quotation marks because it is something much more than, and very different from, just an instruction manual. With this chapter, the descriptions in Chapter 4, and the nature of the first encounter, we have everything we need to proceed. Naturally, there is much more that could be said about many things, and maybe I will do that in subsequent books, but the nut has been shelled. Included in each character group section is a table that contains a condensed form of all the most important information to give you an overview.

How does the overview work?

It is always dangerous to compress times and forms into hard and fast rules because they too easily become restrictive cages and crutches, and excuses and reasons for deficient empathy and creativity. Nevertheless, I will attempt to describe certain concepts in a more concrete way. In the character group overview tables and descriptions of the work, the following concepts and sets of concepts arise.

1. **Reprise, Sequence, Session**   These refer to individual sections of work (see illustration), which can be either short or long, with short or long pauses in between. One session is the entire lesson, the entire period during which the horse is worked. If it is a long session it is of twenty to thirty minutes duration. If it is a short session it is sometimes much less than that; a session can sometimes be concluded after only a few minutes. A session should only be longer than thirty minutes for a very good reason.

Reprises

The individual reprises build the sequence

| Sequence | Sequence | Sequence | Sequence |

Start of session   Session   End of session

A sequence is a set of the same reprises. A reprise is the individual exercise from beginning to end, and in this system it is of the smallest size. With these two concepts too, the respective amount of time spent and the number of exercises is very significant. For example: a horse is learning to trot off from a halt; he is standing in place and waits for the precise instruction. The reprise lasts from the moment of the subtle signal to trot until the next signal, for example another halt. If I now repeat this reprise five times, in order to then proceed to another exercise, one sequence has ended. A reprise can be short or long, and it can be repeated a greater or lesser number of times. The rhythm that thus results within the total session is of fundamental significance and dependent upon the horse's stage of development. A long reprise can last as long as three or four minutes, and a short one is often less than a few seconds. A long sequence can fill nearly the entire session, and a short sequence can be over after a few minutes, or even less. In the tables I give the first particulars of this – knowing full well that these are very rough guidelines that in no way are a substitute for feel or cement.

2. **Fast tempo, slow tempo**   These concepts are to do with the overall character of the session. It can be more rapid and challenging or more restrained and slow. Naturally,

Establishing the right atmosphere. These photos show down-tempo, 'flat' work that is kept within a tight framework.

patience and quiet should always be the foundation.

3. **High or flat**   Particular character types should generally be schooled 'flat' on level terrain without obstacles, and move from there into collection and elevated action. Other character types on the other hand should generally be schooled 'high', that is, in the countryside, for example, or over obstacles, cavaletti, and small jumps.

4. **Domineering or restrained tolerance**   With some of the character groups, the aim is to resolve the question of dominance right from the start; quiet inner strength must serve to restrain any tendency towards encroachment by the horse. Other character groups should be given 'a long rope'; they should be led with reserve and tolerance but, even then, no encroachment by the horse should be accepted.

5. **Within narrow boundaries or playfully free**   Every horse wants to, and must, be led so that he feels secure and can build up trust in the person and in the world around him. Some character groups must, from the very beginning, be given very clear boundaries and structure to their work while others only really bloom when the framework is more open and playful.

6 **Concave riding-in, convex riding-in**   These terms describe another crude tool, which should only be used as a first rule of thumb. The character groups can basically be divided into convex or concave types. Please note the references to this in *Dancing with Horses*. The concave horse has a fundamentally weak back and probably inferior carrying power, therefore a horse like that must first be strengthened with work on the ground and then carefully ridden-in lightly, and on a long rein. A convex horse would more likely be harmed by that method. Naturally, all riding-in must be done with the highest degree of care. All my instructions on this point are of course intended to be used within the context of my sensitive framework.

Further differentiation from 1 to 3   In order to differentiate everything even further, I have given the various sections of the overview tables numbers from 1 to 3. The numbers indicate: 1 – a horse might tend toward a particular factor; 2 and 3 - this factor should be taken seriously or very seriously. For example: concave riding-in – 1, indicates that a horse in this character group occasionally has a weak back, and that you must, therefore, be more careful with the work; concave riding-in – 3, indicates that horses in this character group mostly

The above photos show up-tempo, 'high', playing-free work in the arena and the open countryside.

have very weak backs and that therefore riding-in can present very significant difficulties and should be undertaken only with extreme caution.

The overview tables: a first orientation

If a pair of concepts has numbers assigned to both, it means that the full spectrum of work in that area is possible and helpful. For the Unicorn, for example, down tempo has a number 2, and so the emphasis here is on quiet and down-tempo ways or working (although this horse will occasionally be worked up tempo). For the Dove, however, both up and down tempo have the number 2, therefore, typically, work for the Dove contains tempo variation.

Note Remember to consider all the suggestions in the overview tables as part of the whole picture, and as an additional guide for preparing yourself to work with a particular character type. They are only of value when taken in context with everything else that has been presented in this book. Your sense of 'feel' and your ability to communicate will in the end determine what happens. Every horse, no matter from which character group, is an individual with very special qualities within the fundamental type, and I very much hope that this point in particular has been completely understood.

Conquering Shortcomings en route to High School Work
The Unicorn on the Path to Becoming a Riding Horse

1

The Unicorn seeks clear, respectful closeness more than training. He frequently has a weak back and occasionally dragging quarters. Good nutrition is important; calcium deficiencies, especially in youth, can create an even more negative influence. These deficiencies and the overfacing of this horse can cause problems in the stifles such as over-extension and weakening of the stifle ligament, which make it even more problematical for the horse to use his hindquarters in a good and powerful way. This horse should not be too thin, but because of his stifles, not too fat either.

Regularity

As a rule the Unicorn is a late developer. It is most important that the horse maintains quiet, regular and elegant forward motion, and so under no circumstances should this horse be rushed or put on his hindquarters too soon. This would result in a sluggish horse, unhappy in movement and, possibly, with compromised health.

Bending/flexing

You should approach bending and flexing of all kinds very carefully at the beginning of work on the ground and under saddle. The Unicorn's massive body on a large, but as a rule not very strong, foundation would put too much strain, too

Overview Table for the Unicorn	
Reprise	rather short
Sequence	rather short with pauses
Session	medium to long
Up tempo	–
Down tempo	2
High	1
Flat	2
Domineering	1
Restrained, tolerant	–
Tight boundaries	1
Playing free	–
Concave riding-in	2
Convex riding-in	–

A typical picture of a Unicorn that has not had the smallest signs of discontent taken seriously and the problems resolved.

whether at liberty or being led from another horse, combined with careful work in the picadero and the riding arena including occasional work over poles or low cavaletti, that is the way in which this horse can slowly be developed into a riding horse. A special regularity and quiet 'flat' work over the years keep this sensitive horse balanced in mind and body, healthy, and of a joyful, affectionate nature for his entire life.

Excesses of any kind are to be avoided at all costs with this horse; he is no playmate and not a creature intended for constant hectic activity. Quiet thoughtful seriousness and the careful and regular increasing progression of the exercises are the basis for keeping this horse content. This then leads to the acceptance of the dominance of the owner who must always be very quiet and considerate in his approach to this horse. If the horse develops doubt about the competence of the person, he quickly 'leaves' the relationship.

soon, on joints, ligaments and tendons. This horse needs a good seven or eight years to achieve the start of High School work.

Not infrequently the hooves of these horses are too small and weakly developed for the overall body size, and so good hoof care is of great importance from the very beginning.

'Flat' work

Long-distance rambles in walk and trot, all sorts of outings,

Down-tempo work

The exercise reprises should be quiet and of relatively long duration. Occasionally the rhythm can and should be increased by shifting to a number of tempo changes quickly following one another. As soon as the desired goal has been achieved, longer gaps in the work must follow or, preferably, the session concluded. The smallest signs of discontent or resistance must be taken very seriously, and the causes determined. If the owner does that, and acts maturely and thoughtfully, there should really be no other problems with this horse.

From Fearfulness into Rhythmic Powerful Flight
The Dove on the Path to Becoming a Riding Horse

The entire training of this horse must take into account his background of fearfulness and 'inner fragmentation'. In this case, the owner must constantly expand and secure the bridge of trust.

Feeling free

It is very important that this horse never feels himself constrained. The Dove must, just like a bird, constantly have

the feeling that he can fly freely. That is not always very easy because this horse tends to bolt, to run through the aids, to fidget, and to disquiet. The inexperienced person quickly reaches the end of his tether, and then it is too late; the spiral of misunderstanding is ever increasing, and good advice is expensive at this point. In fact, once the situation has reached this point, this horse can only be turned around by very special horsepeople — of which there are only a very few.

2

First come play and movement

This is how you should proceed with the Dove. Cautiously set about dealing with the phenomenon of the horse's fear, which began in his youth. Before each lesson the horse must be in a state of absolute peace and trust. If the horse is coming straight out of his stable or paddock, he should not be put immediately to work on an exercise; play must come first: movement, snorting, the inspection of the riding arena and surroundings. In other words, the Dove wants to fly, show-off, carry his tail in the air and demonstrate caprioles. If that urge is suppressed, then we are clipping the bird's wings and the Dove dies a little more in our hands each day.

Coming home to roost

Initially the horse wants to find a quiet place in our company, a still point, somewhere to come home to roost. For example, I will groom the horse in the riding arena in a leisurely way, but there are many different possibilities for this quiet time depending on the animal: you can simply stand together admiring the hopefully beautiful landscape, and spend a little time in reflection.

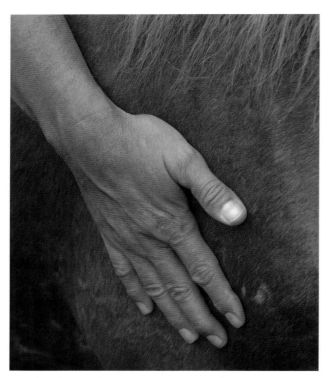

Guarded clarity and trust remove the Dove's fear. See also Chapter 5 on correct touching.

Overview Table for the Dove	
Reprise	very varied
Sequence	very varied
Session	rather short
Up tempo	2
Down tempo	2
High	2
Flat	1
Domineering	–
Restrained, tolerant	1
Tight boundaries	–
Playing free	2
Concave riding-in	3
Convex riding-in	–

Special rituals and variety

It must be remembered that, throughout the Dove's life, you will not be able to simply take this horse out of the stable and ride off as you can with the Friend, for example. This horse will always require special trust-building and calming rituals.

The trust-building exercises always come after the stillness. The horse is gently stroked with a whip, 'wrapped up' in a blanket, led through a constructed tunnel, over the see-saw, and tackles other obstacles or tasks.

I must emphasize that, although the horse will readily participate in all of this after a while, you cannot neglect the fundamental fear of the Dove; he must be kept calm for the whole of his life. That is very important.

The actual exercises will be very varied because the person must feel when a peak can be established, a peak of 'flying' and movement, and when the horse must be calmed with a longer sequence. The fine art in being close to this horse lies in the ability to correctly sense and employ this variety.

The concave shape of the back

Dangers lurk in the basically concave shape of this horse's neck and back. The horse must be kept 'in flight' for a long time by a rider who has the suppleness and ability to support his own weight so that he is barely noticed by the Dove. Under no circumstances should the reins be used to stop or slow the Dove. This horse will begin to check, or steady,

Trust in the person creates trust in the world of human beings and generally diminishes fear. Exercises like these and the ways to them are always part of the life of the Dove.

himself only after he has completely left puberty. Any attempt to force this on him when he is only five or six years old will inevitably force the back downward, the head upward, and the hindquarters to trail out behind; the horse would be permanently ruined in just a few hours.

A few Doves can be brought to the point of being able to perform High School exercises, but in an entirely different way from, for example, the Unicorn, the King, the Tough One, or Pegasus. The Dove must come out of flight, must be gradually grounded in lightness, and must make contact with the earth. That requires much 'feel' on the part of the horseperson. An uncomplicated, light, uncomplaining, and always friendly human nature can well fulfil this assignment.

Order, Form and Great Goals
The Sergeant on the Path to Becoming a Riding Horse

This is a clear horse with clear inner forms that demands clear outer forms. This horse demands regularity, indeed, even punctuality. Janosch has some qualities of this type. When he came to me he was a very pushy animal that was very ready to overstep his bounds.

In particular he did not like farriers at all. In the first year I had him I always had to be present when he was shod. Eventually, Juan, my long-time Spanish farrier was also able to get on with him. He is not only a good farrier but also a reasonable, open person with a quiet and patient nature. One day he came to me and said: 'That is truly the craziest horse I know. He likes absolutely no music. When I shoe him, absolute quiet must prevail, otherwise he will not cooperate. And, I may not chat with anyone else. It is as though we had an agreement. I am permitted, without punishment, to fit him with new shoes as long as I do it as quickly as possible. He punishes every unnecessary delay immediately — with at least a furious face. Then too everything has to occur in an exact sequence. He gives me each hoof on his own, without my having to do anything, but always in the same order'.

Clear rules and fair agreement

With the Sergeant, therefore, everything must happen according to regulations. Changes must always be announced in advance. If a horse like this has been in one paddock for several days and is to be turned out in another one, you would do well to explain that to him in a few words, in advance – have no fear, he will understand!

When I am working Janosch at liberty and, for whatever reason, pause for a bit after having worked him on the left, for example, and then resume work again on the left, this horse that actually understands everything will act as though he understands nothing at all anymore. Then he will, of his own

Overview Table for the Sergeant

Reprise	rather short
Sequence	rather long
Session	short
Up tempo	2
Down tempo	1
High	2
Flat	–
Domineering	2
Restrained, tolerant	–
Tight boundaries	2
Playing free	–
Concave riding-in	1
Convex riding-in	–

accord, turn in the other direction until it dawns on me that I have already worked my little Sergeant in that direction.

Justice

Be absolutely just in the work – when there is a doubt, judge yourself first because such horses have a very strong sense of right and wrong. And if you cross the line, or damage it, then the horse can quickly become estranged from you.

Variety, movement and much praise

The horse needs movement in his work and much praise. Reprimand only very carefully with gentle words and a light

expression. Otherwise what happened to Janosch's previous owner will happen to you: he could not get on the horse's back for eight years.

Give such a horse variety and challenges but do not go too far in the lessons. The horse needs the security of that which he already knows and so you should always begin by quickly running through the things the horse already knows well. That will remind him that he has already learned quite a lot – to his great pleasure and that of his owner. This horse, with genuine affection, wants to do everything he can to please his owner.

Everything must have its reason

The Sergeant is a very clever horse as a rule, and because of that he also needs a reason for doing what he does. With many other character groups this is not particularly important, but in this case it is a pre-requisite for a good relationship and a rich journey together. If possible, have voltes and circles done around trees, and all other exercises should be done in the open air and determined by the terrain. Togetherness with the Sergeant should always be a mixture of play and valid organization. This horse demands much in the way of creativity from his owner.

Sergeants are very sturdy horses and are seldom ill. Depending on their breed, they possess a good, very strong, though fine, skeletal structure.

Overall the training proceeds in a clear, regular, orderly, progressively more challenging, fashion. If these fundamental training principles are recognized and understood, then a light hand will enable this horse to grow into a self-confident, liberated riding horse.

The Sergeant needs clear directions that he can then carry out independently and energetically.

Through Clarity, Dominance, and Trust to Friendship
The Sceptic on the Path to Becoming a Riding Horse

4

This is very certainly not a horse for a beginner. The most important thing is that, at the beginning of his training, and actually the whole time the horse is growing and learning, the dominance relationship is always clear and definitely established. This is not a horse to play with. Here too the rhythm of distance and closeness is one of the keys to success when this horse and his owner work together.

Overview Table for the Sceptic	
Reprise	rather long
Sequence	rather long
Session	medium to long
Up tempo	1
Down tempo	–
High	–
Flat	1
Domineering	3
Restrained, tolerant	–
Tight boundaries	3
Playing free	–
Concave riding-in	1
Convex riding-in	–

The time factor

Everything should happen very slowly, clearly, and at great leisure. After a while, you quietly let the horse begin collection, bring him into trot and later into canter, always bringing him back to the starting point in the middle of the arena in order to slowly and thoughtfully lead him out again. As mentioned in Chapter 4, this horse should definitely have the opportunity to observe other horses at their lessons. That will help every horse, but with this one it is almost a prerequisite. I cannot repeat often enough how important the time factor is with this horse. Only through quiet work and sensible repetition can this horse be put on a path that leads to increasingly friendly familiarity.

Always be on guard

If a horse of this character group appears to have more of a coarse nature, then it is important to always be on your guard. I cannot emphasize this enough. I have dedicated my life to horses, among other things, and my vocation is to deal with horses, even disturbed ones; I am a professional. A professional lives by 'surviving' the encounter, always emerging from it unscathed. I am, therefore, much more careful about interacting with horses than the majority of amateurs. It never ceases to amaze me how naïve, and not infrequently boundlessly careless, people can be when working with horses. The very first thing I do with every new horse that is brought before me is determine what dangers may arise. With a horse of this character group I am always very wary.

With the Sceptic, the Peasant, and also the Fat One, clear dominance must always be in the foreground. The horse in this sequence would not let his head be touched under any circumstances, and to overcome this, again, dominance and trust are imperative.

Once again we see dominance. When two people appear to be doing exactly the same thing with a horse, the horse mirrors the true action of each individual. Here we see a typical problem. In the top three photos the horse reacts to person, whip, and rope negatively and aggressively; he does not yield but fights. But look at the bottom three photos and see with how few means I succeed in getting the horse to yield peaceably. The secret to this is that the inner potency of the person moves the horse and affects him, not the external aids.

Elasticity

As a rule, a horse of this character group, though physically strong, has little elasticity or impulsion. You must be contented with relatively flat gaits and only a moderate forward urge. With such a horse, it is the biggest mistake to expect and demand of him something beyond his natural abilities. That is not a good tack to take with any horse, but with a horse like this one such a mistake can easily result in aggression.

Dominance, once again

If the dominance relationship is correct and the owner is clear, correct, patient and very restrained then the training of this horse will proceed along a quiet, regular track. Then the horse will not demand too much from his owner.

In the course of time, the scepticism in his gaze will diminish and horse and owner will spend many carefree years with one another. No matter what, a person will learn a great deal from interacting with this horse.

From Simplicity thorough Simplicity to Simplicity
The Friend on the Path to Becoming a Riding Horse

5

With this horse too it is very important to recognize and accept his limitations. This horse does not have an overly strong forward urge and his gaits are at best medium and can be flat and dragging. But, if you proceed carefully with, and allow a lot of time for, his training then, eventually, he can present himself in a very attractive light.

Late developer

Horses of this character group are late developers. They should not begin training until about four years of age and even then things should be taken very slowly at the beginning. After a year or two a Friend will greatly surprise his owner by suddenly progressing in leaps and bounds of his own accord. At that point, the training is practically complete. It is not likely that this horse will want to learn very much, but he performs what he has learned well and reliably.

Physically the Friend does not present many problems to the person who trains and partners him. His good short back and constitution make him a good weight carrier. Occasionally, with some representatives of this type, shoeing can be difficult.

Clear, fair, and obliging

So, how do you proceed with a Friend? First, it is important to get very close to him so that you are truly his friend. A sentimental attitude will not achieve this, nor will stroking and cuddling. The main thing is to be clear, fair, and obliging. The dominance relationship is established quickly and simply: this horse relates easily to a strong partner.

Trust and suppleness are developed by changing from work at liberty and light play (which should never lead to over-lively behaviour) to short, concentrated sequences that are never overly demanding. Gentle bending exercises also help – initially done outside the small picadero – as do exercises over low cavaletti.

It is important that this horse be brought very slowly and gently into school work. Suggestions for exercises can be found in *Dancing with Horses*. You can begin with these exercises fairly early in the training, because the horse does not learn too quickly, but very gently, slowly, and carefully.

Overview Table for the Friend

Reprise		medium
Sequence		medium
Session		medium
Up tempo		1
Down tempo		–
High	later in the training	2
Flat		–
Domineering		1
Restrained, tolerant		–
Tight boundaries		1
Playing free		–
Concave riding-in		–
Convex riding-in		1

Being able to do a good shoulder-in is absolutely necessary to his well-being and soundness.

First trust and dominance, then a modest but good foundation

To summarize: first trust and dominance must grow over a relatively long period through a small selection of exercises, then, slowly and gradually a little ground work and ridden work can be built up. Bending and suppleness in particular should be gently introduced and developed through a careful and timely introduction to a good shoulder-in. This horse has no great problems with stamina, which will be satisfactorily developed and consolidated through work at liberty, and long walks in-hand and later under saddle.

Much Patience and Attention Leads to Joy of Movement
The Fat One on the Path to Becoming a Riding Horse

6

Horses of this type pose several challenges to a horseperson. If you want to develop a Fat One into a riding horse, several factors must be considered. That which I describe here can be applied to certain other horses that fundamentally or only occasionally exhibit the same types of behaviour as this character group. Here are some important tips straight out of the 'hot oven of daily practice'.

Never press!

Be very careful with these horses and their problems. In nearly every case, it is the fundamental nature of this type to not want to move very much or, at least, to only want to move when they truly feel an inner urge to do so. The biggest mistake is to press such a horse forward through the use of any aids. That effort will always fail and always end in a battle, with dangerous consequences for the

Dominance is a matter of many details. Correct leading is a repeatedly underestimated fundamental pillar of success. The basic descriptions for these techniques are in *Dancing with Horses.*

owner. If a Fat One bites or kicks, he does not do so as a warning, but with enough force to rid himself of a nuisance once and for all. In other words, he attacks only once – successfully. Afterwards he has no desire to attack a second time. He would rather stand quietly again, rest himself and, if possible, eat.

Dominance and trust must come first

What is the best way to proceed? First of all the dominance and trust relationship must be strongly established. There are many suggestions for ways of doing this in *Dancing with Horses*, but with the Fat One, it can be done only by particularly sensible leading, and through the phenomenon of distance and closeness in the picadero. My instructions here pertain to the extreme case that not so infrequently crops up. Starting from this extreme, you can adjust the work to your particular case. The principle remains the same and that is what we are putting our focus on here.

Moving a 'mountain'

Nothing, absolutely nothing, should be demanded of this horse in the first few months. Any impatience will literally bring about a disaster.

After those first few months, it is important to convince the horse that it is his idea to move and you do that as follows.

Put the horse in the middle of the arena and do nothing. You must always come back to this 'exercise' of doing nothing. Therein lies the secret of making even this horse a halfway reliable 'plodder'. The next step is to always surprise the horse by seemingly never doing what he expects you to. He expects you to ask him to walk forward at some point, and that is why the first step is always so significant. You will

now touch the horse with a whip, so gently that it seems as though a fly were landing on his coat. It must be that gentle. If you want to be successful, then do everything exactly as I describe it to you here. For whatever reason, whether because of your touch or some other motive, your horse will at some point take at least a small step while you are asking him to do that. That is important. The movement should follow your gentle suggestion, even if your gentle suggestion is not the cause of the movement; do try to understand that. Here comes your success and it will immediately be doubled.

1. You praise the horse generously and give him a reward. He will have absolutely no idea why, but that makes no difference.
2. You immediately cease any form of work and take the 'exhausted' student back to the stable or paddock.

Do the same thing the next day. Again the horse will move at some point and, again, the reward is given. By the fourth day, he will most probably think of you in several ways.

1. You want nothing from him and therefore correspond perfectly to what is natural to him.
2. If he just moves, the session is over for the day.
3. If he just moves, there is a reward.

Overview Table for the Fat One

Reprise	extremely short
Sequence	extremely short
Session	extremely short
Up tempo	–
Down tempo	3
High	–
Flat	3
Domineering	3
Restrained, tolerant	–
Tight boundaries	3
Playing free	–
Concave riding-in	–
Convex riding-in	3

On the fifth or sixth day he will come to the riding arena and will immediately move, and he will do that either entirely on his own or at the very slightest suggestion from you. This entrenches itself in the consciousness of the horse. To the uninitiated it looks like laughably little, but in truth it is a cataclysmic success. For we have planted the seeds of ideas in him, namely that movement is connected with something pleasant, and that it is possible to respond to the most subtle of suggestions. These first small signs of green in the desert must now be carefully nurtured and watered, so that ultimately an oasis can grow — and grow it surely will.

Stay absolutely patient

It is important that you always suppress your impatience. Under no circumstances can you now drive your protégé forward, because that is what he actually expects from you, and if you do that, everything will be spoiled. Then the horse will think to himself: 'I knew it. Once I begin to move, then things will get really stressful. So, in the future, I will just avoid it completely'.

If you handle your horse as has been described, he will, in time, willingly trot a number of circles.

Once again, he would also do that if forced, but you would never lead him to be self-motivated. All his life he would have to be forced and pressured, and ultimately you would lose the game — of that you can be certain.

Always in the same spot

The next step is that you look for a spot in the picadero at which the horse should begin to trot. At this spot, always give a clear but never threatening signal. The horse will eventually actually trot and this should be followed by the same reward ceremony as before. Immediately after the first trot step, bring him in to the centre of the arena, reward him, and take him back to his stable or paddock. What has your horse learned? 'In the long run, trotting is easier than walking, because as soon as I trot, I can leave.'

It will proceed the same way with canter too. In extreme cases we are talking about months of work, but ultimately you will have a motivated horse that works with only the softest signals.

Recognizing the principle

If I describe how to deal with this horse in such detail here, it also serves the purpose of giving you a fundamental way of interacting with the most diverse types of horses so that it becomes clear to you what it actually means to work with the horse, not against him.

It is clear that no one will expect very much from such a horse, and so, depending on his particular nature, you can be satisfied if the entire training is only walk, trot, and canter. If, in addition, you can bring the horse to the point of performing a useful and flowing shoulder-in, then you have surely reached the summit of achievement. If you manage to bring such a horse to the point of friendly, lively participation, then you will have achieved much, learned much about yourself and life, and you will have done a great service to your friend and the world. Because true service in this world is never measured in quantity but rather in quality — and that you have achieved, even if no one knows to appreciate it. After all, what is so special about a horse that only walks, trots, and canters? But you know your secret, and, most importantly, your horse knows!

Leading as the basis for dominance and trust.

Contented With the Very Least
The Peasant on the Path to Becoming a Riding Horse

7

As has already been mentioned, this horse is not usually a riding horse, and it is important to clearly and objectively recognize the horse's specific circumstances and to adapt the programme accordingly. If you are working with a Peasant that still shows a grain of promise, and further training does, therefore, seems to make sense, take heed of the following information, even if you will only be able to show this horse the basics of being close to human beings and the basics of being led.

An innocent spirit

This horse is, as a rule, of a childlike, naïve nature. Such a horse will always retain some innocence even when he is older and has completed a course of training.

The childlike naivety should always determine the foundation for the work, along with the fact that this horse needs clear boundaries and clear direction. As far as the conformation is concerned, the foremost question throughout the training is how to raise the forehand and minimize the major fault, which is usually the overdeveloped hindquarters: the too-high and too-massive croup.

Overview Table for the Peasant

Reprise	short
Sequence	short
Session	short
Up tempo	–
Down tempo	2
High	–
Flat	2
Domineering	3
Restrained, tolerant	–
Tight boundaries	2
Playing free	2
Concave riding-in	1
Convex riding-in	–

Play and dominance

How do we proceed? Play, dominance and trust are uppermost at the beginning. Play should not be left out, but it must not, under any circumstances, degenerate into boisterous behaviour that leads to an erosion of our dominance.

With the Peasant you must be careful regarding the use of closeness and distance. This horse will become insecure about his owner and hurt in his childlike nature through too great and too long a separation. This horse needs closeness on the one hand, but clear boundaries on the other. Each person must employ his own 'feel' with this horse, which is not such an easy task for a person with little experience.

Forward impulsion and bending

The next step is to bring the horse to a point where he can execute the first careful, tentative bending exercises with good forward impulsion. It is important that this is done very cautiously. We have several years to achieve the very simplest work goals with this horse. But that is not the only reason for caution. Because of his physical limitations this horse can only be made 'soft' very slowly. Were we to proceed too quickly, the horse would always avoid the bend by falling out with his hindquarters. Therefore, we are careful to make sure that the horse goes absolutely correctly through the corners in the picadero. By shifting our position slightly backwards just before stepping through the corner we will achieve this in time. Ultimately the horse will, of his own volition, begin to offer a shoulder-in after moving correctly through the corner. Then we only need to take it up and refine it (see *Dancing with Horses*).

Time is on our side

If we proceed slowly enough, albeit without marking time, this horse should have a quiet and problem-free course of training, if only to a very low level.

We must take particular care in the choice of a saddle because there are hardly any commonly sold saddles that will fit a horse with this conformation. Nearly all saddles will slip onto the shoulder and further hinder the horse in his movement during the course of a work session. Small California-style western saddles, available in very inexpensive models, frequently fit a Peasant well. A good saddle pad too can be of help here.

From Superficiality into Quality
The Dancer on the Path to Becoming a Riding Horse

8

The Dancer is related to the Unicorn, the Dove, the Child, and the Dandy but, as far as work is concerned, he is more closely related to the Dove and the Unicorn. So, if you want to work with a Dancer, please also refer to the sections for those character types. The Dancer is not as solid as the Unicorn and therefore has different types of difficulties with the work. He is also not as fearful as the Dove. What they all have in common is the tendency towards a weak back, although it is usually most pronounced in the Dove.

Do not overestimate

The main problem with the Dancer is that it is easy to overestimate him physically and underestimate his sensitivity. Therefore he is easily broken down, inwardly as well as outwardly. To ensure that does not happen, pay attention to the following.

The Dancer can only have his back burdened at a relatively advanced age. He will never be a horse of great stamina, and you can never overtax him with great weight for very long. On the whole the work sessions should be kept short. He needs only the correct motivation in order to, in time, 'dance' his way into the qualities of a riding horse. His light, upward-striving natural tendency must be particularly taken into account. With this horse in particular, less is certainly more: sometimes only two or three minutes a day.

Always praise

The Dancer is extraordinarily dependent upon praise. If this horse has done anything at all, even if it is only to have completed a little exercise correctly, you must acknowledge that with, at the very least, a kind word. His self-confidence is not very well established. In contrast to the Minister, King or Pilgrim, for example, this horse is always teetering on a 'precipice' from which he could easily fall. But that must absolutely not be allowed to happen. It can easily be avoided through our careful and always-present attention.

Back, hindquarters, and the correct 'positioning'

The back and hindquarters are our main focus. Indeed, the Dancer should not be worked very strongly, very 'long' or too forward. With moderate impulsion that should not be increased, the horse is guided via subtle aids into the correct bend – through a corner for example – and then later into the shoulder-in. In this type of horse the forehand, back, loins and croup are often held in contraction – they do not swing loosely and lightly as do for example those of the Pilgrim, the Guardian of the Fire and the Friend. It is, therefore,

  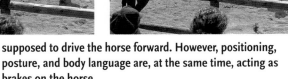

Fundamentally correct positioning is always particularly important. With the Friend and also with the Dancer this factor is even more significant. In this series of three photos the whip is supposed to drive the horse forward. However, positioning, posture, and body language are, at the same time, acting as brakes on the horse.

Here you see that my entire posture is open. My chest is directed towards the withers and, despite the short distance between the horse and me, I am aligned with the croup. This way the horse can go freely forward. Further fundamental aspects of this subject are to be found in *Dancing with Horses*.

Overview Table for the Dancer	
Reprise	short
Sequence	short
Session	short
Up tempo	1
Down tempo	–
High	1
Flat	–
Domineering	–
Restrained, tolerant	1
Tight boundaries	1
Playing free	3
Concave riding-in	2
Convex riding-in	–

imperative that with the Dancer we pay particular attention to something that is always important, namely, the correct positioning.

Under no circumstances should this horse be checked or restrained by the reins or our incorrect body positioning during the work, because then he will fall even further onto the forehand, he will become even more contracted, and the too-high croup will become an insurmountable obstacle on the path to a happy riding horse.

It is particularly important that the Dancer has a lot of space in front of him so that he can express and balance himself while moving forward, without the owner doing much or pressuring him.

People with friendly, light natures are well suited for this task and can help and support this horse. Over the years he will come to move lightly and powerfully, and with continuous attention will build a very close relationship with his owner. He will then be a very impressive horse that, when healthy and well ridden, will draw attention and admiration to himself. But just remember that you should never expect true stamina and high achievement from this horse.

A Little Effort Results in a Lovely Partnership
The Guardian of the Fire on the Path to Becoming a Riding Horse

9

The Guardian of the Fire is related to the Friend, the Pilgrim and the Origin. The way to work with him is dictated very precisely by the description of his nature in Chapter 4. As a matter of fact this horse does not need to be worked that much. If he is properly understood and cherished by his owner, he will move lightly and freely relative to his thoroughly earthbound outer appearance.

Nearly 'completely trained'

Because this horse is comfortable with himself, the hindquarters, back and loins swing freely so everything is relatively supple and soft. As a rule, the horse has a good medium-long to short back. He can carry weight and has stamina. He is, therefore, already relatively 'completely trained' at birth, providing you accept that this horse can never be brought even close to High School work.

Polish the good qualities

Our work with this horse comes down to polishing his good qualities and always keeping him in good spirits. Much of the training should, therefore, take place out in the open, in-hand and also – from the fourth year on – under saddle. An owner with ambition is no good whatsoever for this horse, but those who very gradually, quietly and almost spontaneously devote themselves to the set path in order to shape this horse into a reliable riding horse – up to the point of being able to execute a good shoulder-in – will have a light-hearted and happy time with this horse. In such circumstances, this horse is an ideal companion for daily life.

Slowly getting into the swing

Overall the work reprises, whether in-hand or under saddle, should not be too short – the horse almost needs to get into the swing of things very slowly and patiently. But, I repeat that, under no circumstances should this horse be worked too often or too long.

If a horse like this becomes disobedient in the arena, showing reluctance or unwillingness, which frequently happens and is almost a 'speciality' of this character group, then you must remove the cause of the reluctance. We must remember that these horses are possessed of very old souls. They are far superior to most people and many horses. The owner or trainer of such a horse absolutely must pay attention to these animals' directives. Doing this never leads to a loss of dominance with such a horse; quite the reverse in fact. When the trainer is confronted with such a situation, he

Overview Table for the Guardian of the Fire	
Reprise	long
Sequence	long
Session	short
Up tempo	–
Down tempo	1
High	–
Flat	1
Domineering	1
Restrained, tolerant	–
Tight boundaries	–
Playing free	1
Concave riding-in	–
Convex riding-in	1

should move the training session into the countryside and work more freely with a creative and light touch.

All this will be familiar to owners of Guardians of the Fire and experienced horsepeople.

A good working relationship and the exchange of 'life principles'

Right from the start the Guardian of the Fire demands a good working relationship and a good exchange of ideas. The few things that he can, should and wants to learn he will do practically on his own, with some assistance from the trainer. Do not make the mistake of underestimating this horse; too many people do.

Moulding a Personality
The Origin on the Path to Becoming a Riding Horse

10

With these horses, we must devote a bit more space to the subject of working together. Some people will not be able to fully understand the following ideas. Horses of this type are very commonly found in pleasure-riding circles, but, contrarily, this character type is one that is often misunderstood; this results in much chaos and grief. It is important, therefore, that you try to follow the entire work programme without preconceptions. After that, if you stand back and look at the whole picture, the things that were unclear to you before might now make sense. Even when what is being said goes against conventional wisdom, it is obvious that it is the unconventional that supplies answers to the questions that previously had no satisfactory answers. People have tried, experimented with, and applied the conventional wisdom, but discovered that the harmony they sought with their horses was mostly to be found elsewhere, perhaps by following ideas that were entirely their own. Those who followed their own paths will surely recognize many of the following ideas, and will find confirmation and probably also new support and certainty.

Anything but simple

The character type the Origin is to be found relatively frequently among primitive breeds – similar to the way the Dove, the Dandy or the Child are major character types of Arabian lines.

An Origin is anything but easy to work with. This horse is simply not some sort of 'cuddly wild horse' he is a very sensitive, profound, self-willed spirit of strong character. As was already mentioned in the description in Chapter 4, the Origin is not a children's and beginners' horse.

Horses of the revolution

Over thirty years ago (at about the time of the 1968 student uprisings) there was also a 'revolution' in the riding world: the leisure-riding revolution. But did this actually improve the lives of horses? I think that if it did so at all, it did so only within very narrow boundaries – but in many aspects it actually worsened horses' lives.

The horses that carried these leisure-riding revolutionaries on their backs came and mostly still come from remote areas, from islands and other small and exceptional geographical areas. There, these horses find their ideal environment to which they have been able to adapt over centuries. Then, in their new environments, they suffer from horse-management methods that are in no way appropriate to their origins. This European leisure riding movement was originally started to reawaken in mankind an original experience of nature. Against all intentions it also created a world of shows and competition, which is today responsible for some of the worst examples in this regard and with all its negative and unnatural consequences this environment is the one most unsuited to the Origin. Ideologies always feed upon themselves and end up in opposition to the ideals from which they originated. Politics at the end of the twentieth century, above all in Germany, reflect this all too often.

How do migratory birds find their way?

These horses generally have great power and the most primal urge for freedom. In addition, Origins do not have the very particular characteristics that have, over generations, adapted to a co-existence with human beings, even those horses of this character group that come from riding-horse breeding. What is this deep-rooted, and very typical, problem and what is the solution?

The problem: how do salmon find their spawning grounds up river? How do migratory birds find their way? What drives frogs over the most dangerous obstacles to the place of their birth? How do cats orient themselves over vast distances? Believe me scientists do not have any real answers to even the simplest questions about nature. They only manipulate models and probabilities that they regularly replace with others. In truth, practically nothing is known.

The Origin acts as he must act

We human beings have forgotten how to live in contact with our source. These horses, however, still live so intensely in dependency on natural processes that they can and want to respect and acknowledge the human world less than, for example, domestic pigs, dogs, or pure riding-horse breeds do. It is easy to dismiss this attitude by simply saying that these horses have minds of their own, but that is wrong. The Sceptic, the Peasant, the Fat One, and even, to a degree, the Sergeant are all characters that want to follow their own minds come what may. The Origin, however, does not act the way he wants to act, he acts as he must act.

No horse in any other character group has this quality to this degree, and owners of an Origin must consider this point extremely carefully.

At the end of the long journey many salmon die immediately after the reproductive act. Their path drives them to death. It is hardly a path that they desire; it is a path that they must travel. This trait is of elemental importance in relationships with these horses. Even if there seems to be similarities in the behaviour of Origins and the Fat One, for example, the root cause is completely different, and therefore a person's approach must also be completely different. I describe these long unfamiliar connections here for the first time, and I hope they manage to contribute to the good of both human and horse because so much grief exists because of ignorance of this factor.

Inwardly absolutely unyielding

The solution: any idea of coercion, competition and showing must not be directed at these animals. Even the concept of people sitting on their backs is more alien to these horses than to others. When working with them, therefore, you must be very aware of the fact that these horses will not be won over by us if, like the salmon, they must obey their primal urge. I have witnessed the most shocking torture just because these inwardly unyielding horses cannot give in. As with the salmon, for these horses it is not just a matter of pure survival. This horse can, therefore, only exist with human beings within a completely different kind of relationship. Reason, freedom, space, patience and independence from schedules are as much prerequisites as is the complete absence of ambition on the person's part.

Slowly fathom the secrets

The Origin's training is very time intensive and protracted. For the shortest intervals, and always in a very close personal relationship, the trainer can slowly begin to fathom the secrets of this creature, and it will only work that way: the person must get to know the horse, not the other way around. Perhaps then the trainer will be able to detect something of the eternity that lies just under the skin of these horses, so down-to-earth and direct. Who knows? Perhaps it will be that sort of experience that the founders of the movement once instinctively sensed.

The Icelandic horse

Special consideration must be given to the training of the Icelandic horse and in general to the five-gaited horses.

In times past, tölting horses were gifts for kings – and very valuable gifts at that. That was mainly due to the fact that a correctly tölting horse first had to go through the High School training. Only then was the horse free enough in the forehand, only then could he carry himself sufficiently on the haunches so that he could be faultlessly and cleanly trained in tölt.

In order for a horse to tölt, his forehand must be free. Today that is nearly always produced with many tricks that mostly raise the head and neck without first physically preparing the hindquarters over many years.

It is the same thing even with the so-called natural tölt. In the wild, it occasionally serves to help a horse survive, so it

is employed only in critical situations. A horse that can tölt naturally would still not be able to do it with a rider on his back because the weight of the rider changes the total equilibrium of the horse to his detriment. Up to now I have never met a tölting horse whose rider I could proclaim innocent of any 'underhand' actions. It is only because so many use dubious training methods, and because considerable sensitivity is needed to recognize the agony of a mute creature, that it is not done differently or better. It is much more difficult to train a gaited horse correctly than to take a horse to High School level. Up to now I have not heard of anyone, least of all a professional, who could do justice to the task.

The mass renaissance of tölting horses twenty-five to thirty years ago is one of the sad occurrences in the history of riding. Although tölting horses still exist, there are no masters anymore, no people who are truly sensitive enough and have the strength of character to train them correctly.

About the natural tölt

The natural tölt of a horse develops in regions where the footing allows no headlong galloping flight. On marshy wet ground flight in a gallop would spell death. At a tölt, three legs are always on the ground and therefore the danger of sinking deeply is lessened, that is why a horse tölts.

Another survival technique has developed in marshy

Overview Table for the Origin

Reprise	rather short
Sequence	rather short
Session	rather short
Up tempo	1
Down tempo	1
High	1
Flat	1
Domineering	2
Restrained, tolerant	1
Tight boundaries	2
Playing free	2
Concave riding-in	–
Convex riding-in	1

regions: fighting instead of fleeing. That means that the flight behaviour of certain natural horses, for example Icelandic horses, has fundamentally changed, even regressed. That is a very significant factor in their training, because the entire system of positioning of the trainer's body can be rendered powerless. (See *Dancing with Horses* for more information on the system of positioning.)

Teaching Through Learning, Learning Through Teaching
The Pilgrim on the Path to Becoming a Riding Horse

11

This is a wonderful horse to work with. He has something of the King and the Tough One in his nature. All in all this horse really does not have any faults or weaknesses. He is powerful and of good carrying stature. We find hardly anything in him, inwardly or outwardly, that needs to be corrected during his training. Our task is simply to do justice to the great nature of this horse. Freedom, greatness, independence, loyalty, perspective and composure: these are the qualities that define the horse, and what we can learn from him. What is demanded of us is that we, under no circumstances, should act in any way contrary to this breadth of spirit.

Balance, composure and stamina

Overall the Pilgrim's training proceeds quietly along steady lines. Switching between work in the school and that in open country must be very balanced and moulded to how the horse reacts to things and progresses.

This type of horse tends to be of a fairly big solid stature, and that must be taken into consideration. The Pilgrim is not a quick, jumpy horse; he is the epitome of composure and stamina.

If he is overfaced by speed and spontaneity he can easily shut down and even become aggressive.

Repeated 'loosening' sequences

His strong nature can sometimes express itself in tensions and stiffness. Therefore, it is recommended to periodically loosen the horse with some light cavaletti work, and to 'soften' him with gentle bending both in the ground work and under saddle. The Pilgrim will never have the suppleness of a Dove, a Child, or even a Minister for example; he is a solid, compact animal.

Training on a steady but progressive and quiet track

The work reprises should be short, and the training takes place within a long time frame: over four to seven years. This horse can carry a rider relatively early, between the third and fourth year of life.

The work and the training should proceed along straightforward lines. Experiments of every kind should be avoided. Unlike some other character types, this horse does not need to be 'entertained' by the work. Naturally, the work

Overview Table for the Pilgrim	
Reprise	rather short
Sequence	rather short
Session	rather short
Up tempo	–
Down tempo	1
High	1
Flat	1
Domineering	1
Restrained, tolerant	–
Tight boundaries	1
Playing free	–
Concave riding-in	–
Convex riding-in	1

should always be interesting and rich in variety, but this horse is not especially playful nor does he require a high degree of change. He is an uncomplicated, good horse that is also extremely well suited to breeding.

With Tolerance, Indulgence, and Cheerfulness into Concentration
The Child on the Path to Becoming a Riding Horse

12

This Child is a nice 'person' and good looking, but he is also moody and changeable. He is very different in his nature from, for example, the Pilgrim. When being trained, he reacts very quickly to gestures and body language, and is intelligent and sensitive. But he is a Child, and because of that, certain things have to be taken into account.

Do not overstretch the bow

The reprises at the beginning of a work sequence should be kept short and very varied, and then the trainer's task is to lead this horse carefully and with a great deal of feeling into concentration. While this is being done the bow must never be overstretched, and this is not so easy to accomplish because, if the person lets the framework become too broad, the horse quickly becomes nervous, mistrustful, and might well 'unravel'. If the framework is made too restrictive, the horse quickly becomes depressed, unhappy and finally ill. This is just as it is with a human child: there too much thought must be given to the right framework for growing-up so that the child flourishes.

'Forward freedom'

Like the Dove and the Dancer, the Child needs much 'forward freedom': he must not be held back and above all should not in any case be checked or restrained by the reins. As his back and croup are often somewhat weak it is only relatively late in his life that the horse can carry a rider. It is important to ensure that a horse with a good, harmonious appearance is sufficiently strengthened through his work. Certain things that other horses are born with, must as a rule, be achieved with these horses through sensible gymnastic exercises.

Strengthening the back

By doing work on the ground out in the countryside the horse can strengthen his hindquarters, his back, and improve his entire appearance by working over natural obstacles. At this point I would like to briefly discuss working on sloping ground. Of particular value is a slope with an incline of about 2–4 m (6½–13 ft). The slope should be fairly gradual so that, in going down, the horse does not jump but must walk slowly thereby engaging his haunches. Work at liberty or on the lunge on such a slope is invaluable for building strength, but balance and equilibrium are also improved and supported. You must be careful not to overface the horse, and the work should be adapted depending on age, degree of training, and condition. This slope work is very strenuous and, to start with, it is best to take the horse over it just a few times.

If the horse is over-challenged, not only is nothing

Overview Table for the Child	
Reprise	to begin with, rather short
Sequence	to begin with, rather short
Session	rather short
Up tempo	1
Down tempo	–
High	2
Flat	–
Domineering	–
Restrained, tolerant	1
Tight boundaries	–
Playing free	1
Concave riding-in	2
Convex riding-in	–

This young stallion is very carefully being asked to circle around for the first time, on a loosely draping rope. The horse follows the clear body language. One circle is enough. What is important is that the horse learns to leave the centre and then return to the person in a

nice bend, all in precise response to subtle signals. It is not only with the Child that less is more but with this character group limiting the work is a fundamental requirement. The work framework should, however, be neither to restrictive nor too broad.

accomplished, but the horse also actually regresses to a worse state from the one he was in at the beginning of the exercises. Even with a well-trained horse, this exercise should be conducted for only a few minutes. That way it will create a love of movement and the desire to move in an unrestrained way.

A horse of this character group can practically never be asked to do demanding tasks. If you can acknowledge and nurse the fragility, complexity and short-term attention span of the childlike nature, then the Child will be a pleasant, playful and intimate friend.

A Sensitive Journey towards a Second Birth
The Half-born One on the Path to Becoming a Riding Horse

13

This is a very special horse and interaction with him should be undertaken in a very special manner. If you can become close to such a horse, then a unique and very deep bond can be formed. These horses are very clinging, and in their own way they are very sensitive, even if they do not always appear to be. They frequently seem 'absent', which, quite frankly, also makes them seem 'dopey'.

Tight boundaries

Because they are only 'half born', these horses need a great deal of assistance from human beings. It is as though they are not really in this world. Their overall expression is ethereal as, so often, is their behaviour. The very first thing we must do is recognize and acknowledge that very tight boundaries are set for these horses in every way. They are usually quite weak physically and in addition they come equipped with a concave

body structure. In this they are similar to the Dove, the Dancer, and in certain respects also the Child. So, take note of the work instructions for those character groups as well. Spiritually the Half-born One is similar to the North Wind, the Frog, Pegasus, the Unicorn, and the Child.

Always keep his particular qualities in mind

These horses are always of a simple, naïve, innocent nature, and so they have a particular charm of their own, despite their weak constitutions and their sometimes intense 'absence'. If you want to train a Half-born One, you must keep the particular qualities of these horses firmly in mind. In a certain way, these horses are like children who have been 'left behind' in school. If a child, who is thoroughly creative, independent and full of life, tends to be 'absent', because he is living in a world of his own,

The bond of closeness and trust with these horses must not under any circumstances be allowed to break; this is of vital importance.

trust must under no circumstances ever be broken. Training this horse always involves watchfulness, guarding the time spent together to make certain it is spent in the most pleasant way. The work should not be concentrated; the exercises to build physical strength can be offered only in small, bite-size portions and must be woven into the quiet play of togetherness. To do this, a great deal of intuitive 'feel' is necessary. It is to be hoped that you want nothing from the Half-born One, but certainly less than you would expect from another type of horse. That is why every little bit of progress is a great gift.

he is labelled as having learning difficulties. If that is not taken into consideration the child will be mercilessly ground down in this world. That, not infrequently, also happens with horses of this character group.

This horse is easily made happy by, and will show his contentment to, a person who understands him. Enjoy that, and encourage and allow growth of any aspect of this horse's nature and training that should and wants to grow. That is the path to fulfilment for this horse.

Carefully improve carrying power

Please read the sections on the other character groups just mentioned and, in particular, read *Dancing with Horses* to see how the strength, suppleness and above all the carrying power of this horse can be improved. The carrying power and elasticity of the horse must be carefully increased. It should be unnecessary to mention that, as a riding horse, this horse can only be worked at the very lowest levels. If, at the age of seven to nine years, this horse can comfortably carry a lightweight person through the countryside at all gaits over a not-too-long distance, without being compromised either mentally or physically, then the training has succeeded extremely well.

The bond of closeness and trust

As to what is required in the spiritual component of training, please take note of the following. The bond of closeness and

Overview Table for the Half-born One

Reprise	medium
Sequence	short
Session	short
Up tempo	1
Down tempo	1
High	2
Flat	1
Domineering	1
Restrained, tolerant	1
Tight boundaries	1
Playing free	2
Concave riding-in	3
Convex riding-in	–

Warmth and Trust Arise Out of Distance, Weakness and Cold The North Wind on the Path to Becoming a Riding Horse

14

This horse is similar to the Half-born One both inwardly and outwardly, but the causes of the similarities are not the same, and therefore you must handle and train this horse differently, at least in certain respects. In contrast to the nature of the Half-born One the North Wind's nature lies in this world, it is an element we can experience, even though we cannot see it, even though we cannot hold it in our hands.

Intelligent and mentally agile

The North Wind is, in one moment, thoroughly intense, present and visible, but then in the next moment it is scattered in all directions, diffuse, and of an insubstantial, weak appearance. This horse is not like the child with learning difficulties to whom we compared the Half-born One; he is often quite intelligent and, at least mentally, of astounding agility.

More self-contained and independent

Now we will see how, upon closer examination, initial similarities conceal great and significant differences. The North Wind does not seek closeness as much as the Half-born One does; he is, in a certain respect, more self-contained and independent. This horse is more distanced by nature, sometimes very distanced indeed.

His physical characteristics are very similar to the Dove, the Dancer and the Child. This horse also has a concave body shape that is by nature barely able to carry weight. The same training rules written for the character groups just mentioned also apply to the North Wind.

Concentration is difficult

With regard to his spiritual inner nature, however, we must proceed differently, and pay attention to the following.

It is only with great difficulty that the North Wind can concentrate on us and on the exercises. It is as though you want to put the north wind in a paper bag and carry it home.

A particular steadfastness is demanded of the trainer, therefore; to a large degree, he must become the axis, the centre point around which the horse can orient himself.

This horse is frequently quite full of fury and can be dangerous. He is quick to kick and bite, aims precisely, and wants the strike to hit home. In that respect the North Wind is not a noble horse.

He is in his nature a cold horse, like the north wind. Here again, this horse can and must be trained at only the lowest levels, if at all.

When the cold subsides

In a certain respect this is a horse that barely expresses and barely reciprocates feelings. Unfortunately, therefore, any bonds often remain superficial and sterile. Only over a period of years does an understanding and a sense of true togetherness evolve. And over the years, even the wind can subside and with it the unrest, the absence and the coldness. It is the small details, however, those that are overlooked by the uninitiated, that establish and reinforce understanding and mutual exchange. Man and horse seem to agree and to

Overview Table for the North Wind	
Reprise	medium
Sequence	short
Session	medium
Up tempo	1
Down tempo	1
High	1
Flat	1
Domineering	2
Restrained, tolerant	–
Tight boundaries	2
Playing free	–
Concave riding-in	3
Convex riding-in	–

Once the ice is broken with the North Wind, he will stand loyally by his owner. This young mare of the North Wind character group remains resolutely by me, even when I put the saddle pad on her back for the first time and tighten the girth.

understand one another with a sort of minimal secret language. This type of relationship does not suit everyone, but even in this kind of encounter there is happiness to be found, and happiness, thank God, is as many-faceted as the creatures themselves. There can be no question, therefore, that even on the back of this horse all the happiness in the world can be found, at least for he who makes the effort to look for it.

Back Into the World of Horses
The Lonely One on the Path to Becoming a Riding Horse

15

In my view, working with these horses is sometimes quite difficult. Other people, who want something quite different from these horses, see things very differently. But this book, as a reflection of my work and my procedures, sees the existence of horses and horsepeople from another viewpoint: that of the horse, and from that perspective, organizing this horse's training is not simple. Here I must reiterate that the character group of the Lonely One, as with all the groups, is definitely not breed specific, even though a lot of warmbloods are to be found in this group.

Horses of this type are relatively 'absent' and, depending upon the individual, they have lost some or even many of their natural qualities. Seen in this way, they are practically numb and stunted.

Passed on through generations
Broodmares pass on much of their behaviour to their foals. If, through work with human beings, a mare has been frightened or brutalized, then the foal and the young horse will display

some of the same behaviour, as though they had themselves been frightened or brutalized. The carriage necessary for a specific competitive system is in the blood of these horses, having been passed on from generation to generation.

How these horses move

Now we have to take into consideration the way these horses move. The wide frame and the ground-covering movement actually require a much larger training area. This horse can be schooled in the picadero only at a very late stage. It is also much more difficult to bring such a horse into a truly balanced series of movements. My work is based on the principal idea of continuously giving a horse different tasks, on a relatively small training area, which encourages him to constantly re-establish his balance, thereby consolidating it. The horse is asked to adapt to a series of changes in balance that quickly follow one another with the spaces between the different tasks becoming progressively shorter. In this way the horse eventually becomes like a spring, and is enabled to successfully complete the tasks of a nimble work horse. These working methods are not in the catalogue of requirements these horses normally must satisfy and therefore, as a rule, depending on their breeding, also not in their nature.

The question of distance

How do we proceed? As with every horse, and exactly as described in Chapter 5, we seek trust and closeness in the first encounter. In doing that, it is particularly important to pay attention to the question of the distance between trainer and horse. As a rule, I initially let a Lonely One remain at a distance for a longer time than other types. You must also take into account the aggression level at any given moment, because many of these horses have a relatively high potential for aggression. Aggression, however, lies concealed in the fundamental nature of loneliness. Frequently, therefore, sudden attacks occur without prior warning. From the horse's point of view these are inevitable, but for the trainer they are nevertheless exceedingly unpleasant.

Diligence and nervousness

As a rule, these horses are inclined to nervousness, and have

The Lonely One usually has to be brought back into the world of horses by being free, playing and being 'allowed to be a horse'.

a tendency not to enjoy work, and the underlying reasons are often misunderstood. These horses are often far less capable of doing demanding work, and have far less ability to perform, than would initially appear to be the case. Compared to some other character groups these horses tend to be lazy, and that is why they require the constant, prolonged 'fire alarm' type aids that are avoided in every

Overview Table for the Lonely One		
Reprise	at the beginning medium to long, then shortened	
Sequence	at the beginning short, then longer	
Session	at the beginning short, then medium to long	
Up tempo		1
Down tempo		–
High		1
Flat		1
Domineering		2
Restrained, tolerant		–
Tight boundaries		1
Playing free		1
Concave riding-in		2
Convex riding-in		–

other form of riding simply because they tire the rider too much. Nevertheless, these horses must and should perform, because performance is what fuels and drives the entire breeding industry. Unfortunately, many of these horses carry within them jumpy and nervous elements that do not arise from, and are not appropriate to, their true nature. Thus Lonely Ones appear very dramatic and temperamental, but it is only the fear and anxiety of being overfaced being expressed. With appropriate, horse-oriented interaction they lose this tendency to overreact and their true nature comes to the fore; then we must reconcile ourselves to the fact that in fact there is hardly any 'fire and temperament' lurking in these horses.

Condense the rhythm

We can continue with the training by, amongst other things, getting the horse to move forward in a medium stride, wide reprises in a large space that are not too challenging, and to progress, over time, to shorter reprises in gradually longer sequences. The tempo is gradually increased and the overall time spent working, the length of the session, increases. That means that in the beginning this horse should be worked only two to four minutes after an initial phase of playing and letting off steam. After many weeks and months the sessions can increase in length to from ten to twenty minutes or more. If all this is based on my gentle principles, which are discussed in my publications, then you will have a horse that willingly participates in the sessions and will be able to attain, according to his abilities, balance in his movement and satisfactory lateral suppleness. In this way withdrawn animals will become creatures that, though they can never recover entirely from their 'breeding-determined disability' will, with our help, be able to learn to live well and happily with these disabilities. That would be a beautiful achievement.

From Apathy to Creativity
The Used One on the Path to Becoming a Riding Horse

16

This is a character group that is very isolated. There is some similarity to the Lonely One and in a very distant way to the Friend and also the Pilgrim. In a certain respect the last two are also rays of hope, because the nature of Used Ones can lean in that direction, if we awaken the creativity that lies within them.

My position

Let me make my position clear immediately. Just as with the Lonely One, my indignation and, in a certain way, my abhorrence with respect to this character group is never in any way directed at the horses themselves. They are the victims of 'politics of degeneration' created by human hands. My indignation and my abhorrence are for the merciless human systems that breed rabbits to suit the show judges, cats that can barely move, dogs that bring serious eye, ear and hip ailments into the world with them at birth, and horses solely and uniquely designed for winning sporting events, and other occupations that more or less exploit nature.

Riding 'downhill'

The most noticeable physical characteristic of these horses is the heavy, too-high croup coupled with the underdeveloped forehand. This immediately throws the horses onto the forehand and creates the deeply set on neck and the dragging, stumbling gait so prized by those riders who quickly arouse the suspicion that they are not capable of sitting the trot of a sound horse. Every horseperson can only be advised to study the history of riding and horsemanship. Then not much will remain of the illusion of the glorious western hero and his horsemanship, because that never existed. From the very beginning too many of these horses were bred for exploitation, for often uneducated or badly educated employees who enjoyed a reputation that accorded with their origins. A gigantic film industry beautified the image of this group of people, making them into stars.

The horse's self-confidence

It goes without saying that the conformation of these horses makes them completely unsuitable for any form of High

School work, but that is the least of their problems. In *Dancing with Horses* I describe the connection between spiritual power and presence with the ability of the horse to engage the hindquarters in order to unburden the forehand. A horse balancing itself on deeply engaged hindquarters is the archetypal symbol and image of natural power. It is quite simply the pose of the self-conquering conqueror, of the victorious modest 'hero'. This horse often embodies the opposite of this image, but not in his original nature, he is a product of twisted thought. And that is the dilemma.

Trust, bonding, and a firm framework

This is how I usually proceed.

- In a first encounter with a static, settled, and thoroughly 'slow' emphasis, I first create quiet trusting distance. I keep these horses at a distance for a relatively long time, even for as long as 10-15 minutes. When the horse does come to me, I allow him to stand by me a very, very long time. Then it is as though I form a sort of different, more primal, structure during this time. It seems to me as though the horse is going back, 'remembering'. Any thought of pressurizing the horse in any way must be immediately torn up by the roots. From the first second the horse must experience the complete opposite of that which he genetically carries within himself: that he exists to be exploited.
- Careful and clear dominance that is enforced on the one hand, but on the other hand never exerts pressure or in any way appeases, is the path to progress and the guide for the training. This horse must be led to himself as though on invisible tracks. Later on the tracks can be abandoned and,

in the ideal case, we will have before us a liberated horse, and one that also did not come to harm during the process of liberation. With these horses there is a very fine line between 'letting him have his way' and the support, stability and leading that are necessary. In this respect, horses of this character group are a great exception. Only very sensitive and open human beings can manage this.

Naturally I can hear some people saying, 'I do not know what more he wants, they are the best functioning horses'. And I also know that there is hardly anything in this world that will lead the thoughts of such a person to recognize that this is exactly what I am talking about.

Overview Table for the Used One

Reprise	in the beginning short with very long pauses
Sequence	long
Session	in the beginning short
Up tempo	1
Down tempo	–
High	1
Flat	1
Domineering	2
Restrained, tolerant	1
Tight boundaries	1
Playing free	1
Concave riding-in	2
Convex riding-in	–

Between Freedom and a Clear Framework
The Gypsy on the Path to Becoming a Riding Horse

17

The Gypsy is a catlike, very exciting horse. A horse of this character group is normally light, supple, and possesses a certain outer delicacy that does not correspond either to his nature or to his great capacity for work. Being of a good, harmonious conformation, this horse gives the trainer few challenges with respect to correcting possible weaknesses.

Freedom and play within a solid framework

Because of his very specific nature this horse always poses new tests for the trainer, who should be extremely

Between freedom and a clear framework. Exercises like the ones I am doing here with my stallion Almendro are very suited to the Gypsy. The horse appears free, yet he is restrained, appears independent, yet he is led. The draping rope lying loosely around his neck does not serve to hold the horse but only to transmit subtle signals and indicate direction.

empathetic, composed, and thoroughly grounded if he wants to work with a horse like this. The training, as such, takes place on clear, simple tracks. If the trainer understands how to proceed in accordance with this horse's special nature, he will follow the individual training levels in textbook fashion. You should be particularly aware of the following.

- This horse requires freedom and play but at the same time a thoroughly broad but nevertheless clearly defined framework. The reactions of the horse must be repeatedly checked to see that the equilibrium is correct. If the framework is too narrow, the horse will become depressed and/or aggressive. If the framework is too wide, he becomes rebellious and aggressive. He becomes unfocused, wild, nervous, and insufferable, even to other horses.

- Also to help with the above problem it is important to always let the horse 'breathe' in his movements, both inwardly and outwardly. The trainer must understand and know how to utilize the spiritual and physical inhaling and exhaling, that is the natural rhythms of a natural creature.

- It is not so easy to bore a Gypsy. Although it is not immediately obvious, this horse can be asked to perform tasks requiring concentration on longer sequences. This horse wants to plumb the depths and achieve mastery of his work. If he understands the purpose of a particular exercise and where it can lead then the Gypsy will develop great ambition. If you always preserve and protect this quality through play and sequences performed at liberty then you and your horse will go far.

Overview Table for the Gypsy	
Reprise	short to long
Sequence	short to long
Session	short to medium
Up tempo	1
Down tempo	1
High	2
Flat	2
Domineering	2
Restrained, tolerant	–
Tight boundaries	1
Playing free	2
Concave riding-in	1
Convex riding-in	–

- Only in a very few cases can this horse reach High School level. He is a quick supple horse with stamina that, given the discipline of certain fundamental exercises, will be kept healthy and sound. The horse can easily master shoulder-in and the lateral movements that shoulder-in leads to. Please note that it is important to do this work slowly, in-hand for example, and with much impulsion. For this horse a medium tempo that lacks impulsion is dangerous; it has the effect of 'choking' the exercise but also, in a way, the horse.

- This is a freedom-loving horse with an uncomplicated nature, and the exercises should be constructed accordingly. You can really dance with this horse. Enjoy his freshness, his inner agility, and his temperament. Naturally, that all has some consequences which occasionally test our patience but that can aid our growth. Fortunate is he who has at his disposal all that this horse has to offer.

From Superficiality into Depth
The Dandy on the Path to Becoming a Riding Horse

18

The Gypsy is related to the Minister, and the Dandy is related to the Dove and the Child. At first glance, the Gypsy and the Dandy seem similar to one another, but the influence of the other relationships clearly shows the differences between the two. While the Gypsy possesses all the seriousness of the Minister, with a sense of freedom and a joie de vivre, in the Dandy we can see both the weakness of the Dove and the superficiality of the Child. These factors are something we must consider in the work with this horse.

Compact

The Dandy is a good, compact, very impressive horse. However, it is part of his nature not to want to dig too deeply or to soar too high. Unlike the Gypsy who truly strives for inner qualities, the Dandy leans more towards seeking the external appearance. He is not as tough, clear or as grounded as the Gypsy.

He is, however, of a simple nature. He bonds with human beings more quickly and in a less complex way, and does not demand nearly as much from them as the Gypsy does. Therefore, this is a horse that even a beginner can get on with. First, however, he is a horse that you must simply love. The Dandy is particularly well-proportioned and attractive, and has a simple, uncomplicated nature, which makes it easy for someone to build a good relationship with him.

The shape of the back

These horses have differing back shapes. As a rule, a character group also defines relatively clearly the exterior shape of a horse but that is not the case here when it comes to the back. It can be either wonderfully short, compact, and of good carrying power, or long and relatively weak. If the back is short, then this horse can be taken up to High School level.

Overview Table for the Dandy	
Reprise	medium
Sequence	medium
Session	medium
Up tempo	2
Down tempo	1
High	2
Flat	1
Domineering	–
Restrained, tolerant	1
Tight boundaries	–
Playing free	1
Concave riding-in	1
Convex riding-in	–

Then the result will be an outstanding, powerful horse that can be enormously impressive. However, if the back is longer, then it can mean a distinct overall weakness and if this is the case we must concentrate particularly on those exercises that directly support the carrying power of the back.

Fear and nervousness

Fear and nervousness sometimes play a role in the nature of the Dandy and so some of the training procedures for the Dove may also prove useful when training a Dandy. Because of the nervousness, it is also important that this horse is always spoken to in a quiet and calm way. A friendly playing-rough way of interacting such as can be cultivated with the King, the Pilgrim, the Friend and the Gypsy will poison a relationship with the Dandy.

Horses of this character group want to be taken seriously to a very special degree. This is significant for every horse, but with the Dandy this point must be given particular attention. This desire to be taken seriously is probably rooted in the horse's desire to impress, to have an effect, particularly externally.

A rather wide framework

The individual reprises in the work should be of medium length and very varied. The horse likes to feel he is 'free' and, consequently, his work framework should be wide rather than too narrow. In contrast to the Gypsy, the Dandy will not take advantage of this wide framework to overstep his bounds. He wants to please people, one way or another, and makes an effort to be acknowledged, which means he will, of his own accord, make the framework narrower again. If the trainer is sensitive enough and patient, if he allows the horse a wide framework and gives him interesting exercises and opportunities within the framework to find and prove himself, then a relationship with this horse is very inspiring.

Lingering in the Simplicity and Enjoying the Ease
The Modest One on the Path to Becoming a Riding Horse

19

This character group is related to the Guardian of the Fire, the Friend, the Pilgrim, the Unicorn, and in a certain respect also to the King, all of which indicate the type of work framework required for this horse.

The Modest One is a very earnest, very clear horse. Even in the work with human beings he displays his modest aspect. Similarly to the Guardian of the Fire, this horse brings with him – within his physical limitations – very many fundamental qualities necessary to becoming a riding horse. There is really not very much more that he has to learn. His behaviour is quiet and grounded, and he has great trust both in himself and in the world.

Developing simple but good talents

The task for the person who wants to develop this horse into a riding and/or driving horse is to help him develop his natural abilities in a quiet way. The quality that, above all, is demanded of the person doing this training is fairness. Modesty goes into forceful resistance against incorrectness and unfair handling. This horse forgives many mistakes and some ignorance, but if he is continually unfairly handled he resists surprisingly forcefully.

Recognizing the limits

Physically this horse is limited and you can demand only minor riding tasks of him. That little is, however, usually completely sufficient and fills this horse with purpose and dependability.

The Modest One can carry a rider at a relatively young age, as early as three or four years old, providing the backing is done with care. Overall, the training takes place in clear, not very spectacular, steps, and the horse will grow steadily into his new life as a riding horse. The individual reprises are not too short, and the work should not be too richly varied. This horse enjoys spending a longer time on an exercise when he has understood its purpose. With too much variation and any great change he becomes insecure and his contentment is disrupted.

This horse has relatively good endurance and is useful as a driving horse.

The broadly designed basic training

Physically this horse does not possess particularly outstanding qualities, but neither does he have particular weaknesses, and so we do not need special exercises for this horse, but rather a broadly structured training in the basics. Overall, the Modest One is a bit awkward and stiff and, typically, the underside of his neck and his jaws and jowls are quite tight. The remedy of choice for this is, for example, to change the direction of the shoulder-in down the centre line after a few strides. Through the careful and consistent changing of the bend of the shoulder-in, this horse will become soft and supple in the shoulder and neck, and he will develop more impulsion. An exercise like this can only be

Overview Table for the Modest One	
Reprise	rather long
Sequence	rather long
Session	medium
Up tempo	–
Down tempo	1
High	–
Flat	1
Domineering	–
Restrained, tolerant	1
Tight boundaries	1
Playing free	–
Concave riding-in	–
Convex riding-in	1

started, at the earliest, in the second year of training – and then very carefully; it is important that, because of the nature of the horse, no mishandling causes him to become anxious.

This horse is a wonderful pleasure-riding horse. With a quiet and fair owner, he can live many problem-free and therefore happy years.

The Head and Neck Rise and Self-confidence Grows
The Frog on the Path to Becoming a Riding Horse

20

This is a very difficult case, and so let us start with the simplest part. This horse has a very loyal and good nature; he is a very grateful creature and very willing to bond with the right person. He knows his weaknesses and has become reconciled to them and has learned to live with them quite well. And that is the starting point for the training.

Strengthening – but carefully and correctly!

This horse is sensitive and realistic, and he is also extremely likeable. If we take all this into account and keep the physical demands at a very low level, then hardly anything can go wrong. The most important thing is to strengthen the horse and to boost his self-esteem. He always needs to have

experienced success and to feel that he is constantly getting stronger and more able to work.

Between play and clarity

In the beginning the work together should be arranged around playful activities and short, but very clear, sequences. Early in the training, the Frog's strength should be built up by long walks or by being led from another horse. This horse will not protest if he is physically overfaced, and so it is, therefore, very important that we take responsibility for keeping the demands at a very low level. Work in medium length reprises at liberty on an initially large circle, and repeatedly on the straight, followed by work over poles and low cavaletti, will fundamentally strengthen the horse.

Overview Table for the Frog

Reprise	medium
Sequence	short
Session	short
Up tempo	1
Down tempo	–
High	1
Flat	1
Domineering	–
Restrained, tolerant	1
Tight boundaries	–
Playing free	2
Concave riding-in	3
Convex riding-in	–

Saddling-up before the walks

Although the following directions are very specifically for the Frog, many can well be used for other character groups that also have weak backs.

A light saddle can be put on very early while the Frog is still young. If you always do that, then the young, as yet unridden, horse will connect a saddle only with something positive. The saddle then becomes a harbinger of a 'trip out'; however, this horse can only be ridden very late in his training – if at all. If the Frog is to be ridden, two things are especially important.

- This horse must, without question, be encouraged to step his hind legs well under his body by the use of extensive lateral movements in-hand and work on the circle. That will shorten the long horse from back to front and will raise the head. Now the horse presents a completely different image: the hindquarters become fuller and more muscular and the back is gradually raised.

- The Frog must also be ridden-in on a light rein and in a long frame at first. Through the movement and the light fluid impulsion the first offerings of shoulder-in will come as the horse's hind legs step under him through the corners. The rider can then increasingly attend to the bend and the carriage of the horse, which will eventually develop the collection enough, so that the horse can remain sound while carrying a rider well and for a bit longer.

That is how a Frog is responsibly brought along the path to become a riding horse. I know that many people complete this process much more quickly.

There is not much to Say
The Prince on the Path to Becoming a Riding Horse

Overview Table for the Prince

Reprise	medium
Sequence	medium
Session	medium
Up tempo	1
Down tempo	1
High	1
Flat	1
Domineering	1
Restrained, tolerant	1
Tight boundaries	–
Playing free	1
Concave riding-in	–
Convex riding-in	1

Any problems with this horse generally remain very minor. Physically as well as mentally this horse follows a simple and uncomplicated track. Similarly to the Pilgrim and the Friend this horse can, from the very start, go through a quiet and regular training programme. During the first encounter this horse will easily find his place near the trainer and from then on will effortlessly follow him through the individual stages, as long as he behaves clearly, sensitively, and fairly. Even the horse's back does not, as a rule, pose any problems. You should definitely not demand great outward displays of affection or closeness from this horse because his affection always remains hidden behind a sort of 'aristocratic' aloofness. Occasionally, there is a tendency to timidity which can be prevented though appropriate preparatory exercises. Once in a while the

Prince's hooves will pose problems and they should receive good care and shoeing right from the start. Sometimes this horse seems a bit immature, even, and particularly, in his

youth. If that is the case, it is important to allow plenty of time for his training, without any sort of external pressure.

Through Controlled Explosions to Consistency
The Victor on the Path to Becoming a Riding Horse

22

With these horses you should first direct your attention to one of their physical weaknesses, namely their weak backs, and also on their sensitive characters.

you raise will be only partially under your control, or not at all.

Quiet

It is important to always work these horses in a very quiet way. By nature this horse will want to go forward and he will want to let off a little steam one way or another, and it is imperative that he always has a safe and harmonious training regime in which to do that. That is why the reprises, for example, tend to be shorter, but the sequences longer. In between there are always relatively long pauses so that the horse can concentrate better, and can take the opportunity to gather himself. Caution is advised if you in any way whatsoever 'heat up' this horse. It is a character peculiarity of this horse to become easily over-excited, and you must be very careful not to allow this to happen because the 'spirits'

Easily dominated

The Victor is usually easy to dominate without having to resort to extraordinary measures. Because he is very sensitive, you must be very careful not to be overbearing or intrusive; that will, quite justifiably, make him rebel and resist everything we are trying to do. Dominance is easily achieved through dignity, clarity, and the subtle movement between closeness and distance. The spiritual depth of this animal must always be taken into account and all communication with him should take place on a high plane. The work should take place in a peaceful atmosphere but, nevertheless, should be interesting and rich in variety.

Upwardly directed action

The horse should never, under any circumstances, be overworked when attempts are being made to strengthen the back, but he should always work with a good 'swing' through the back. A flat, dragging trot is of no use whatsoever to the Victor, but he will benefit from shoulder-in, performed with impulsion down the long side (20-30 m) of the riding arena. The rider's seat in shoulder-in should be light and yielding, and must not interfere with the horse's action. From a shoulder-in reprise, the horse can be allowed to canter and, after a few collected strides, come to a stop. In this way the horse learns to be round, collected, and calm even in the first few canter strides. If the rider does not throw the horse onto the forehand through harsh use of the reins, he will learn to use his energy to direct the action upwards with a good head carriage and his hind legs stepping well under the weight of his body. I repeat that

Overview Table for the Victor

Reprise	rather short
Sequence	rather long
Session	medium
Up tempo	1
Down tempo	1
High	1
Flat	1
Domineering	1
Restrained, tolerant	–
Tight boundaries	1
Playing free	–
Concave riding-in	3
Convex riding-in	–

these quiet, but short and very precisely executed reprises always serve to collect the horse and enable him to find a convex shape. If the reprises are too long, then the danger is that the horse will 'fall apart' again.

A Wise One Among Us
The Minister on the Path to Becoming a Riding Horse

This spiritually very superior, very sensitive and companionable horse is probably the most intelligent of all the character groups. The Gypsy is artful, the Dandy is clever, the Sergeant is mentally extremely quick, and the King is shrewd, sensible and very practical in his thinking. But the Minister is intelligent and, above all, wise, and it is precisely that which is often his undoing because most human beings cannot and will not hold a candle to this horse.

From violation to aggression

To simply exploit such a creature is not only a great insult but, if this happens, this animal will also then try any means to make himself understood; ultimately he becomes aggressive, very aggressive indeed. At the point when the horse employs his intelligence and dexterity against a person, the person has already lost. In fact, both horse and person have lost. Even if some people succeed in parrying the attacks of horses of other character groups, it is hardly ever possible with these horses because they fight with total cunning, bite as well as kick, and usually at the same time. The person is nearly always defeated.

Discussion and response

The Minister seeks and needs a direct discussion. This horse is the first to forgive at least a person's smaller mistakes, but should you wish to train this horse you must not put yourself on a pedestal. You must reconcile yourself to coming to an agreement with the Minister about everything that takes place; you must do this. Every small reaction of the horse will tell you whether or not what you are doing is correct. The Minister needs variety in his exercises which should also suit his cleverness and intelligence. Mentally this horse can do everything and, in addition, he has stamina, is able to work hard, and is very disciplined and focused in his work. The Minister does not only want to learn, but he must also always learn a little extra in order to stay in equilibrium. We must keep that in mind.

The particularities of the Minister

- This horse occasionally has a weak back or weak hindquarters. That means that his training regime must include exercises that strengthen these areas. For this reason the horse should generally not carry a rider at too young an age. He is a relatively late developer.
- These horses are more often than not poor-doers, but despite their sometimes gaunt outward appearance, they have a powerful and massive skeletal structure. The Minister is often significantly heavier than he appears. That too is something we must take into consideration in his training. This structural weight means that the horse is deprived of some suppleness, speed and sprinting ability, and he should never be overstretched in these areas.
- If you come to the point where you no longer know how to proceed – and with a Minister you can come to this point very quickly – then simply ask him. That might seem silly or naïve, but you will get an answer. Do not just carry on

23

Overview Table for the Minister

Reprise	long
Sequence	long
Session	long
Up tempo	1
Down tempo	1
High	1
Flat	1
Domineering	1
Restrained, tolerant	1
Tight boundaries	–
Playing free	1
Concave riding-in	1
Convex riding-in	–

with the old routine. It is much better to spend a creative interlude 'playing' than to upset the nature of this horse by replacing the discussion with an argument.

- If you remain clear, quiet, and above all modest, if you observe the horse and opt to temporarily stop the work rather than stubbornly press on to the end, if you want to learn at least as much as you are supposed to teach, then you can be happy with this horse.

- All in all, the Minister's training should proceed simply, in a straight line, and relatively normally, taking into consideration the weak back. The palette of exercises, in the arena as well as in the countryside, should cover quite a broad range.

Powerful and Stately
The King on the Path to Becoming a Riding Horse

24

The King's training regime consists of short, clearly delineated sequences. Few preparations are necessary. The programme is built up from the simple work on the ground, through the first lateral movements, and on to the collecting of the strides and beyond. With great power this horse can, and seemingly of his own volition, have his gaits collected to hint at passage and piaffe with the first elevated steps very quickly.

Occasional youthful nervousness and overly high spirits subside at from eight to ten years of age. Until then, canter strides can be explosive and sometimes uncontrolled, but one should not restrain the horse with the reins. With very little, if any, help, that power will increasingly shift to the hindquarters, creating elevation and lightness of movement that can only be described as majestic.

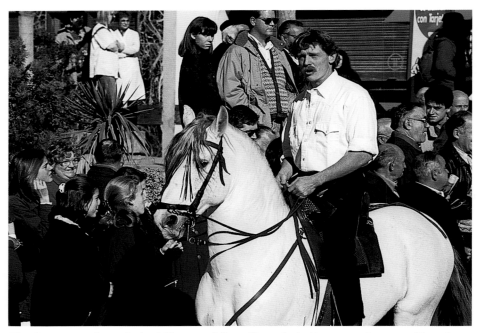

The King wants to be worked quickly, powerfully and intensively. He wants to impress, shine, show off, and hold court.

A capacity for very hard work for short periods of time

The King and the Tough One are physically even more powerful than the Pilgrim. They are by far the most powerful of all horses. They can, therefore, be asked to do very hard work, not necessarily for long, but certainly for short, periods of time. From this quality comes the fundamental principle of training, also characteristic of the classic Iberian style. Here horses are asked to perform their work quickly and very intensively. Unfortunately, for many years

this has been done by some with great brutality and with the horses at much too early an age. But, particularly for horses in this character group, the original principle is still correct. It is through short, intense reprises that the horse is optimally physically developed, and he 'expands' and rounds in shape, and then as a mature stallion he presents an impressive and compact power that leaves you in awe of his ability.

The King and his court

The King is a war-horse and parade horse. He needs his owner around him for many hours of the day. He needs his 'court' and he wants to hold court. This horse sees himself as the centre of his particular universe and he wants to be acknowledged as such. There is so much potency and energy in him which, if unused, dissolves into a corrosive mixture that eats away at the horse inside. This horse is meant for a person who lives with horses – ideally with just one horse, this one.

Overview Table for the King

Reprise	short
Sequence	short
Session	short
Up tempo	2
Down tempo	1
High	1
Flat	2
Domineering	2
Restrained, tolerant	–
Tight boundaries	2
Playing free	–
Concave riding-in	–
Convex riding-in	3

Born Piaffing

The Tough One on the Path to Becoming a Riding Horse

25

Much of what was said about the King also applies to the work with the Tough One. But, the Tough One is sometimes even more compact, more severe, and more down to earth. Possibly he lacks the aristocratic, thoroughly thoughtful quality of the King. Also this horse wants to do his work and be led through life in short, intense reprises and sequences, but this should not be done too soon in his training; a young horse should always be allowed plenty of time, particularly one of this character group. Even the sessions should be comparatively short. The horse learns quickly, he comes piaffing into the world. That sounds strange, but I mean it

exactly that way. At the beginning of his training the major focus should be on the care of the young horse, but he should be taken to the schooling arena in order to become accustomed to it, followed by work at liberty at a distance. The Tough One will then quickly progress to performing ever tighter turns and lateral movements in-hand next to his trainer.

Anyone who still believes he needs to indulge in unnecessary chatter with his horse, anyone who has not yet learned very much about himself, or learned about and experienced the nature of life and the world, should keep his hands off this horse. You can only get together with this horse as though for morning or afternoon tea, to pass the time with one another like two gentlemen, like nobles or knights, and to share. Nothing superficial, nothing contemptible, nothing idle should disturb this noble circle. Remember this: 'Art for art's sake – and life for the sake of life'.

You must only dominate through character

The inner strength and power of the trainer must dominate the Tough One from the very beginning. This horse needs a lord who leads without being dictatorial. The person's character is what must win over this horse. If, out of weakness, the person instigates the least little battle, he must either brutally beat and break the horse down (as I have witnessed) or live in constant danger.

A horse for High School work

From the beginning the training of the Tough One must be designed to introduce him to collection and High School work immediately. Lateral movements in-hand and concentrated work in a tight space and in place alternate with

Overview Table for the Tough One	
Reprise	short
Sequence	short
Session	short
Up tempo	2
Down tempo	1
High	–
Flat	2
Domineering	2
Restrained, tolerant	–
Tight boundaries	2
Playing free	–
Concave riding-in	–
Convex riding-in	3

reprises full of impulsion and dynamic 'liberation'. In this way the urge for movement and forward momentum is always maintained, together with the motivation and the strength to move expressively, even on the spot. The art of training this horse lies in this interchanging of one type of work with the other.

Sensitive Messenger from Another World
Pegasus on the Path to Becoming a Riding Horse

26

In this creature, creation has embodied itself in a unique way. St. Paul fell off this horse countless times. Even Caravaggio, master of light in the black void, could, in a particular instance, do nothing but paint to the edge of the canvas, filling it with one single horse. Rubens knew only this horse, figure of light and timeless symbol in the most radiant light. Michelangelo put him in the centre of his St. Paul's opus and let the figure that is meant to represent God point forcefully to it.

If a painter no longer thinks about painting but only creates, if a singer no longer sees notes and there is only sound and space, if a horseman no longer seeks external rules, proportion, form and tempo but simply allows it to come from within himself – that is the highest degree of mastery. To experience that with a person is what this horse strives for.

Pegasus is independent and seeks a special kind of closeness with a person. He should mostly be worked at a medium level with comparatively easy challenges.

It is not, however, the actual training that is most important, but rather an experience that proceeds along paths different from the usual ones, and that sets itself entirely different goals. Performance, comparison, ambition, recognition, reputation, and other self-centred goals, should never define a relationship with this horse.

Into High School but in a different way

Like the Tough One and the King this horse can, of course, be trained to High School level, but in an entirely different way. Pegasus is physically not as sturdy, shows weakness in the hindquarters, the stifles and tendons, and

Overview Table for Pegasus	
Reprise	medium
Sequence	medium
Session	medium
Up tempo	–
Down tempo	1
High	–
Flat	1
Domineering	–
Restrained, tolerant	1
Tight boundaries	1
Playing free	1
Concave riding-in	–
Convex riding-in	1

occasionally also has a too-long and too-weak back. Overall Pegasus's skeletal structure is not as solid as that of both the Tough One and the King, and so his short exercises should be distinctly less challenging, and he needs exercises that gently and moderately build up the hindquarters, begin to collect the horse, and lift and strengthen the back.

A 'silent' horse

When working with this horse it is always very important to take his psyche into consideration. This horse is, in a way, a 'stranger to the world' and he basically does not want to be confronted with the banalities of existence. A very quiet and calm atmosphere is the pre-requisite for training to proceed well. Anything hectic or distracting should remain outside the schooling arena. Despite all his creativity, this horse does not need play, and despite all his power, he does not really need to release excess energy. He needs a lot of time to experience the wonder of nature on long rides with his owner, and time to experience harmony with nature, the human being, and himself. In this sense he is a 'silent', extremely sensitive and also thoroughly 'romantic' horse.

Phenomena that are becoming extinct

I know that there are those who will smirk at my way of writing about and describing horses. I, however, do not anthropomorphize them; my approach, and probably also the dignity and earnestness of it, simply allows to happen what does happen when I am at one with horses. What I experience is that many seemingly impenetrable boundaries melt away, and that seems to be the experience of the horses as well. Probably because of that, the world to me is one where everything is interconnected. Modern human beings long ago severed this interconnectedness and thereby fired the starting pistol for the assault on the physical existence of this world. For a long time now, the world has not been considered as a flowing whole, and nor have horses. Because of that my descriptions and demonstrations often seem like messages from another world. Pegasus is such a messenger from another world. Is he also a phenomenon soon to be extinct?

Conclusion
What are you going to do with what you have learnt?

You can exploit everything you have learned from this book. You can cut out and separate from the whole those pieces that will enable you to exploit horses better. With what you have discovered here you can, in fact, perpetuate an outrage and oppress your horse even more effectively than you have until now. That happened as a result of people misusing the information in my other books, and will probably be the case with this one.

But time separates the soft from the hard, and here the circle closes with the words I spoke at the beginning. They who only exploit and seek salvation in that sort of world view, they who first and foremost seek to put themselves in the centre of everything, they for whom the need for gratification of their insatiable desires is the main purpose of life – they punish themselves with each new deed.

The others, however, can use that which they have learnt to continue constructing or to further adorn their palace of inner joy, true contentment and vibrant silence. That which I have written can be only a part of that, a few building blocks perhaps, a beautiful piece of furniture, a stimulus. He who is aware will everywhere find something that can enrich and beautify his own palace of a fulfilled life. He will all too gladly hide the resulting glow beneath a veil. He unites with the silence, with the mystery of this world that otherwise indulges only the loud and the notorious.

Two people will sit on a horse in seemingly the same manner; two people will speak of God in seemingly the same way, and yet, they could not be more different. This worldly difference between things that seem as alike as two peas in a pod is symbolized by the horse. It is in your hands whether your horse is for you the devil incarnate or a winged Pegasus.

The mean-spirited person rails against the splendid festivities and extravaganzas in the palace only so long as he is not himself invited. The wise person does not rail against the festivities, but neither does he dance at them when he is invited.

In this spirit, my greeting is the same for the one person as for the other.

Denmark, autumn 2002
Klaus Ferdinand Hempfling

Klaus Ferdinand and Karsten Hempfling